THE STRONGHOLD

The author in Cretan dress

THE STRONGHOLD

*Four Seasons in the
White Mountains of Crete*

XAN FIELDING

*Foreword by Robert Messenger
With photographs by Daphne Bath*

PAUL DRY BOOKS
Philadelphia 2013

First Paul Dry Books Edition, 2013

Paul Dry Books, Inc.
Philadelphia, Pennsylvania
www.pauldrybooks.com

Printed in the United States of America

Library of Congress Cataloging-in-Publication Data
Fielding, Xan.
     The stronghold : four seasons in the White Mountains of Crete / Xan Fielding ;
foreword by Robert Messenger. — First Paul Dry Books edition.
          pages cm
     First published: London : Secker & Warburg, 1953.
     Includes bibliographical references.
     ISBN 978-1-58988-085-6 (alk. paper)
     1. Crete (Greece)—Description and travel. 2. Fielding, Xan—Travel—
Greece—Crete. I. Title.
     DF901.C8F54 2013
     914.95—dc23
                                                                        2013003230

To the Memory of
my Cretan Friends
Who Lost their Lives
during the German Occupation
of their Island
1941–1945

Contents

PART FOUR

Spring–Summer

List of Photographs

Xan Fielding: A Brief Life
(1918–1991)

by Robert Messenger

Xan Fielding was ever the supporting player. His first wife, Daphne, was a famous Bright Young Thing and even more famously married to the Marquess of Bath. His second wife, Magouche, was the painter Arshile Gorky's widow.

A member of the British Special Operations Executive during World War II, Fielding was the main on-the-ground organizer of the resistance movement on Crete, but it was his great friend Patrick Leigh Fermor who got the popular acclaim thanks to his kidnapping a German general and spiriting him away to Cairo in 1944. Fielding had been Fermor's first choice as a partner in the mission, but it was felt that his small stature and swarthy looks made him a poor candidate to impersonate a German officer. The job went to W. Stanley ("Billy") Moss, who wrote a best-selling book in 1950 about the exploit, *Ill Met by Moonlight*.

If Fielding is remembered today, it is likely because of Fermor's renowned accounts of walking across Europe in the 1930s, *A Time of Gifts* (1977) and *Between the Woods and the Water* (1986). These evocations of a vanished world begin with a letter to "Dear Xan." And with good reason. Fielding had walked the same roads, with the same picaresque urgings. "Like him, I had tramped across Europe to reach Greece," Fielding wrote in his wartime memoirs. "Like him, I had been almost penniless during that long arduous holiday—but there the similarity between our travels ended, for whereas I was often forced to sleep out of doors, in ditches, haystacks or on public benches, Paddy's charm and resourcefulness had made him a welcome guest wherever he went."

After Crete, Fielding served in occupied France. When he was arrested at a German checkpoint in southern France in August 1944, he was reprieved from death by the bold action of another SOE agent, Christine Granville. On the Italian border organizing the defection of a Polish unit pressed into Wehrmacht service, she heard that Fielding and two companions had been captured in Digne and were likely to be tortured and shot. She drove straight to the town and confronted the French policeman who had made the arrest. Identifying herself as a British agent (and so forfeiting her life if the gambit failed), Granville pointed out that the Allies had just landed on the Riviera, that the town would soon be liberated, and that he would surely die in reprisals for causing the deaths of three important agents. (She also claimed to be the niece of British General Bernard Montgomery for good measure.)

The Frenchman helped her bribe the guards, and when Fielding was taken out of his cell expecting to face a firing squad, he was instead led to a car where Granville sat behind the wheel. Yet even so extraordinary an adventure was merely one more accident of Fielding's life. Granville had acted to save another of the prisoners, Francis Cammaerts (codename "Roger"), one of the most important resistance organizers. "Had Roger not been arrested with us," Fielding wrote, "Christine would have been perfectly justified in taking no action if action meant jeopardizing herself. Indirectly, then, I owe my life to him as much as I do, directly, to her."

In the late 1960s, Fielding even learned that his "mother" was actually his grandmother. His real mother had died in childbirth. The newborn was adopted into the older generation, and his father, Major Alexander Wallace of the 52nd Sikh Frontier Force, was simply never mentioned again. His brothers and sisters turned out to be aunts and uncles. According to Fermor, he related this tale with "considerable humor and bewilderment."

Alexander Percival Feilman Wallace was born in 1918 in India—at Ootacamund, one of the summer capitals of the Raj, where the British hid from the relentless Indian heat. He was adopted by his grandparents and raised at the Chateau Fielding in Nice. He followed an education at Charterhouse with a peripatetic career at the universities in Bonn, Munich, and Freiburg in the late 1930s. These

years added to his set of European languages and gave him a clear
sense of the evil of Nazism. (He was so appalled by Chamberlain's
appeasement policies that he contemplated becoming a communist
and tried to enlist on the Republican side in Spain.) Fielding thought
about a career as a painter, but was restless more than determined
and set out across Europe on foot.

September 1939 found him in Cyprus. He'd been sacked from
the local English newspaper and was running a bar. He said it took
him "almost a year to decide what attitude to adopt towards the
war." He wasn't "afraid of fighting," but he was "appalled by the
prospect of the army." The news in the summer of 1940 that Greek-
speaking Englishmen were wanted to help raise a Cypriot regiment finally brought him to volunteer, and three months shy of his
twenty-second birthday he was commissioned a lieutenant.

Far from the fearful martinets he expected, the officers of the
1st Cyprus Battalion proved to be misfits. Life revolved around the
commanding officer's desire to organize a regimental sports day to
encourage his unenthusiastic soldiers. "The Cypriots have never had
a military tradition, and it soon became clear that they were not
going to break a habit formed before the first century by taking
kindly to soldiering in the twentieth." Fielding found these among
the most carefree months of his life: "The incidence of venereal disease among the men rose to a height which was only surpassed by
the officers' drunkenness."

The fall of Crete in May 1941 changed everything. Cyprus was
thought the next German target, and a defense had to be organized.
Fielding was drawn into the creation of a fake "Seventh Division"
whose presence on the island might deter the Germans. Numerous
regimental headquarters were made to communicate with one another in ways that German agents in Turkey were expected to notice. "Since all these phantom units were represented only by myself,
I spent most of every day travelling between them on a motor-bicycle
in order to put in an appearance at each."

It was Fielding's first taste of intelligence work, and it appealed—
both for its excitement and the relief from regimental chores. When
the threat to Cyprus passed in the wake of the German invasion of
Russia, he was offered a chance at real clandestine work on Crete.
In December 1942, he reported to the Cairo headquarters of the
SOE. The first question his new boss, Jack Smith-Hughes, asked
was "Have you any personal objection to committing murder?"

The SOE had been founded after the fall of France in 1940 to aid
the resistance movements of conquered Europe and to perform acts
of sabotage and propaganda. Smith-Hughes was captured during
the Battle of Crete. After escaping, he was hidden by Cretan guerillas in the fortress-like White Mountains and taken off the island by
submarine in August. In October, he was sent back to "feel out the
country to see who had influence." Having made preliminary contact with potential resistance leaders, he returned to Cairo and recruited men who could pass as Cretans. Fielding could not have
been better suited to the work and was landed on Crete on January
11, 1942.

His first task was to make contact with the two British officers
Smith-Hughes had left there with a wireless set, and then begin
organizing the evacuation of the British and Commonwealth soldiers still on the island. He also started building intelligence networks in the White Mountains and in the Canea region, especially
near the airfield at Maleme and the port at Souda Bay. By the time
Crete became the staging ground for the German Afrika Corps
offensives in the spring of 1942, Fielding's network was providing
constant reports to Cairo of the enemy supply chain and timetables.
The Germans certainly felt the weight of these activities—their new
airfield at Tymbaki was bombed by the R.A.F. "on the very day the
runways were completed."

German troops poured into the hills searching for the agents, and
Fielding played a tense cat-and-mouse game. He particularly enjoyed
visiting his networks in the towns and rubbing shoulders with the
enemy. Endless days of waiting and exhausting treks were punctuated by headlong flights to hideouts. In August, Fielding was taken
off Crete and had a month's leave in Syria and two weeks of parachute training. Returning to the island at the end of November, he
spent fourteen grueling months organizing the resistance to aid the
hoped-for Allied landings to liberate Greece.

Back in Cairo in January 1944, he was discouraged by what he
learned. He realized that "the Second Front would be opened in
Western Europe. Crete was therefore doomed to remain in enemy
hands until the end of the war, when the Germans stationed there
would simply lay down their arms." With an increasing distaste for
the internal politics of the Greek struggle—the communists and na-
tionalists were already beginning their civil war—and feeling that
his efforts in Crete had all been in vain, Fielding asked for transfer

to SOE France, where he hoped his native knowledge might be an asset. "Since I had been brought up in the South of France and knew the language and the country from childhood, I had little hope of being accepted," he wrote, reflecting on the surreal habits of army bureaucracy. "To my surprise, however, I was."

There followed his misadventure in Digne and rescue by Christine Granville. In 1945, he spent two more months in Greece (seeing the liberation of Athens and revisiting Crete), all the while growing disenchanted with the postwar settling of scores and the failure of resistance heroes to be rewarded as opportunists gained power. (The new local leader appointed in Vaphes, where Fielding had long been headquartered on Crete, was a man so afraid of the Germans that he had threatened to inform them of Fielding's presence in the village.) Like many SOE veterans, Fielding then transferred east where the war against Japan continued, and he saw brief service in Indochina. Short stints in occupied Germany and as an observer at the postwar elections in Greece and the Balkans brought his military career to an end. He held the rank of major.

Demobbed, Fielding fit no better into metropolitan life than he had in the 1930s. A last attempt at university failed—at Oxford, where he chafed at English strictures. A job on the Express newspapers was even less congenial. These were years of wild parties in London. Fielding and Fermor shared an apartment above the Heywood Hill bookstore and could be found nightly drunk with the likes of Dylan Thomas and Stephen Spender, the painters Ben Nicholson and Lucien Freud, and the philosopher Freddie Ayer. Barbara Skelton, soon to marry Cyril Connolly, noted in her diary in 1950, "Xan dislikes any form of work more than most. What a pity he can't be kept by the state for doin' nothin'." He had appeared on her doorstep that morning to borrow a typewriter, as he had a job helping with an Egyptian's memoirs.

Fielding placed an ad in the *London Times* of July 31, 1950: "Tough but sensitive ex-classical scholar, ex-secret agent, ex-guerrilla leader, 31, recently reduced to penury through incompatibility with the post-war world: Mediterranean lover, gambler, and general dabbler: fluent French and Greek speaker, some German, inevitable Italian: would do anything unreasonable and unexpected if sufficiently rewarding and legitimate."

In 1951–52, he returned to Crete to revisit his wartime haunts, and his wanderings resulted in a pioneering travel book, *The Strong-*

hold: Four Seasons in the White Mountains of Crete (1953). It's a documentary-like record of days among Cretan peasants blended with history and literature. *Hide and Seek*, a vibrant account of his SOE service, followed the next year and is a classic of World War II literature.

He married Daphne on July 11, 1953. They first lived in Cornwall before a long sojourn in Tangier. *Corsair Country* (1958) recounts a journey from Tangier to Tripoli in search of traces of the Barbary Pirates—"a year driving slowly," Fielding called it. It's another blend of history and encounters with a local culture, this time focused on the "unchanging and perhaps unchangeable qualities of North Africa." Fielding found immense interest in the meeting of Islam, colonialism, and modernity. The strict Islam of Djerba was welcome, for instance, for discouraging the riff-raff who attached themselves to all tourists. At the trip's end, Fielding admitted—"at the risk of appearing a chauvinistic Pharisee"—that "after these months spent in the shadow of Islam I've never before been so conscious and proud of my European and Christian background."

There followed six years in Portugal before the Fieldings finally settled in Uzès, in southern France, when they thought they would finally receive the proceeds of a protracted lawsuit. The Fielding family property in Nice had been misappropriated when the Corniche road was expanded, but the suit dragged on endlessly. The couple had to mortgage their house and work to keep afloat. He became a prolific translator of popular novels from the French, most famously Pierre Boulle's *Planet of the Apes* and *The Bridge on the River Kwai* and Jean Larteguy's *The Centurions* and *The Praetorians*; Daphne wrote her memoirs and a novel (the roman-à-clef-like *The Adonis Garden* featuring a very Xan-like hero and a particularly barbed portrait of Cyril Connolly). He also worked during this time on his history of the casino in Monte Carlo, *The Money Spinner* (1977)—a subject the inveterate gambler in Fielding greatly enjoyed.

In 1978, he and Daphne divorced, and he married Magouche the following year. They lived in Andalusia, and his last decade was spent on a biography of his wartime comrade Billy Maclean—whose SOE career in the Mideast and Albania was out of a John Buchan novel—an edition of the letters of Gerald Brenan and Ralph Partridge (two more friends and Bloomsbury stalwarts both), and a personal study of the winds in myth, *Aeolus Displayed*. (It appeared in German in 1988 and was privately printed in English in 1991.)

Fielding was stricken with cancer in 1991, but he was able to travel to Crete in May for the celebrations of the fiftieth anniversary of the battle. He spent ten days visiting wartime comrades and, with six other Allied officers, was awarded the Greek commemorative medal of the resistance. He died three months later on August 19. "Xan Fielding," Fermor wrote in a memorial, "was a gifted, many-sided, courageous and romantic figure, at the same time civilized and Bohemian, and his thoughtful cast of mind was leavened by humour, spontaneous gaiety and a dash of recklessness. Almost any stretch of his life might be described as a picaresque interlude." Magouche and Fermor carried his ashes to Crete.

The biographer Roger Jinkinson describes meeting Magouche in 2008: "I asked if anyone was writing her biography and she put me carefully in my place: 'No, I appear in other peoples'.'" The statement would be equally true of her husband, who has brilliant cameos in books about figures as diverse as Lawrence Durrell, Dirk Bogarde, and Bruce Chatwin.

Fielding met Bogarde in 1957 during the filming of the movie of *Ill Met by Moonlight.* The actor was cast as Fermor in the depiction of the wartime kidnapping of General Heinrich Kreipe in Crete, and Fielding had been hired as the technical adviser. Expecting a stern military hero, Bogarde at first avoided any meeting, but they became fast friends. Filming done, Bogarde and his partner and the Fieldings drove north for Paris together. They stopped for the night in Digne at a favorite hotel of Bogarde's. It was only at dinner that Fielding mentioned that the building next door to the hotel was the one where he had been held awaiting execution during the war. Bogarde was shocked and apologetic, but Fielding dismissed the concern: "I don't mind a bit. In fact I'm glad to be back here in such different circumstances. After all this time. Twelve years . . . Good heavens, it's twelve years exactly, to the very day!"

"This calls for a bottle of champagne," said Bogarde.

Foreword

by Robert Messenger

GEOGRAPHY WAS the key. In 1945, C. M. Woodhouse, who led the resistance forces in occupied Greece during World War II, declared, "Nothing matters so much in this story as the Greek mountains. The rolling downs of Olympus, the precipitous ravines of Agrapha, the orchards of Pelion, the staggering crags of Smolikas, the long, thin ridge of Taygetos, the pine forests of Giona, are almost individual characters in the story, their roles perpetually changed by sun and snow and rain. Without them no guerilla movement could have been born." He was writing of mainland Greece, where he had headed the Allied mission, but Woodhouse had also been part of the first Special Operations Executive mission to Greece—to Crete in October 1941, where the question of whether British officers could operate under the Nazi yoke was answered affirmatively thanks to the White Mountains.

Xan Fielding joined Woodhouse in Crete in January 1942. The twenty-three-year-old, Greek-speaking lieutenant first saw the island in a full gale from a submarine off the south-central coast. He was being landed at Treis Ekklisies, tasked with building intelligence networks in the western part of the island and supporting the local resistance. He spent twenty-one of the next twenty-four months living in various hideouts in the White Mountains—caves were the most popular, but in the summer he happily slept in an orchard for many weeks. It was a time of close escapes from German soldiers and long treks through the rugged landscape.

Fielding formed intense friendships on the island, and when the war ended (he had also served in France and Indochina), he longed to return: "Although I must have tramped several thousands of miles during the three years I was there, I felt I had taken in less of the countryside than an observant visitor would in the course of three weeks." A decade after he landed in that gale, he returned to Crete planning to spend a year seeing the places he knew only furtively and to write a book about the mountain fastness that had kept him safe.

Crete is an island of four parts: Lasithi in the east, Herakleion (taking its name from the capital) in the center, Retimo with the heights of Mount Ida, and farthest west, Canea, which holds the high massif that is the White Mountains. Fielding titled his book *The Stronghold*, for these mountains form a semicircular "walled city rising from plains that fringe its circumference, with the sea as a moat along its diameter." There are only a small number of entrances into this fortress, and Fielding "planned to use them all in turn before leaving Crete."

While Crete is central to classical mythology—the birthplace of Zeus, for instance, and the home of the Minotaur—Fielding was not interested in its ancient history or archaeology. He was interested in the island's relations with the dominant modern powers of the eastern Mediterranean: Venice and the Ottoman Turks. When the Roman Empire was divided in the third century, Crete came under Byzantine control. There followed an age of Christianization and church-building—though witnessing a christening in the early 1950s, Fielding felt certain that "anyone with doubts about the pagan source of peasant Christianity should attend an Orthodox feast." By the twelfth century, Crete was a pawn in the rivalry between Byzantium and the rising power of Venice. When crusaders sacked Constantinople in 1204, the Venetians (who were funding the campaign) claimed Crete. They held sway for four and a half centuries.

Rebellion is the Cretan's hobby—Fielding found the island's history "mainly a chronicle of alternating phases of insurrection and retribution, as repetitive and indigestible as a pickled onion." And the revolts began in the White Mountains. The Cretans rose frequently against their Italian overlords. They were just as difficult for their Ottoman rulers. (The all-conquering Turks landed on the island in 1645, though it wasn't until 1715 that the last Venetian redoubts fell.) Crete remained under Ottoman control when Greece gained independence in 1832. Huge revolts in 1889, 1895, and 1897 brought Britain, France, and Russia to intervene and free Crete. But not until 1913 was the island finally recognized as part of Greece. The credit goes to Eleftherios Venizelos, who went on to become the founding father of the modern Greek state. Born just outside of Canea, Venizelos is still revered in Crete (and himself took refuge in the White Mountains when he was declared an outlaw in 1901).

This is the history that interests Fielding in *The Stronghold*, and he searches out the places associated with the major revolts and their leaders, trying to understand the resilience of these islanders in the face of two millennia of invaders. "The people and the soil seem to have conspired against construction and preservation. Villages razed to the ground in war have been repeatedly re-built, only to be destroyed again by disastrous earthquakes which have shaken the island almost as frequently as the numerous insurrections against foreign oppression." Yet, for all his explication of the island's history, Fielding is traveling at a time of transition. He cannot but notice how much life is changing in the mountains. These were shepherds for hundreds of years, but during the war too many of the flocks disappeared, "stolen by thieves when their owners were away at the war, or confiscated and commandeered by the Germans; or . . . slaughtered to provide food for Allied missions such as mine." Without money to replace what was lost, men headed to the plains and coasts for work. The mountain life was passing away.

Fielding records it from personal experience. He dosses down in any old spot, on a roof or terrace, endures the bites of fleas and bedbugs whenever he finds the mild comfort of a bed, and uses the bushes as plumbing. ("The place," as the Cretans call it, is kept clean by pigs, though in Souyia on the coast, chickens are used and "proved to be equally enthusiastic scavengers and forced me to straighten up with literally indecent haste in order to get out of range of their beaks.") He enjoys the old customs: Soap is "never handed directly by one person to another for fear of its washing away friendship between them." Napkins must not be refolded at table, which would insult the host. A woman who has recently given birth must not cross her neighbors' threshold for forty days or their wine will turn to vinegar. A child whimpering "fretfully" at the nocturnal intrusion of guests is ignored and, "realizing that it could not make its voice heard above ours, went to sleep again." Fathers with too many daughters are almost literally starved to death as they use more and more of their land for dowries—they are "a curse which, more slowly than a plague of locusts but just as inexorably, devours all his crops." Fielding meets a priest whose wife has died young and so has been condemned to celibacy, as the Orthodox church forbids re-marriage. "For him, then, sex was not a closed book but something far more frustrating: a book that had been confiscated when he was less than halfway through it."

It is a primitive life, and Fielding revels in it. Welcomed into a cheese-maker's hut high on the plateau of Omalo, he recognizes how "The smoke and glare of the flames at once transformed this simple interior, heightening the air of mystery which always surrounds—at least, so it seems to me—such elemental activities as bread-baking or cheese-making. Bread, the symbol of life; and the miracle of milk—I was more than ever conscious of their mystic significance in the fire-lit atmosphere of the hut, compounded of church and clinic and laboratory; I felt that I was attending a divine service, assisting at a birth and witnessing a chemical experiment at one and the same time."

He was joined on some parts of the trip by his future wife Daphne, who wanted to photograph the places he had told her about. In her memoirs, she remembered steep climbs up to remote villages and the shrugging replies she got to her queries about where they might be spending the night. "With my godbrother" was Fielding's standard reply. And everywhere they went, they received a warm welcome punctuated by round after round of drinks and the death sentence of a chicken or two. "For during the war, when he organized the resistance movement in this area, he . . . stood as godfather to countless baptisms—a position which in the Orthodox Church bound him and the parents of the child he christened closely together in a sacred and eternal union."

Their arrival brings no surprise in these remote villages and requires no advance warning. Heading into Ayia Roumeli in search of an old comrade, Fielding asks directions at the first house, only to be told that there were "three or four" men of that name in the village. He describes his friend, and the old woman reports it is her nephew but that he's away in Canea. "In his absence," she insists, "we must do our duty to his friends." Drinks and chairs are set out for the visitors, but the next person to appear is the very friend Fielding was told was away. His description had confused two cousins. Even so, the old woman insists the guests remain in her house, and she feeds them delicious food—"pancakes filled with cream-cheese floating in honey." The accommodations Fielding finds are almost always on the down side of spartan, but "wine and weariness are twin guarantees of deep sleep: under any condition; and we had plenty of both."

Yet there is more to Fielding's welcome than just the Cretan tradition of hospitality. There is an air of anticipation. He is greeted by wartime companions who assume they will soon again be called upon to fight. (The Greek civil war had only ended in 1949, with the nationalist victory over the communists.) The banal café conversations that begin "What do you think about the situation?" or "What are the Russians up to?" are indications of "expectancy for the next war to come."

Many are also certain he can help them in some official capacity: with a family member arrested or with a pension for wartime service. In Canea, the endless arguments over who had actually headed the resistance (and so could vouch for the activities of any individual) had led the government to deny service pensions to everyone. It is assumed that Fielding can fix this. He protests his lack of influence, and when he tries writing a letter to the editor calling attention to the pension injustice, he manages only to enrage those he fails to mention by name. As a friend tells him, "You tried to make the Sign of the Cross and all you've done is poke your own eyes out."

The Cretans generally refuse to believe that Fielding isn't still working for the British government—writing a book is just too absurd a reason to have traveled from London to Crete in the early 1950s—and they grow suspicious. "[P]eople, who had remembered me as an officer with apparently unlimited funds, now saw me return as a civilian whose purse was quite clearly restricted—a highly suspicious transformation!" They persist in calling his trip a "mission," and "since they would not believe in my inability to help them, they concluded that I was denying them assistance simply out of laziness or malice."

Far more intolerable, though, is the lack of independence or solitude. "There was no way of dealing with the villagers' aggressive friendship, except to submit to it; completely in their hands, I sometimes felt that I was their prisoner. Nor was there any way of returning their hospitality, no chance of standing them a second round—money could buy nothing where there was nothing for sale. Companionship was all that one had to offer; and they could never have enough of it." The Cretans value talk above all else, but not in its variety, simply in its existence. At times, Fielding finds it hard

"to spend whole days in a crowded room cheek-by-jowl with people whose only recreation was eternal talk, talk confined to political
discussions, war-time reminiscences and peasant humor. . . . Silence
was never golden; not a moment for reading or reflection."

He and Daphne hope to see the Chapel of St. Paul, supposedly
sinking due to erosion, on the coast between Ayia Roumeli and
Loutro. It acts as a grail for many chapters. But it is Loutro, a town
Fielding had not known during the war, that is the revelation. They
are housed by the kindly proprietor of the local café, where they
have some privacy and where no effort is made to entertain them.
The population of the seaside town is made up of "charming idlers."
Only one man even bothers to fish, and the English couple are
allowed to swim and read and sit silent without comment. It is "an
attitude to life unique in Crete," Fielding believes, and he is "disturbed to find that I much preferred it to the more primitive peasant outlook which I had hitherto romantically championed. I began
to have doubts about the bliss of an Arcadia uncontaminated by
the touch of civilization." He is ten years older and discovering how
much has changed in him since the war, how different life seems
without the presence of danger.

His journey ends in Kallikrati, where he exits the White Mountains through the last of the gateways as he heads north to Canea
and England. He spends his final night in the hut of another cheese-
maker, a friend from the war now on the lam from the Greek police
rather than German soldiers. It's an ordinary night in every way, but
Fielding finds it "charged with a different, deeper meaning. . . . Sentimentality, provoked by impending departure, had blunted my critical faculty." He longs for all the things that have bored him over the
last year. The Crete that had haunted him since the war's end has
"given place to reality; the ghost had been laid in the daylight of tangible fact." But as he prepares to leave, the "phantom" has returned,
"even before the darkness of absence and distance had fallen."

The Stronghold is one in a long line of English travel books about
Greece—the country has loomed large in the English imagination
since Lord Byron died in 1824 aiding the Greek struggle against
Ottoman rule. Robert Byron (who, though no relation of the poet,
found the name stood him in good stead in Greece) was the most
influential English Hellenophile in modern times. In books like *The
Station* (1928), *The Byzantine Achievement* (1929), and *The Birth of
Western Painting* (1930), he put forth a new interpretation of the

Aegean world, one that stressed the Byzantine ages over the classical ones and invented a semi-mystical form of travelogue that mixes history, culture, and personal experience. He was a heavy influence on postwar travel writing, and his two greatest heirs, Lawrence Durrell and Patrick Leigh Fermor, were also Fielding's two greatest friends. But while *The Stronghold* wanders among history and culture—and certainly reflects Byron with its stress on Byzantium, Venice, and the Ottoman Turks—it is different in both tone and artistry.

Byron's was an upper-class world, one of elegance and intellect, and there is much of this in both Durrell's and Fermor's books. *The Stronghold* is an account of peasant life. Fielding did not glamorize days and weeks without running water, rudimentary plumbing, or beds. He is plagued by the same fleas in peacetime as he was during the war. Roads vanish due to the rains and rockslides. The diet is unvaried. The Cretans he goes to see are mostly uneducated and incurious about any history beyond their own doorstep. The book remains an outstanding picture, for Fielding was truly welcome in these homes. The hours are spent in conversation circles that, with the constant rounds of drinking, become song contests and eventually lead to guns being fired off in sheer joy of life. These are not the days of a visitor, but of a brother.

Fielding, moreover, made no attempt to shape his material into a larger story. This is where his book diverges from the artful casualness of Byron's books and from the even more innovative type of travel book that Fermor and Bruce Chatwin (another friend of Fielding's) would pioneer in the 1960s and 1970s. In these, the traveler's experience is filtered and edited and improved, drawing on cultural sources to build out an idealized journey of self-realization. Fermor and Chatwin were dramatists in search of the telling scene. Either would have made much of the moment in Asi Gonia when Fielding pours over a photograph of his wartime comrades, unable to name one of them. "In this unpleasant portrait of an unpleasant person I seemed to recognize someone whom I had known years before." His future wife "loyally" refuses to believe he could ever have looked like that, while his Cretan friend despairs at his new, clean-shaven look: "You've certainly deteriorated." It is a scene that, written twenty-five years later, would have formed the denouement of the book. But for Fielding it is just a passing moment.

The Stronghold is a signpost toward *In Patagonia* and *A Time of Gifts* (both 1977), blending in history and culture with experience, but one wedded to fidelity. Fielding never arrives; there is no great journey of self. There is just a question answered about the war and youth. He is a different man ten years later. But he can't shake Crete, as no man can shake the formative experience of his youth. The mayor of Anopolis replies when Fielding tries to thank him for "an additional crowning gesture of hospitality": "'Words are superfluous; the only way you can thank us is by coming to stay with us again.'"

Preface

The rocky southern shores of Crete advance in luminous
salients and recede again in dark grottoes where the goats'
eyes flash; roofed by the asbestos-white limestone sierras of
Sphakia. Those toppling iconographic crags are the world of
minotaurs and the blood feud, of thorns and twisted goat-
horns and fierce epics and daemonic energy . . .

Patrick Leigh Fermor

I FIRST SAW CRETE on the 12th of January, 1942, through the
periscope of a submarine.

The strip of cliff visible in the lens was magnified to such an extent, the texture of its stone was so apparent, that it seemed within
arm's reach; I imagined I only had to stretch out my hand and touch
those rocks to know how they would feel under my fingers. Yet this
first sight of the island was as unsatisfactory and disconcerting as a
telescopic view of the moon or a high-altitude aerial photograph. It
needed interpretation. I had been told by the submarine-commander
that this was "my beach"; I was to land there in a few hours' time, as
soon as it was dark. I took another look and tried to picture myself
landing there in the dark, but what I could see was no more inspir-
ing than an old-fashioned lantern-slide illustrating a lecture on geology, entirely unrelated in my mind to the enemy-occupied territory
into which I was to be secretly infiltrated.

My war-time experience in Crete could not have been very different from that of other agents operating elsewhere in Greece; I un-
derwent the same danger, discomfort and disappointment, enjoyed
the same stimulation and excitement, formed the same friendships.
But war-time fun and tragedy were not all that Crete had to offer;
the appeal of the island persisted long after the war was over and

1

I found myself, constantly and almost desperately, anxious to return there.

It was not a sentimental pilgrimage that I wanted to make. I had not the mourner's yearning to visit the grave of a loved one, nor even the murderer's urge to return to the scene of his crime. My reason for wanting to see Crete again was, I think, more prosaic; it was simply that my experience of the island, being limited to war-time, was inevitably incomplete, and irritating me like an unfinished sentence or a catechetical question which could only be answered by a return visit in time of peace.

I had left Crete in 1945, when it was still in a state of exception caused by the German occupation, a state which brought out to an astonishing degree the reckless hospitality for which its inhabitants are renowned. But I had known those inhabitants only on a temporary, artificial basis, as a commander knows his troops, or an ambassador the country in which he happens to be serving. (Literally so; for although I was a junior officer with no diplomatic training when I first went to Crete, the fact of my being an Allied representative gave me an inflated position of importance which was out of all proportion to my natural qualifications or practical experience.) I had known the Cretans, at best, as a comrade-in-arms; I wanted to know them, if possible, as a fellow-citizen.

In the same way, I had only seen the island when I was in a state of exception myself. Although I must have tramped several thousands of miles during the three years I was there, I felt I had taken in less of the countryside than an observant visitor would in the course of three weeks; for I had usually been too busy and travelling too fast to look at the landscape; and when I had noticed it, it had been for tactical reasons rather than for pleasure. It was to remedy these deficiencies in my knowledge of Crete that I wished to return to the island, and particularly to that part of it where I had spent most of my three years' service and which I knew best: the White Mountains. My wish was eventually granted; thanks to my publishers, I was back in those mountains exactly ten years after I had first seen them.

On a small-scale map of Crete the altitude tints representing the main mountain features form three distinct geometrical patterns: a rough circle for the Lassithi range in the eastern prefecture of the same name; a rectangle which is nearly a square for Mount Ida on the boundary between the two central prefectures of Herakleion and Rethymnon; and an almost perfect semicircle for the White Mountains in the western prefecture of Canea.

This semi-circle includes the whole of the province of Sphakia; its diameter is the thirty miles of southern coast stretching eastwards from Souyia; its circumference runs through the neighbouring Canea provinces of Selino in the west, Kydonia and Apokoronas in the north, and along the borders between Canea and Rethymnon in the east. Looking at the map and studying the contours in relation to these geographical boundaries, one gets the impression that the mountains were originally intended to be confined within the limits of Sphakia but, through sheer weight and power, burst these bounds and overflowed into the adjoining provinces, spilling their rocky content into the chestnut-plantations and vineyards, the orange- and olive-groves of the surrounding fertile plains.

The current *Guide Bleue* to Greece, which devotes twenty-five pages to Crete, dismisses Sphakia in three lines: "*Cette province est la plus sauvage de la Crète et n'a jamais été entièrement soumise par les Vénitiens ni par les Turcs; c'est là que se sont le mieux conservées les anciennes traditions crétoises.*" This area, in fact, contains no Knossos to attract the tourist. It has, however, sometimes attracted more serious travellers, particularly naturalists. As early as 1422 a Florentine priest, Buondelmonte, came back from Crete with accounts of a fabulous "moon herb" which gilded the teeth of the sheep feeding on it; and the new horizons opened up later by the discovery of America inspired travellers to examine and study other distant lands, including those of the Near East which had been a closed book to naturalists since the time of Pliny. A few, but very few, of these scientists and scholars penetrated into the White Mountains, and their visit sometimes provided a small part of the material for the various *Voyages*, *Travels*, *Researches*, *Descriptions*, *Peregrinations* and *Rambles* which loaded the bookshelves of Western Europe from the sixteenth to the nineteenth centuries. But these were isolated chapters; and even the tide of less learned travel books which has flooded the public libraries during the present century has so far failed to wash up a single volume devoted to this area.

I am not surprised. No traveller has spent sufficient time in the White Mountains to give an adequate account of them; they are too wild for the lotus-eater in search of the womb-pocket atmosphere which is usually associated with Mediterranean islands, too tame for the zealot in search of physical adventure. What is surprising is that their inhabitants, particularly the Sphakians, have escaped the notice of the social anthropologist. Almost every reference to them gives a tantalizing hint of an ethnological group which would repay closer study. No one has taken the hint.

The field is still clear. This book of mine does not claim to be a serious sociological work; it is simply the account of a more or less carefree year spent among people who seem to fit so perfectly into their startling surroundings that at times I imagined it was not the landscape that had conditioned their lives but their personalities that had conditioned the landscape. I cannot myself regard them as objects for scientific observation; this would demand a cold and calculated approach. My view of them is subjective, and no doubt biased, since their friendship has infected me with their own uninhibited enthusiasm and tendency to exaggerate. But it is no exaggeration to say that whenever I think of them, they appear to me larger than life in their isolation, occupying in the human race the same unique and inaccessible position as the ibex[1] holds in the animal kingdom or dittany in the world of plants.

———

My thanks, then, are chiefly due to the villagers of Crete, but to so many of them that I cannot mention all by name; nor can I single out a few since I am equally indebted to each, both for the hospitality they lavished on me in their homes and for the material they unconsciously provided in themselves. The main contributors to the making of this book must therefore remain anonymous.

1. Since I shall refer elsewhere to this animal (*capra aegagrus*) I feel I should at the outset forestall the criticism of any zoological purist who might question my terminology. I am told that what is known in Crete today as the *agrimi* cannot properly be called an ibex, this genus being limited to the Alps, the Caucasus, Persia and Upper Egypt. But even professional naturalists seem incapable of deciding on a name for it: in France alone it has at various times been described as *bouc estain* (Belon), *chèvre sauvage* (Tournefort) and *bouquetin*. Pashley plays safe by referring to it as "wild goat"; Spratt compromises by qualifying "ibex" with the epithet "Cretan." In the face of such expert disagreement I trust a layman like myself may be allowed his own version, however inaccurate. So many so-called tame goats strike me as being wild that I am disinclined to adopt Pashley's term, while to insist on the qualification "Cretan" in a book about Crete seems to me redundant. I shall stick to "ibex," plain and simple.

More objective contributions came from Canea, the capital, and for these I am particularly indebted to Manoussos Manoussakis, Petros Hadzidakis, Yiannis Vandoulas and Mercy Seiradaki, all of whom provided valuable suggestions and advice. I also record my gratitude to Michael Botonakis, Curator of the Historical Archives, and to his staff.

In Athens, my greatest debt is to George Katsimbalis and Thanos Veloudios, both of them apparently inexhaustible mines of incidental information; and to Dr. Shirley Webber of the Gennadeion Library.

While I was still in Crete, and even before I went there, I received much considerate help from various people in England. Professor Richard Dawkins, Sir John Myres and Sir Harold Nicolson generously provided material which was hitherto unknown to me and kindly consented to let me incorporate the results of their learning and experience in this book. Michael Powell put at my disposal his unpublished diary of a recent journey to Crete, and Louis MacNeice gave me permission to include his expert translation of the songs quoted in the first chapter. To all of these I gratefully acknowledge my debt and record my thanks, while remembering with particular warmth my obligation to Patrick Leigh Fermor who, as a source of encouragement, stands in a category of his own.

Special thanks are due to my travelling companions on the island: to Anthony Baynes, then Director of the English School in Canea, and to Hugh Farmar, a visiting friend from England, each of whom accompanied me on a long march through the mountains which, on both occasions, was over all too soon. But if thanks can be measured in terms of distance covered, then most of mine are due to Daphne Bath who, in order to take the photographs which illustrate this book, twice flew out to Crete and patiently put up with continual discomfort and occasional boredom for mile after mile and for months on end.

This list of creditors would be incomplete without the names of those who facilitated the actual writing of this book. Last, then, but by no means least of those to whom I am gratefully indebted, are Mary and Robin Campbell and Malcolm Munthe.

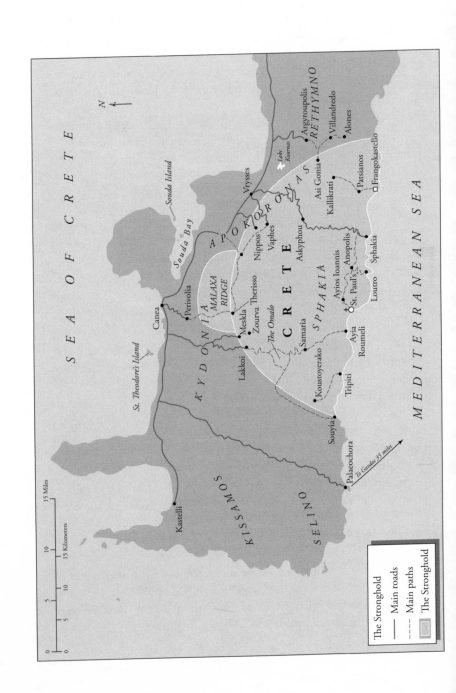

SEA OF CRETE

Souda Island

Souda Bay

St. Theodore's Island

Canea

Perivolia

KYDONIA

Lakkoi

Kastelli

KISSAMOS

SELINO

Palaeochora

Souyia

Koustoyerako

Tripiti

Ayia Roumeli

Samaria

The Omalo

Meskla

Zourva Therisso

MALAXA RIDGE

APOKORONAS

Vrysses

Lake Kournas

Nippos

Vaphes

Askyphou

CRETE

SPHAKIA

Ayios Ioannis

St. Paul's

Anopolis

Sphakia

Loutro

Asi Gonia

Kallikrati

Argyroupolis

RETHYMNO

Villandredo

Alones

Patsianos

Frangokastello

MEDITERRANEAN SEA

N

15 Miles

15 Kilometers

To Gavdos 35 miles

The Stronghold

——— Main roads

– – – Main paths

▢ The Stronghold

PART ONE

Summer–Autumn

The wildest and most picturesque part of the coast of Crete commences to the eastward of Suia; for the roots of the Omalo Mountains, and also those of the higher group of the Madara Vouna or White Mountains, following them to the eastward, press upon the shore here in remarkably bold and precipitous ridges, which are separated or cleft by deep valleys and steep gorges that are almost inaccessible except by sea.

Spratt

I

SOUYIA

LOOKING AT THE skyline from Canea, I felt as a housebreaker must feel when he studies for the first time by day the front of a building which he once entered by a back window at night. The façade was familiar, not because I had seen it before but because I had been behind it, inside, and so knew that its external appearance could not be otherwise. Here was the main entrance to the mountains: over the rock-green ridge which half concealed the range as neatly as a garden wall, or across the cultivated plain which flanked it on either side. I preferred a less orthodox approach and decided to sail straight into the highlands from the sea by landing on the south coast.

I hardly expected to recapture the sensations of my war-time landing, when the smell of wild herbs was wafted from the midnight-shrouded cliffs towards the collapsible canoe I was paddling a mile off-shore; but I did hope somehow to create an artificial channel between Sphakia and the rest of Crete, so that in reaching the White Mountains by boat I would have the same pleasure that I always feel when reaching the Continent from England. I therefore planned to make for Palaeochora[1] as one might for Dover, and from

---

1. I do not believe there is any set rule for transliterating Greek names. If there is, I certainly have not followed it. I have simply tried to retain as closely as possible the sound of the Greek while simultaneously guarding against too outlandish an appearance in the English spelling. On War Office maps *Palaeochora* is written

there take a caique to Souyia, the nearest point on the coast where the mountains meet the sea.

I did not give much thought as to how I was to get there—I assumed it would be by bus—since I was not particularly interested in this part of the journey; in fact I was prepared to sleep all the way. I wanted to avoid a gradual re-introduction to the Cretan landscape; to close my eyes to the villages and villagers encountered on the road; and to wake up to the full impact of the Crete that I knew best by remaining unconscious until I was in the mountains of the south. I almost succeeded, even though I did not board a bus and fall asleep. Instead, I was invited to accompany the five local Liberal candidates on an electioneering drive which would take me to my destination.

We left Canea early in the morning. By midday I was sufficiently comatose not to notice the details of the drive: we had stopped at every village en route, where each candidate had delivered a speech while I had drunk his health in *tsikoudia*.[2] I have a faint recollection of luncheon under a plane tree where the *tsikoudia* was supplemented by beakers of blunt red wine. We stopped at other villages throughout the afternoon—more speeches were made, more *tsikoudia* was drunk—and at dusk attended a baptism, about which I remember nothing save that the child who was to be totally immersed in the font was a boy of five who was shy of appearing naked in public and kept screaming for his trousers. It was almost dawn by the time we reached the end of the road and settled down to sleep on the floor of a crowded room overlooking a sandy beach.

The promontory which pierces the sea at Palaeochora must have delighted the Venetian engineers who fortified it in 1282; it is an almost perfect archetype of the characteristic heart-shaped Venetian bastion. Yet for all its natural defences Fort Selino, as Palaeochora was then called, was completely destroyed by Barbarossa[3] in

---

Palaiokhora—an accurate enough rendering but clumsy to look at; moreover this system, if universally applied, would make *archaeology* read *arkhaiology*. The problem of transliterating the name of the capital of Crete does not arise: *Canea*, like *Munich*, is an established anglicism.

2. The local name for raki, similar to the *tsipouro* of Epirus, which is distilled from what is left of the grape after it has been pressed for wine.

3. The name given by the Christians to Khizr and Hassan Khair-ed-Din. This note is for the benefit of those who persist in confusing the Turkish pirate with the Holy Roman Emperor, Frederick I, who was known to the Italians by the same name.

1559. For the next three centuries the promontory, like the rest of
the Selino coast, remained deserted, the fine summer roadstead and
anchorage in the bays on either side being used only by successive
fleets of Turkish, Maltese and Algerine pirates based on the island
of Gavdos. By 1890 a handful of fishermen—the statistics for that
year give their number as 39—had settled at the foot of the old
Venetian walls; today Palaeochora is the largest, and ugliest, village
in the province. The level summit where the fort once stood is as
bare as it ever was—more bare indeed than fifty years ago, for what
remained then of the ruins of the fort has since been used as building material for the modern houses lining the main road, the road
to which the village owes its present-day existence. This kilometre-
long strip of grim grey stone is, I believe, the only example of rib-
bon-development in the whole of the Cretan countryside. I was glad
to leave it.

My hangover began to lift as soon as the caique started, despite
the miasma of Diesel oil which rose from the deck a few inches
under my nose as I lay flat on my stomach watching the coast. Eastwards the sand of the bay gave place to a low ridge of rock which in
the heat-haze shimmered and slithered over the waterline like mercury under pressure; above, but apparently not beyond it, hung a
sun-bleached backcloth of mist and hill. As suddenly as the beach
ended the backcloth vanished. Cliffs, which seemed to drop from
the sky rather than rise from the sea, intervened as effectively as
a safety-curtain and the view was protected by a palisade of stone
which, less distant now and shaded by itself, brazenly displayed its
structure and tincture. A few miles further on this barrier came to
an abrupt end. Like a motor-car turning a blind corner, the caique
nosed inland round a sharp angle of the cliffs; and I found myself
facing Souyia bay.

The sight of the shingle crescent caused a pang of recognition, the
first I had felt since my return. Yet I had never before been inside
the bay. I only remembered that it was visible from a certain spot in
the mountains where I had once stopped during the war; so now,
even though I could not pick out that spot from the sea, I knew by
heart more than by eye that I was near it. Memory merged the past
into the present and, although I was conscious of my body flattened
against the deck and throbbing to the movement of the engine as
we approached the shore, in imagination I was sitting on the hillside overlooking the same shore, surrounded by the Selino guerillas.

And so it seemed quite natural to find them surrounding me again as soon as I landed; it never occurred to me to ask how they came to be there to meet me; I had long ago ceased to wonder at the workings of their grape-vine telegraph. Their leader, Vasilis Paterakis, was the first to step forward and kiss me on both cheeks, with the ceremonial greeting:

"It is well you have come."

"It is well I have found you," I replied.

"So you have remembered us?"

I avoided a direct answer to his question for, apart from Vasilis and his brothers, I could not remember any of the others by name, though their faces were all familiar. (I have one of those capricious memories on which anyone I meet leaves an indelible, but unsigned, impression of his features; the portrait lasts forever while the sitter remains unidentified.)

"I have never forgotten Crete," I said; and embraced them all in turn.

As we moved from the water's edge towards the single row of houses fifty yards inland, the inevitable question was put to me: "What news?" These two words, in Greek, are charged with undertones of meaning which are lost in the cool formality of the English phrase. I realised that the curiosity of my companions could not much longer be held in check by their natural courtesy; they were longing to discover, without asking, why I had come back. I explained that I wanted to write a book about them.

"You have done well to come first to our parts," said Vasilis.

Once again I divined a deeper significance in his words. It did indeed seem logical to come first to this western corner of the range before moving eastwards through the mountains—as logical as starting at the beginning of a line and reading from left to right—but I felt this was not what Vasilis had in mind. By "our parts" he meant the broad valley behind Souyia, which contracts into a narrow gorge a short distance inland and leads to Moni, Livadas and Koustoyerako. These three villages were the backbone of the Selino resistance movement throughout the occupation; and all three paid a heavy price for their heroism. On the 28th of September 1943 they were burnt to the ground in a German punitive expedition and, while the women and children took refuge with relatives outside the area, the men took to the hills to form the nucleus of the guerilla band which Vasilis eventually commanded.

"I could call on the men again," he now added, "tomorrow, if necessary."

Only then did I understand that for him, for all of them, the last war had not yet ended; or else a new war had already begun.

Like one or two other refugees from the burnt-out villages, Vasilis had left the mountains when the Germans left the island, and had come to live on the coast. Since then he had married, sired a son and become the owner of the coffee-shop[4] which catered for the fifteen other houses in the bay. He now wore trousers instead of breeches—a concession, no doubt, to his new occupation—but he still could never be taken for anything but a mountaineer, especially when in motion. Years of walking along uneven paths and over rough country where no paths exist had developed in him the necessary balance for bounding from stone to stone, which gave him a curiously stealthy gait on the flat. Yet he did not seem out of place in Souyia, where the foothills dwarf the beach; he was as well established there as any of its original inhabitants. His wife, Prokopia, had transformed the two rooms and terrace above the shop into a comfortable house; he had achieved the Cretan ambition of having a son-and-heir as his first child; and his business provided him with an adequate living. Even so he gave the impression of being unsettled, as though he was waiting for a signal to take to the hills again.

I noticed the same restlessness in everyone else I met as I sat outside Vasilis's shop talking to his customers; it was as if these men were living not as inhabitants of their own village but as displaced persons in a transit camp.

I woke up next morning as soon as the sun swept the shadow of the hills off my bed on the terrace. Vasilis was already downstairs.

"Come and have some coffee," he shouted when he heard me getting up.

4. I have purposely refrained from using the word *café*, which might conjure up a picture of striped awnings, Riviera parasols and marble-topped tables. The Cretan equivalent of such an establishment is even more uncomfortable and hideous than the average English pub and usually consists of a single white-washed room decorated with political posters, furnished with kitchen chairs and tables and equipped with a small charcoal stove for boiling coffee. Besides spirits, wine and cigarettes, it also sells anything from cotton-reels to playing-cards and, in the mountain villages at least, is generally referred to not as the *kapheneion* or *café*, but simply as the *magazi* or "shop."

"Just a minute," I answered, "I'm going outside."

"Then try the bushes over to the right."

What the Cretans euphemistically call "the place"—and this, in many villages, means "any place"—is normally kept clean by the pigs, which still perform their task, as Professor Raulin observed some eighty years ago, "*avec une prestesse incommode.*" There were no pigs in Souyia; but the chickens, which immediately invaded the clump of lentisk I had chosen, proved to be equally enthusiastic scavengers and forced me to straighten up with literally indecent haste in order to get out of range of their beaks.

By the time I got back the shop was beginning to fill up for the day. On an ancient pair of brass and iron scales, which must have been far heavier than any load that it had ever had to measure, Vasilis was weighing a pitifully small catch brought in by a crew of fishermen who did not look like fishermen; their bare calves protruded not from rolled-up seamen's jeans but, unnaturally, from the ends of breeches which seemed to be crying for a pair of boots to cover them. These were the limbs of mountaineers out of their element. After a quick cup of coffee I went off to explore the bay; I knew that if I stayed in the shop a moment longer I would find myself involved in conversation for the rest of the morning.

The smell outside, which I had not noticed before, gave me my first proper clue to Souyia. It was the sight of the catch being weighed, I suppose, that had prepared my nostrils for an effluvium of fish: instead I inhaled the sickly, unexpected sweetness of carob. It was the pungency of those beans drying in the sun which, more than anything else, more than the meagreness of the catch, more than the inefficiency of the crew, made me realize that although Souyia was on the sea it was not a seaside village.

The empty beach was littered with coils of wire netting which had once been intended for building purposes but had long ago rusted into uselessness; they had now become mere decoration, dissolute-looking maritime props, brittle replicas of the rust-coloured fishing-nets which should have been lying there instead. The only craft afloat was a small blue rowing-boat anchored in the shallows a few feet off-shore, in which an old man called Yiorgaki spent all his waking hours—and his sleeping hours as well, for at night he would put away the line he had been dangling over the side all day and curl up on the floor-boards until dawn. He was the one person in Souyia who seemed happy to be on the sea, and his happiness was reflected in the smile which he wore on his lips as permanently as the straw hat on his head.

"Caught anything?" I asked him.

"I have never caught anything," he cheerfully replied.

I had a similar conversation with another man whom I met a few minutes later in the untidy little plain immediately behind the village. He was carrying a shotgun, and his game-bag was as empty as old Yiorgaki's fishing-basket.

"We are doomed," he added, as though to explain his lack of success, "we are all doomed down here, completely cut off from the world in this out-of-the-way corner."

Like old Yiorgaki, he smiled quite proudly as he spoke, so that the words sounded more like a conventional phrase than a genuine complaint.

"Do you think there is still any treasure in Souyia?" he suddenly asked.

I told him that I had no idea.

"But all Englishmen know about treasure," he persisted.

I was delighted to have come across a man—and not even an old one—who still subscribed to the theory that every foreigner who visits Crete, whether he calls himself an archaeologist, a botanist or a butterfly-collector, is in reality a treasure-hunter in search of buried gold. He went on to tell me a story which, I suppose, only served to strengthen his belief.

"Some time ago an English man-of-war put into the bay. The captain and the officers came ashore and everyone turned out to welcome them. A terrific party started, for the Englishmen had brought with them a large barrel of rum, and everyone in Souyia was soon dead drunk. When they saw they had achieved their purpose, the officers signalled to the ship and presently a group of sailors, armed with picks and shovels, pulled into the shore. By the time the villagers had sobered up next morning, it was already too late. The Englishmen had left with the treasure they had dug up during the night."

"When did this happen?" I asked.

"Many years ago. Many, many years ago."

It was impossible to pin him down even to an approximate date. If his story was true in every detail the theft of the treasure must have occurred after 1885, for before then Souyia did not exist as a village, and therefore contained no villagers, drunk or otherwise. Robert Pashley, a Cambridge don who visited the bay in 1834, found only ruins; but in his search for antiquities he records: "I learn that, till a few years ago, there was here a large marble slab covered with an inscription. A kaík (*sic*) came and took it away." It would require little effort of the imagination to transform the marble slab into gold bullion, and the caique (unidentified) into a British battleship. The man who had apparently made that effort seemed pleased with the way in which his tale had been received and straightaway embarked upon another:

"Do you know why we're building a new church on the beach? I'll tell you.

"We would never have thought of it if old Yiorgaki hadn't had a dream. It was when the Germans were here. To be on the safe side we all used to sleep out of doors—we were never sure those cuckolds wouldn't surround our houses in the middle of the night and take us off to forced labour. Well, one night Yiorgaki went to sleep at the end of the beach over there, and God appeared to him in a dream. 'Why are you sleeping outside, Yiorgaki?' He said, 'there's no need for it. No harm will ever come to the people of Souyia, least of all to you, for on the very spot you are sleeping there once stood a church. Dig for it and you will find it.'

"God is great. Souyia was spared. And as soon as the Germans left we dug on the spot where old Yiorgaki had slept. Sure enough, just below the surface we unearthed the remains of an ancient church. So we decided to build a new one exactly where the old one used to be. Come along, I'll show you."

At the far end of a row of tamarisk planted along the line of demarcation between the shingle of the beach and the soil of the plain, we came upon a half-finished building which already promised to look, when complete, as ugly as the other houses in the bay. We went through a hole in the newly-made wall where the door would eventually be and I found we were treading on a rough tesselated pavement of multi-coloured pebbles which, to my untutored eye, looked more like the floor of a Roman villa than that of a Christian church. As though sensing my disappointment, my guide pointed out two squat marble pillars lying in the dust, the first with the words: "Saint Basil, help us" carved upon it in Byzantine characters, the other engraved with the same prayer addressed to Saint Panteleimon.

"Those were dug up at the same time," he explained.

He was clearly so impressed by this humble excavation that I was tempted to tell him that he too could probably unearth something similar; he did not have to wait for the site to be revealed in a dream, he only had to dig in one of the many spots which furnished ample evidence of ancient remains. But I felt sure that he would not have believed me—it sounded too easy—so I asked him, instead, if there was any other church in Souyia.

"Not in the bay itself," he replied, "but if you climb the cliff over there you'll come to the chapel of St. Irene—a tiny thing and very old, not worth the walk."

But I wanted a walk, so I set off at once in the direction he had pointed. I soon reached the top of the cliff and, after following the path along its edge for a few hundred yards, caught sight of what appeared to be a perfect little cruciform church perched on a natural belvedere high above the sea. It looked so lovely at a distance that the discovery I made as I came closer, of a reinforced concrete excrescence built on to its far side, shocked me as much as an unsuspected goitre on the neck of a beautiful woman.

Inside, it was disfigured as well. The walls had been recently whitewashed so that the Byzantine frescoes which once adorned them from floor to ceiling were now barely visible. A few patches of orange-gold pigment showed through the coating of lime but none of these was large enough or clear enough to indicate the nature of the painting underneath; Christian peasants with their caustic-laden brushes had destroyed the faces of the saints more thoroughly than Moslem conquerors had ever done with the point of their yatagans. Only the very top of the dome had been spared—presumably because it was out of reach—and from there the eyes of the Pantocrator emerged as though from a cloud, staring down with disapproval on the vestments lying in tatters behind the worm-eaten iconostasis and on the candles drooping limply over the crumbling window-sills.

I tried to straighten one of these obscene-looking bars of yellow wax, intending to light it and place it on the candle-stand; but as soon as I picked it up it slithered through my fingers, oozed out of my fist and dangled over my knuckles like a slug that was not quite dead. I dropped it and made for the door, instinctively wiping the palm of my hand on the seat of my trousers. I had done enough sight-seeing for the time being.

There was fish for luncheon—not the skin-and-bone red mullet that I had seen being weighed, but a plump blue-brown beauty crowned with a heavy dorsal fin. When I asked Vasilis what it was he replied by quoting a few lines of doggerel verse to illustrate as well how it should be cooked, served and eaten:

My name is *scharos*, cook me on a grill[5]
And place me on a dish in oil-and-vinegar,
Then you can eat me up, my guts and all.

Vasilis had prepared it according to this formula and it tasted as delicious as it looked; the fumes of the charcoal on which it had been cooked seemed to have been trapped inside its flesh and sealed by the *sauce vinaigrette*, so that a flavour of smoked pinewood accompanied every mouthful. I subsequently learnt that the *scharos* was considered a great delicacy by the Romans, who were fortunate to find it in large quantities off the whole of the south coast of the island. I imagine that they must have fished for it then, as the Cretans do today, not with nets but with lobster-pots baited with a certain kind of green vegetable which, apart from small crabs, is the *scharos*'s staple diet.

With it we had greens to eat ourselves, though I could not tell which of the many local varieties they were since all are referred to simply as *khorta*, a name which embraces not only the edible wild grasses but also the leaves of kidney-beans, chick-peas, pumpkin, horseradish, mustard-plant, mallow, chicory and dandelion as well as various campanulas and valerians. And to think that the British housewife is content with boiled cabbage!

Vasilis and I had just finished the jug of wine, and Prokopia was clearing the table, when a tubby man in uniform with silver-white hair and a red moustache burst into the room, seized me by the arm and announced:

"I am responsible for you here. I am responsible for all the villagers in this valley. I'm a very important man. Don't look at my hair, look at my moustache—it's twenty years younger, and so am I. You ought to see me dance—when I jump into the air I don't

5. The play on the Greek words *scharos* (the fish) and *schara* (a grill) cannot be reproduced in translation.

come down for days. I'm the best dancer in Crete. I'm also the best singer in Crete. I can see that you too are a very dashing fellow—let us drink to each other's health—no, not now, this evening—when there's more to eat. I can't drink unless I eat, and I can't sing or dance unless I drink. All I can do now is sleep. Good-night, good-night, sleep tight."

He saluted, winked, and tripped out of the room.

"That was Stavros, our police-sergeant," Vasilis explained. "The funny thing is that he really can dance—which is quite an achievement considering that belly of his—and he does sing beautifully. We must get him drunk tonight; he's splendid company when he's drunk."

Stavros was drunk long before dinner-time. When I returned from my evening bathe I found him in the shop playing cards with Vasilis's brother, Manolis, who had come down from Koustoyerako to invite me to the wedding of one of the numerous Paterakis cousins. The skeletons of red mullet and the olive-stones which littered the floor round their table testified to the amount of wine they must have consumed to warrant so much food; the recognized *mezes*—the titbits which throughout Greece are served free with every drink—was one small fish or a couple of olives.

I could not follow the rules of the game, which seemed to consist mainly of slapping each card down on the table-top with a triumphant, or defiant, cry of "Cuckold!" Nor did I discover who finally won. I had been told that the loser was to provide a chicken, which we were to eat for dinner; but when the game ended both players went out and presently returned, each with a headless hen in his bloodstained hands. I never learnt whom the birds belonged to—certainly neither to Stavros nor to Manolis—but I believe that they must have been the mayor's, for it was in his house that we ate them, boiled with rice. They were extremely tough and, considering their diet, mercifully tasteless, but that was not important; they were only there, as Stavros hastened to explain, "for the wine."

Four of us sat down to dinner, Stavros, Manolis, the mayor and myself—we had had to leave Vasilis behind to look after the shop—but as soon as the singing started neighbours began to drift in, the men joining us at the table, their wives remaining as usual in the background. Stavros was obviously the attraction of the evening.

A "good singer," in Crete, generally means someone who can make more noise than anybody else in the room, so I was prepared for several sustained bursts of tuneless thunder. But Stavros was an artist, with a well-controlled baritone voice which was perfectly suited to the songs he selected—not the frenzied and lachrymose *rizitika*, or songs of the foothills, but the simple *mantinades*, the rhyming couplets which are sung all over Crete though not everywhere to the same tune. Almost everyone in the island has an apparently inexhaustible repertoire of these songs, some of them centuries old, others made up on the spot; for like the *calypso*, the *mantinada* lends itself to impromptu composition and improvisation. Stavros preferred the traditional form, and his face assumed an almost devout expression as he sang:

> *Crete, O my love, my beautiful, Crete to whom we're beholden. . . .*

He raised his eyebrows, closed his eyes and drained his glass as we burst in with the chorus:

> *Ela, ela, Crete to whom we're beholden.*

Then, like a speaker after a round of applause, he continued:

> *All of your rocks are diamonds, all of your earth is golden!*

> *Lives there a man who will not fight, letting himself be beaten?*
> *He has no right to dwell in Crete, he is no more a Cretan!*

> *Dig where you will the soil of Crete, even with a needle rake it.*
> *Blood of a hero stains the point, bones of a hero break it!*

> *Crete, but your brave sons fare abroad, why, oh why can't you keep them?*
> *Far, far away their valour shines, you—you are left to weep them!*

At the end of each distich Stavros knocked back more wine and murmured: "Long live Crete!" while we yelled the words after him and drained our glasses simultaneously. Soon the toast, suggested by himself, was "Long live Stavros!", for he had now begun to sing about love:

> *Love, but your lips are red, so red—kiss me, I cannot doubt it.*
> *Give me your lips and I'll need no wine—you'll make me drunk*
>   *without it.*

("Oh no, you won't," he muttered. "Long live Stavros!")
"Long live Stavros!" we echoed.

I shall become a nine-foot snake, all round your waist I'll wind me,
And the next time that you say No, I'll leave you dead behind me!

("But they never do say No, not to me; all the widows in the world are after me. Long live Stavros!")
"Long live Stavros!"

Hyacinths, rose and violet, cyclamen and carnation,
All who can find a fault in you go to their own damnation!

Shamed is the rising red-cheeked sun, shamed is he as he advances.
Drunken and dazed with your beauty, love, dazzled by your glances!

We might have sat there all night if the wine had not run out. I forget how many times the large stone jug had been filled and refilled before the mayor turned it upside down after pouring out the final round; I only remember regretting the quantity we had prodigally splashed all over the table-cloth or carelessly spilt down our shirt-fronts. My face must have betrayed my thoughts, for Stavros thumped me on the back and yelled:

"Never mind. There's nothing left to eat here anyway. We'll go back to Vasilis."

Nobody objected to the noise that we made as we stumbled past the silent shuttered houses; most of the men in Souyia were with us outside contributing to the din, and none of the women inside would have dared to complain. In any case they were not sleeping or trying to sleep; they were waiting, as usual, for their husbands to come back before going to bed themselves.

Prokopia was ready to receive us, as though it was noon instead of well past midnight. Her only concession to the late hour had been to let down her hair, which now fell in two long plaits over her shoulders. With a happy grin she nodded at Vasilis who, with the child in his arms, was fast asleep in the only bed in the house. I thought that she was going to ask us to make less noise; instead she crossed the room, shook him and shouted:

"Wake up! Here are the guests."

No one apologised for disturbing him; he apologised himself for being asleep, got up at once to fill the glasses which had been set in readiness on the table, and told Prokopia to bring in some bread and cheese. The child, which, like all Cretan children, was used to this sort of nocturnal intrusion, whimpered fretfully for a few minutes;

then, realising that it could not make its voice heard above ours, went to sleep again.

It would have been so easy, and quite reasonable, to use the child as an excuse for breaking up the party, but if the idea even entered Vasilis's head, he did not voice it. It was only when he saw me yawning that he tentatively ventured: "Whenever you like . . . ?", leaving it to me to decide when we should go to bed. I nodded.

Extra blankets were put out on the terrace beside mine, for Manolis had to have somewhere to sleep and Stavros did not feel like walking the few yards to the police-station; and we lay down together under the stars. As I dozed off I found myself silently laughing. It was not the idea of the three of us lying out there in the open, happily drunk and fully dressed, that amused me; what made me laugh was the thought that we could have done nothing else had we even been sober—for there was no other bed and none of us had pyjamas—though we might, I dreamily conjectured, have taken off our boots.

If it had not been for the beach I would soon have got tired of Souyia, where the only distraction was listening to the conversation of Vasilis's customers. This was limited—except when Stavros mercifully intervened with his inevitable fanfaronade—to two topics: the German occupation, which was still discussed in every detail as though it had ended only yesterday; and the long-awaited road from Canea to the coast.

That road! Everything, it appeared, depended on it. It had been pushed forward since the war as far as Kambanos, a village up the valley, only five miles away as the crow flies but several hours' distant as the mule walks; and there it had stopped. So Kambanos had collared the trade between the capital and the more remote villages in the area, which Souyia had previously handled through Palaeochora. How was Souyia to recapture that trade? Its inhabitants pinned their hopes on bringing the road down to the bay; they had turned their backs on the sea, which had given them their original *raison d'être*, and were now looking inland for their salvation, waiting for prosperity to trundle down to them on four wheels. No wonder they were restless.

Their endless talk about the economic and engineering problems involved soon drove me out onto the beach which they so studiously avoided. My favourite bathing-place was at the far end of the shingle, where an outcrop of rock provided privacy and shade. Here I used to spend every morning, reading and feeling grateful for the absence of this road which was expected to turn Souyia into a second Palaeochora—not that the buildings of the former were any less hideous than those of the latter; they were simply less numerous. But I did not really believe in that road. I kept thinking of the words of the man with the empty game-bag: "We are all of us doomed in this out-of-the-way corner." Perhaps they were literally true. Less than a hundred years ago the only buildings standing in this bay were the ruins of an ancient harbour—I could still see the remains of a Roman aqueduct through the carob-trees a short distance inland. In a hundred years from now what would there be left of the present-day trading-station? Perhaps these houses too—Vasilis's and the rest—having long since served their purpose and been abandoned, would be in ruins; and Souyia be sunk again in centuries of oblivion. It had happened before.

Throughout the history of Crete, the people and the soil seem to have conspired against construction and preservation. Villages razed to the ground in war have been repeatedly re-built, only to be destroyed again by disastrous earthquakes which have shaken the island almost as frequently as the numerous insurrections against foreign oppression. During one of these terrestrial upheavals which, according to Dephner, occurred in 66 b.c.—a date which I am in no position to dispute though it seems to me almost as difficult to establish as that of the Deucalionic deluge or of the subsidence of Atlantis—the whole island shifted on its axis, so that while the eastern edge was submerged, the western was raised twenty feet above the old sea-level (I could see the water-mark which still showed on the cliffs as plainly as the dado on a bedroom wall). The harbour of Souyia, which then served the city of Elyros,[6] was consequently drained. There is no record of its buildings being destroyed. Rendered useless, they were simply abandoned; and remained abandoned until the end of the last century when the present houses were built to fulfill, in a minor way, the task performed by the original buildings two thousand years before. As far as I could see, that task had now come to an end. Souyia was certainly doomed.

6. The site of this ancient city is now occupied by the village of Rodovani which, until the construction of the road to Kambanos, was served in the same way by present-day Souyia.

I did not really believe this, of course, any more than I believed in the hypothetical advantages of the road; but arguing with myself on these lines helped to relieve the restlessness with which I was beginning to be infected. I found myself contemplating these isolated box-like buildings on the beach almost with hatred, and, almost with satisfaction, imagining how they would look when they were covered by several centuries' deposit. And what of the half-finished church? Would some future Yiorgaki, I wondered, dream of its previous existence when it was buried just below him in the sand?

As though the cataclysm was already upon us, I felt like telling Vasilis to escape while the going was good, to take to the hills again, now, at once. But when, in a saner mood, I suggested that it was time for me to be moving, he replied in that gentle voice of his:

"You've come all the way from England to see us. Stay a little longer. Wait till the guests arrive for my cousin's wedding. Then we can all go up to Koustoyerako together."

2

KOUSTOYERAKO

THE WEDDING WAS to take place on Sunday, not only so as to enable as many guests as possible to be present, but also because, in Crete, this particular day of the week is regarded as the most propitious for the ceremony. The time of year, too, was favourable: it was now the season of the grape-harvest which, after Christmas and Easter, is considered more auspicious than any other period. For some reason, which I could never fathom, May is always avoided as the most ill-omened month of all: a May bride or bridegroom is expected to die within a few weeks—"and no wonder," said Vasilis when I asked him about this superstition, "only donkeys mate in the month of May."

On Sunday morning, then, Souyia was astir even earlier than usual. From my vantage-point on the terrace I could see the occupants of the other houses preparing themselves for the party: a couple of men washing their feet at the water's edge; a woman fanning a charcoal brazier into life outside her front door; another combing her hair which she had just soaked in water; a youth harnessing his mule; a little girl being shaken into a new white dress by her elder sister.

In honour of the day I shaved for the first time since my arrival and put on my only clean shirt. Even so I felt conspicuously underdressed when I went downstairs and found the usual crowd of ragged drinkers transformed by their Sunday best into a conversation piece of tailor's dummies. Encased in suits of pale grey, beige and indigo, which looked and must have felt as stiff as armour, they sat uncom-

fortably but complacently waiting for their hair to be cut by Christos, a sheep-shearer, who during the occupation had enlarged his
scope by experimenting on the heads of the Selino guerillas. Now
the self-appointed barber of the district, he still used the scissors
and clippers that had been dropped to us by parachute in 1943; but
I doubt if he had sharpened them since then, for while he was in
action his customers winced as though they were being scalped, and
when he had finished they almost looked as if they had been.

Stavros came in shortly after me for his early-morning *tsikoudia*,
"to kill the microbe." He refused the offer of a hair-cut since he
had already dealt with his hair himself; scraped back and flattened
down, it fitted his head as closely as a skull-cap. Before sitting next
to me he spread a clean handkerchief on the seat of his chair for fear
of soiling the broad expanse of spotless khaki drill which covered his
own seat; and after finishing his drink he wiped his mouth on the
back of his hand with exaggerated care so as not to disturb the symmetry of his moustache, which had been curled up from his lip to
form twin flames on either side of his nose.

"Why this gallant get-up?" I asked him. "Didn't you tell me you
weren't coming to the wedding?"

"Of course I did, of course I did. But how can I resist a party?
Dancing! Singing! It'll be my downfall. I know I shouldn't come.
Don't you see what's going to happen? They'll all get drunk, then—
dang! dang! dang! dang! dang!—pistols, rifles, everything! Virgin
Mary, if they had a cannon they'd let it off. Then what do I do?
Think of my position—a man of my importance! I would have
to report them. And I don't want to report them, I only want to
sing and dance, hoopa! hoopa! But I can't pretend I didn't hear—I
shall just have to leave if the cuckolds start shooting—leave, do you
hear?" he went on, addressing the rest of the room, "If I hear a single shot fired, even if it's only a pistol, I'll leave at once. You wouldn't
want me to do that, would you? Think of it—making Stavros leave
in the middle of a dance!"

The caique bringing the guests from Palaeochora did not arrive
until after luncheon; it was in the blazing sun of siesta-time that we
set off for the hills. We crossed the dry river-bed which divides the
plain, the men sweating under their smart jackets which they refused
to discard, the women stubbing their bare toes on the rocks—for the
sake of economy or comfort they were carrying, not wearing, their
shoes. Stavros, who was walking just ahead of me, tripped dain-

tily along from boulder to boulder, his body bouncing with every step like an inflated rubber beach-toy; after one particularly impressive *salto* he glanced back at me for approval and chortled with self-satisfaction when I grunted: "Long live Stavros!" I kept up with him and by the time we started climbing we were both far ahead of the rest of the cortège.

With maddening deliberation he increased his speed as soon as we struck the slope. "I go much better uphill," he sadistically explained, "but put me on a main road and I burst at once." There was a perfectly good path to follow, a paved path so well preserved that it looked as late as Venetian though it must have been Roman; but Stavros avoided the flat slabs of stone laid at an easy angle along the side of the valley and blazed a trail by a series of short cuts straight up the face of the hill. After half an hour of crazy racing, tearing through scrub and stumbling over loose earth, I insisted on stopping for a cigarette.

Below us I could see our companions slowly ascending in a single serpentine file, singing as they climbed up the path, advancing with such military precision that I half expected to hear the banal beat of a marching song instead of the piercing wail of the *tragoudia tis stratas*. The weird semi-tones and broken rhythm of these "songs of the road"—a ritualistic rather than logical accompaniment to walking—seemed to give that commonplace motion an almost mystic significance; the approaching crowd of guests appeared to be transformed into a procession of devotees. Stavros and I waited for them to catch up with us, and a little later we reached the outskirts of Livadas all together.

As we passed through the village I again had the impression that I was witnessing some solemn rite. From every house along the path young girls emerged carrying trays laden with *tsikoudia*, water and walnuts—the simplest of refreshments, yet ceremoniously presented as though they were votive offerings. The houses here had been re-built and the freshly-worked stone gleamed in the sun, a suitably ordinary setting for the ordinary travellers laughing and chatting on the footpath as they drank to each other and to their hosts of the moment; but a few yards away pilasters of burnt masonry stood black and broken among the olive trees; against this background of ruin, the gesture of the girls raising their trays to offer us a last drink before we moved off was, unconsciously but absolutely, the gesture of a chorus of suppliants.

Koustoyerako lay hidden a little higher up, in the shadow of Mount Psilaphi whose grey dome nudged the sky less than four miles inland but over six thousand feet above the sea. Vasilis had told me that the village had been completely rebuilt and I wondered if I would recognise it. "You won't see much difference," he assured me, "it's not the first time the place has been burnt, but it always comes up again, the same as ever." When I entered the village I saw that this was true: each house had risen, phoenix-like, from its most recent ashes, in its previous position and original shape. The only change that I noticed was the use of reinforced concrete instead of dried mud for the roofs, and this was due not to any progressive architectural spirit—for even the latest holocaust had, it seemed, made no impression on the strict conservatism of the peasant designers—but to Marshall Aid, which had provided the modern material.

The present buildings, then, are almost exact reproductions of those burnt down by the Germans, which no doubt were faithful replicas of those razed to the ground by the Turks, which in their turn had probably been copied from the original models destroyed by the Venetians; so that Koustoyerako today would be almost as recognisable to the Bey of the Sublime Porte who thought he had wiped it out in the early eighteenth century, or indeed to the Public Representative of the Most Serene Republic who imagined he had done so two centuries before that, as it was to me now. I would have had no difficulty in finding the Paterakis house, even without Vasilis as a guide.

It was as if I had never left it. Without being told, I avoided the front door, which I remembered as the entrance to the kitchen, and climbed the steps outside on to a terrace leading into the main room. The nagging emptiness of most Cretan homes seems almost as distressing as a hollow tooth, but in the Paterakis house the cavity had, as it were, been filled—I could scarcely enter the room because of the furniture and, once inside, I found myself trapped between the heavy iron bedsteads lining the walls and the long wooden table that occupied the remaining space. Like every other family in the village, the Paterakis brothers had killed a goat in honour of their cousin's wedding and the smell of meat from the kitchen below was so overpowering that I half expected it to take visible form and issue like jets of steam through the cracks in the floorboards. A sudden undertow of nausea almost swept me off my feet; as I closed my eyes in the struggle to keep upright, I fancied that I was standing in the hot-room of a Turkish bath which, as though in a nightmare, was being used as a slaughter-house.

———

The nightmare recurred several times during the day, each time, in fact, that I entered a house—and my duty, as a guest, required me to visit every house in the village. I soon felt I would never be able to look a goat in the face again, yet I found myself repeatedly having to do so; for a goat's head, boiled and horribly beardless, stared blindly at me from the centre of every table. Mercifully, it was not allowed to remain intact for long. As soon as the mountains of meat surrounding it were brought down to plate-level, it was cracked open and divided. The real gourmets then helped themselves to the eyes, which looked, and no doubt tasted, like slightly flattened squash-balls; others were content with a less exotic mouthful of the brain; and the remainder either sucked the cheekbones clean or tackled the unrewarding jaw-bones with a gusto that made the animals' teeth and their own chatter together like castanets. Feeling utterly insufficient and ashamed of my squeamishness, which I could not help regarding as an unvoiced insult to my hosts, I grappled with successive waves of nausea and primly nibbled bits of cheese made, I gratefully realised, from sheep's milk and not from goat's.

After almost a dozen of these meals I began to wonder what time the wedding was going to take place. No one seemed to know or care. "Don't worry," I was told, "the priest hasn't turned up yet." But the priest, I presently discovered, had turned up. He had turned up hours ago; the wedding was already over; it was time to go to the bridegroom's house and offer our congratulations. By now I was too dazed with food and drink to ask why nobody, as far as I could tell, had attended the ceremony. I passively followed the crowd, like a somnambulist in a dream, a dream that turned into the now familiar nightmare as soon as I was inside the house; for there on the table—and I was not yet seeing double—was not one goat's head, but four.

Once again the feasting started, a repetition of the previous meals, only on a larger scale. At the top of the table sat the bridal pair, looking as dazed as I felt, while the crowd pressing round them drank to their health and wished them "Long life!" There were not enough chairs for everyone in the room, so the few that were available were used as supports for two long planks placed on either side of the table; on these makeshift benches the abnormally large number of guests could be more easily accommodated. In a flash of alcoholic clarity I found the answer to a question which I had often asked myself: why are the songs that are sung by the guests at weddings, baptisms and similar ceremonies always called *tragoudia tis tavlas* or "songs of the board"? Now I knew.

One side of the room was masked by what appeared to be a vividly-coloured punkah. This was part of the bride's dowry: handwoven blankets draped over a long pole suspended on wires from the ceiling. A dowry is essential in Crete; without it a girl cannot marry. And so, in her youth, she spends all her spare time at the loom or over needlework; for, besides blankets and bedclothes, she is also expected to provide shirts and a suit for the bridegroom. All these are kept in a large wooden chest until her wedding day, when they are brought out and proudly displayed as an example of her industry. But her real value can only be assessed in terms of land. Before her prospective father-in-law allows his son to marry her, he will ask her parents how many okes of oil she is worth; and if he considers insufficient the annual yield from the olive trees that her parents are willing to give her, the marriage does not take place. For this reason the father of a large family of girls looks upon his daughters as a curse which, more slowly than a plague of locusts but just as inexorably, devours all his crops.

Consequently, a girl whose other sisters have already married, or whose parents owned little or no land in the first place, has hardly any chance of finding a husband, however great her personal charms. And so she relies on other charms. I am not sure if love potions are still widely used in Crete, but I discovered existing recipes for two of them, which show to what lengths a girl will go in order to get her man.

The first, known as "mothers' milk," requires ingredients which certainly cannot always be available in a small mountain village. Moreover, four female accomplices are needed for the preparation of the potion—two women with the same Christian name, and two others who must be a mother and her married daughter. Such a quartet would not be hard to find, but the recipe lays down an additional condition: the mother and the daughter must each have an unweaned child. They are made to sit down, back to back and facing east and west respectively, and are then milked simultaneously by the two women of the same name. The milk extracted is given to the would-be bride, who mixes it with water and whispers: "As a mother loves her child, so may—" (and here she names the youth of her choice)—"love me." The liquid is finally used to make bread, which is offered to the youth at the earliest opportunity. After eating it—but how long afterwards, nobody knows—the youth is enflamed with uncontrollable passion for the girl, which makes him blind to the poverty of her parents and deaf to the counsel of his own.

The second potion, which is said to be equally effective, is simpler to prepare. Only the basic ingredients of elementary sorcery are needed: nail-parings and hair—and these do not even have to come from the victim; the young girl uses her own. She plucks one hair from her right temple, to which she adds a bit of her left thumb-nail; then—and the order is important—one hair from her left temple and a bit of her right thumb-nail. This mixture is enriched by the addition of one hair from her right arm-pit, followed by a bit of nail from the big toe of her left foot; and one hair from her left arm-pit with a bit of nail from the big toe of her right foot. These precious odds and ends are then set on fire and, while they burn, the girl utters her spell: "May I shine in his eyes like the sun, may I beam on him like the moon." The ashes are finally collected and carefully set aside until an opportunity occurs for them to be put in a cup of coffee, which is promptly offered to the unsuspecting suitor.

No wonder mothers here warn their unmarried sons against accepting food and drink from the hands of a virgin!

Until quite recently a village wedding ceremony used to last at least a week. It must have been a real endurance test for, apart from the compulsory eating and drinking to excess, the only time the revellers were allowed to go to sleep was when they passed out. Nowadays the feasting is almost always limited to forty-eight hours, but even that was too much for me. Bludgeoned by wine and the noise of singing, I left the bridegroom's house and tottered off to bed before the fiddler and the lutanist, specially summoned from another village, had even started to play.

The house I was staying in belonged to my *synteknos*, Manolis Yedekakis. Eight years before, during the occupation, I had stood as sponsor at the baptism of one of his children. Since then we had been morally bound together for life. In the Greek church the bond between the natural and the spiritual father of a child is considered stronger than any that could exist between two members of the same family[1]; my *synteknos* and I were, in fact, brothers-in-God, a relationship more sacred than one due simply to common parentage. It was therefore unthinkable that I should sleep under anyone else's roof. Manolis (known as "Black Manolis," to distinguish him from his cousin of the same name) was one of the poorest men in the village. There was hardly any furniture in his newly-built house, and the only bed that he had was put at my disposal. I was grateful, for I wanted to sleep; but I got no sleep that night.

Just before I lay down the shooting started. A single pistol-shot at first; then, after two or three minutes, a *feu-de-joie* from half a dozen rifles. I concluded that, in the interval between the first shot and the fusilade, Stavros had jumped up and rushed off, as he had threatened to do, and now that he had gone the firing, which I could still hear, was being safely continued. I discovered next morning that my conclusion was correct. Poor Stavros! His sense of duty had deprived him of his song and dance.

It is almost impossible for a village policeman to be both punctilious and popular. Serving in a lawless area, Stavros wisely observed the spirit rather than the letter of the law; he knew exactly how many unlicensed fire-arms were kept in Koustoyerako, since their owners made no attempt to conceal them; but so long as they were not flourished in his face, nor fired in his presence, his professional conscience was satisfied. He maintained his popularity, not by relaxing the rules—this would have earned him nothing but scorn—but by working on the villagers' *philotimo*,[2] trusting them to play the game according to his own rules. This method, the only one that could possibly be applied, was fairly successful—until any celebration was held, when the villagers' childish passion for noise (which,

---

1. This relationship, which Pashley translates "gossipred," is also considered as complete a bar to marriage as the closest consanguinity. If a Greek were to marry his godfather's daughter, or even one of his godfather's god-daughters, the marriage would be incestuous.

2. A difficult word to translate, since there is no English equivalent of this essentially Greek personal attribute; "sense of honour" is a fairly accurate etymological rendering, though the word has the additional connotation of "self-respect." *Philotimo* and *philodoxia*—also untranslatable; the nearest approach to it in English would be "ambition," but ambition in the mildly derogatory sense of "love of glory"—are the chief characteristics of the Cretan peasant.

I imagine, is the only thing the Cretans have in common with the Chinese) invariably had to be vented.

Many theories have been put forward to explain this Cretan mania for weapons, the most common being the romantic's "a man's best friend is his gun"; the traditionalist's "an inheritance from the War of Independence and, more recently, the German occupation"; and the rationalist's "an obvious means of self-defence against sheep-thieves and personal enemies." None of these, to my mind, is completely valid. I believe the real reason to be something which, for want of a better word, I shall call the *pallikari*-complex, a form of hero-worship inculcated by village education. History, as taught in the village schools, is limited to the centuries of resistance against Turkish domination, a period during which every active patriot was an outlaw, an outlaw whom the passage of time has glamourized into a figure at once trite and improbably noble. This is the *pallikari*, a man as strong as a horse and as brave as a lion. Beetle-browed, hook-nosed and heavily-moustachioed, he is usually represented armed with a breech-loading musket as tall as himself, and caparisoned with crossed bandoliers, a piratical pistol and a brace of silver-sheathed, ivory-hilted yatagans. A hero to the Cretan schoolboy, to the adult he remains a hero, a superannuated and hellenized form of Robin Hood, a man to be emulated.

So, as I listened to the desultory firing all night, I realised that this was no more than a grown-up version of a child's game: a noisy game, admittedly, which kept me awake, but one which I was far from resenting. For the sound of the shots echoing round the hills made me feel more than ever at home in Koustoyerako—a stimulating sound which sent the adrenalin surging through my veins and allowed me to indulge in a delightful sense of danger, safe in the knowledge that there was none.

But not for long. At first light the peripatetic revelry of the previous afternoon was resumed and my room was soon invaded by a crowd of happy drunkards shouting for "Potato-shape." This was the nickname given to Black Manolis's wife, who presently came in and at once started to lay the table for yet another meal. Since my bed would be needed I reluctantly left it, silently praying for a shortage of goat.

"Potato-shape" deserved the name she had earned, and recognised it as the compliment that it was intended to be—thin women are not much admired in Crete. But she made no attempt to exploit her charms; her hips swayed almost apologetically as she waddled, goose-like, round the room; her thighs and stomach heaved with sympathetic self-reproach; while her breasts, as though ashamed of their involuntary provocativeness, tried to hide their tumescence beneath the black cloth which enfolded her body from throat to ankle. A black cotton kerchief round her head completed this anaphrodisiac uniform, which is worn by every woman in the mountains. It must have been adopted at a fairly recent date, for earlier travellers give a quite different account of female peasant dress.

In 1610, for instance, George Sandys, the youngest son of the Archbishop of York, observed with a commendably pious shudder "the women only wearing loofe Veils on their heads, the breasts and shoulders perpetually naked, and died by the Sun into a loathfom tawny." Half a century earlier, Belon had also noticed these evidently ubiquitous breasts *"toutes noires et hallées du soleil"*; and two centuries later they were still to be found immodestly revealed, for Tournefort mentions the women wearing *"une jupe de drap rouge tirant sur le grisdelin, fort plissée, suspendue sur les épaules par deux gros cordons, et qui leur laisse le sein tout découvert."* Even as late as 1869, their dress must have been comparatively careless; Raulin describes it as *"une chemise . . . à large manches, nouée a la ceinture et laissant souvent voir les seins qui, excepté dans le jeune âge, ne se font pas remarquer par leur fermeté."*

To which, speaking of today, I can only add: *"ni par leur nudité non plus."*

By midday I was wilting again from the combined effects of sun and wine. A hangover is a condition unknown to these villagers— the most they will admit to is "spoilt stomach"—so I received little sympathy. Although none of them had gone to bed (even the newly-married couple had unselfishly stayed up all night) they all looked capable of continuing the party indefinitely. I, who had never felt less like a *pallikari*, was glad that it would soon be over. The constant shifting from house to house, and the nonstop eating and drinking in each, had reduced me to a state of fecklessness which would have been frightening had it not been irritating. But there was one consolation: no more goat. Instead, bowlfuls of comforting rice-soup were provided—and yoghourt, better in Crete than anywhere else in the world.

I have often wondered how Cretans would react to the present-day pseudo-science of dietetics. Admittedly, they have their own

superstitions about food; but none of these seems to me as mediaeval in conception as the modern mumbo-jumbo of calories,
proteins, vitamins and all the other abstract props of the twentieth-century witch-doctor. (Is a calorie more credible than a sala-
mander, a protein more palpable than a sylph?) Though their food
may be primitive, they themselves would be far too civilised to
indulge in the new-fangled heresy of "a balanced diet." Meanwhile
they remain true to the ancient tenets of their own, and every other,
established religion, which sensibly impose alternate periods of fasting and feasting.

That I was incapable of their excess, was simply an indication of
my physical inadequacy; and their full-blooded enjoyment, like a
challenge which I knew that I could never accept, made me anxiously conscious of this. In the atmosphere of almost aggressive virility which they engendered, I even felt that my appearance also was
somehow sub-standard; and I realised with a shock that in the whole
of Koustoyerako I was the only adult male without a moustache.
What in England I had scorned as a sign of inferiority complex, in
Crete now appeared as a symbol of heroic stamina.

My favourite view of Koustoyerako was from the crown of a small
hill behind the Paterakis' house, the only accessible point from which
the whole village is visible. The roofs of the houses below repeat the
pattern of the terraced fields on the slope, creating a momentary
illusion of a properly-planned architectural unit. Beyond them, on
a broad saddle where, if this were Italy or France, the village square
would be sited, the stony earth is camouflaged by a number of olive
trees too sparse to be considered a grove but sufficiently abundant
to mask the roots of a second, steeper hill opposite. Built out of this
almost perpendicular crag-surmounted surface, but by distance flattened against it, are the remaining houses of the village. From this
angle, only their front walls can be seen so that the general view,
which includes the roofs in the foreground, gives the impression of a
plan and elevation combined.

I could never make up my mind whether Koustoyerako looked
more like a dungeon or a citadel. In the early morning or late evening, when the shadow of the higher peaks pressed down upon this
basin like a lid, and at midday when the sun seemed to halt overhead, hemmed in by the surrounding hills, the village appeared to

be enclosed on all sides: a basin in which nothing simmered. But the slightest breeze from the Souyia valley would shake the olive trees inside out and expose the silver lining of their dark green leaves; a stronger wind would plough a visible furrow through them, like a shaft of light on shot silk or a finger-mark on velvet: the basin bubbled over then with elemental life and the village looked as stripped and unprotected as a lighthouse.

Apart from the view it afforded, I had a secondary, and to me more important, reason for frequenting my vantage-point: the hill was invariably deserted. The path which zigzagged through the trees and up the opposite cliff led first to the nearest water-supply, the Koutsounara spring, then on to the summer pastures in the topmost folds of the mountains; at every hour of the day women with pitchers on their shoulders and donkeys laden with casks could be seen ascending and descending, sometimes through the dust-storm raised by a flock of startled goats. But no one at this time of year climbed the track I used to take through the terraces; for it led only to a small church, which was scarcely ever used since the village had no priest of its own.

It was outside this church that I came across a direct link between Koustoyerako and Byzantium: the grave of a certain Kandanoleon, killed by the Germans when they burnt down the village. A short synoptic history of mediaeval Crete will show how that link was forged:

In 832 the island, which then formed part of the Byzantine Empire, was invaded by a force of Saracens under the chieftain Abu Kaab who, in order to exploit his success, burnt all his ships immediately after landing and so denied his troops the opportunity of eventual withdrawal. Summarily divorced from their wives and children, the Moslem invaders were forced to found new homes and families by intermarrying with the Christian islanders, many of whom at once embraced the faith of Islam and so no doubt provided in their descendents, the so-called Abadiotes, living encouragement for the wholesale apostasy that took place eight hundred years later under the Turks.

During the century and more of Saracenic occupation, while Crete was being used as a fortified base for piratical raids against the mainland, and serving at the same time as a slave-mart for the rest of the Eastern Mediterranean, at least two serious attempts were made to recover the island. But it was not until 960, and then only after a long blockade in which the victorious general Nikephoros Phokas bombarded the beleaguered garrison by catapult with the chopped-off heads of his Moslem prisoners, that Crete once more reverted to Byzantine rule.

A eugenic experiment in the form of compulsory immigration was then introduced. In order to repopulate the ravaged island, and to purify the islanders debased by infidel blood, Armenians and Slavs, and other "barbarian" Christians who owed allegiance to the Empire, were brought in as permanent settlers (they subsequently founded the several village-colonies which still bear their name). Shortly afterwards, the Emperor Alexis Comnenos sent over the *Archontopouloi*, twelve families of Byzantine nobles, to act as a ruling class.

At the partition of the Empire which followed the fall of Constantinople in 1204, Crete was allotted to Boniface, Marquis of Montferrat, who for a small sum sold this share of crusaders' loot to the Venetians. Occupied with more urgent strategic commitments elsewhere, Venice did not immediately garrison the island, which consequently degenerated for a number of years into a slippery foothold for a succession of Genoese marauders. But by 1210 these semi-official adventurers had been driven off for good, and the standard of Saint Mark was firmly planted on Cretan soil with the appointment of Jacob Tiepolo as the first *Duca*, or Governor-General.

Meanwhile the *Archontopouloi* had increased in number and in power. One family alone, the Argyroupolos, administered the whole district now known as Selino; another, the Skordylis, controlled Sphakia (which was then a much larger area than the modern province of that name) with three hundred men-at-arms organised into five companies. The latter family figures prominently throughout Cretan history, especially as leader of the successive rebellions that took place during the first three centuries of Venetian occupation.

These well-organised uprisings were quite different in nature, and even in purpose, from the more notorious peasant revolts which occurred under the Turks. In the Ottoman Empire, as in other Moslem States, religion and not race was the criterion which determined the respective status of the conqueror and the conquered; new converts to Islam *ipso facto* acquired all the rights and privileges of the ruling class—hence, with the exception of Sphakia, the wholesale apostasy in Crete, as everywhere else in the Empire. The revolts during the Turkish occupation were based, therefore, not on racial prejudice but on class warfare, in which the Cretan *rayahs*, or Christian subjects, were matched against their islamized compatriots.

No such apostasy occurred during Venetian rule,[3] for there was nothing to be gained by it; conversion to Catholicism would not imply a change of class—in any case large sections of the Orthodox community, represented by the *Archontopouloi*, were in such a strong position as to require no change. They directly controlled extensive areas of the island and so, in relation to the Venetian authorities, resembled a rival political faction rather than a subject race. By the middle of the sixteenth century, indeed, the Pateropouloi of Sphakia (whose independence had remained unchallenged throughout the occupation) supported by other *Archontopouloi* in charge of the surrounding mountain districts, had grown sufficiently confident in their strength to establish an opposition government, and this at a time when, in the prefecture of Canea alone, the Venetians could call on over thirteen thousand *huomini de fattione* based on the forts which they had built along the coast in addition to that of Canea: Castel-Chissamo in the bay of Kastelli, Castel-Selino at Palaeochora, Castel della Sfachia at Sphakia and Castel-Franco, an isolated fortification near Sphakia known today as Frankogastello. Plans for the erection of yet another fortress—the one that now stands on Souda island—precipitated the formation of the Cretan revolutionary government.

This bid for independence almost succeeded. In addition to the populations of Selino and Sphakia, the inhabitants of the Riza—the foothill district on the northern slopes of the White Mountains, which includes some villages situated almost on the very plain of Canea—also united together and refused to obey the representatives of Venice; instead, they formed a new administration of their own and serviced it with officers appointed by themselves. Duties and taxes were now paid not to Venetian but to Cretan authorities, so that for some time two independent powers co-existed in the island. From the scanty material available it is difficult to conjecture what the outcome of this situation would have been had not a strange episode occurred, causing the abrupt and final downfall of the rebel administration which might otherwise have achieved some degree

3. In fact the very opposite occurred on one occasion: in 1363 the Venetian colonists themselves rebelled against their mother country, united with the Cretan subjects and joined the Orthodox Church.

of official recognition. The hero, or perhaps the villain, of this episode was a native of Koustoyerako, a certain George Kandanoleon.

His name does not appear on the list of the twelve original *Archontopouloi*, though it is almost certain that he was a direct descendant of one of them, probably of the famous Skordylis family.[4] By 1573, at any rate, he had achieved a sufficiently important position in the island to warrant his appointment as Rector, or Governor, of the independent provinces under Cretan control. Nothing is known of his public administration; and the little that is known of his private life is based on Trivan's isolated account of the Rector's downfall and death. If, then, Kandanoleon is remembered in Crete today, it is only because of his one recorded action, which remains as inexplicable as it must have been dramatic. The Venetian chronicler gives us no clue to the man's character from which we might deduce the motives behind his unaccountable and fatal behaviour. All that we have are the facts, which are these:

One day Kandanoleon suddenly descended from his mountain headquarters at Meskla and called at a country house in Alikianou which belonged to a Venetian noble called Francesco Damolino. The only apparent reason that he had for this unexpected visit was to propose a marriage between the Venetian's daughter Sophia and his own son Petros; but what was the reason behind such an unpredictable proposal? Had Kandanoleon already been in touch with Damolino, or with any other Venetian official? If so, on what basis and for what purpose? These questions have to be answered if he is to be cleared of the charges, imputed to him by certain historians, of treachery and double-dealing. Was Kandanoleon, in fact, the Ephialtes of his time—that sinister figure which crops up throughout Greek history and tarnishes its most brilliant moments? In the absence of reliable information, any answer is bound to be speculative.

---

4. The problem of tracing the descendants of the *Archontopouloi* is aggravated by the change of name which often occurred as and when they developed new branches. Thus the Mousouros family, one of the original twelve, hardly ever appears in official documents, though I have come across the name in a folk-song; this family is believed to have adopted the Sphakian name of Vlachos at a very early stage in its career. On the other hand, Kallergis, though recurring constantly in the history of Crete, is not one of the original names; those bearing it are said to be descended from the family of Phokas. The Skordylis family, outside Sphakia, appears variously under the name of Pateros, Papadopoulos and Kandanoleon.

I am personally induced to believe the best of him, and so attribute his motives either to *philodoxia*, that typically Greek failing of personal ambition, or to a genuine, though naive, belief that by relating himself to the Venetian *feudator* by marriage—which in Crete is still quite a common method of reconciling two enemies—he could somehow come to terms with the Venetian authorities. This, to my mind, is a reasonable surmise, for in his proposal the Rector added a rider that he would resign his office in favour of his son as soon as the marriage took place.

Damolino appears to have welcomed the suggestion—and here again Kandanoleon lays himself open to a number of charges, the least of them being that of blind innocence. Why, in fact, having made such a wild proposal, did he fail to suspect the readiness with which it was accepted? Surely he must have known that the Venetian's aversion to the Orthodox church was no less strong than the animosity which he himself felt, or should have felt, for Catholicism?[5] Again, these questions remain unanswered.

It is worth describing the wedding ceremony in detail, not only because it is one of the few recorded episodes in a relatively unknown period of Cretan history, but also because it illustrates a certain aspect of Venetian policy, which tends to be overlooked by most Cretan historians in their Christian zeal to focus attention on atrocities perpetrated at a later date by the infidels of Turkey and Egypt.

The wedding, then, took place at Damolino's country-house on the Sunday week after the Rector's visit. The Venetian invited fifty of his friends from Canea to attend the celebration, for which a hundred sheep and oxen had been slaughtered, and Kandanoleon arrived accompanied by three hundred and fifty men and about a hundred women. The ceremony was duly performed, and the rest of the day devoted, as usual, to festivity. The generous host sedulously plied his guests with wine, so that by sunset they were all

---

5. This animosity persisted long after the Venetian occupation. In 1833 the Reverend John Hartley observed that "if a Roman Catholic confirms to the Greek Church, as is not unusual for the sake of marriage, he is rebaptised: and it is asserted that he is sometimes retained in the water for a very considerable space of time, in order that the Papal infection may be more completely effaced." In spite of the basic similarity between the Eastern and Western Churches, the animosity between them persists even now. The sixteen-hundred-year-old memory of Nicaea is not as easily effaced as an individual's "Papal infection."

quite drunk—too drunk, anyway, to realise the significance of a rocket that suddenly went up above Canea.

This was a private signal to Damolino, who had notified the Venetian Governor of Kandanoleon's proposal and had asked for official co-operation in obtaining satisfaction for the indignity which he claimed to have suffered. The authorities had cooperated by assembling a raiding-force of a hundred and fifty horsemen and seventeen hundred foot-soldiers; the rocket now announced their approach.

When the troops arrived they found all the Cretans overpowered by wine and sleep, and too bewildered to resist or run away. It was therefore an easy matter to bind them hand-and-foot and let them wait there till day-break. At dawn Damolino himself hung the Rector, the bridegroom, and one of his younger brothers. Three of the Mousouros family were shot, and the rest hanged[6] on trees, as were also eight of the Kondos family, the remainder being sent to the galleys in chains. All the other prisoners were then formed up into four separate columns and marched away under escort. The first group was hanged at the gate of Canea, the second at the castle of Apokoronas, the third in the mountains above Meskla, and the fourth in Kandanoleon's birthplace, Koustoyerako. By their death, Trivan assures us, "all men who were faithful and devoted to God and their Prince were comforted and consoled."

The alleged indignity was thus avenged; there still remained another account to settle, one beyond the power of the local authorities. The matter was therefore referred to the Senate at Venice and a certain Cavalli was elected as *Proveditor*,[7] with orders to exterminate the rest of the rebels. Cavalli's method was swift, simple and effective. He began by burning down a village, hanging a dozen priests and disembowelling four pregnant women. With threats of more to come, he then confiscated all rebel property, put a price on the head of every inhabitant of the district which he had proscribed, but undertook to pardon any one of them who would make

6. The extermination of this family probably accounts for the omission of its name on all subsequent documents. See footnote, p. 39.

7. This post seems to have been somewhat similar to that of Commissar in the modern Soviet system. A *proveditor* was not answerable to local authority, but reported direct to Venice, and was appointed at indefinite intervals for a tour of duty which sometimes lasted as long as eighteen months. In Crete there were usually two of these officials serving simultaneously.

a sign of submission by producing in Canea "the head of his father, or brother, or cousin, or nephew." Strangely enough, many of them did, and the sight of these bleeding offerings moved even the representatives of Venice to compassion. Cavalli's law was abolished—but not before the rebellion had been quelled through the never-failing system of hostages and reprisals.

What is now known as the Kandanoleon Rebellion was the Cretans' last attempt to assert their independence of Venice, an attempt which might have succeeded but for the strange behaviour of a single individual. The Kandanoleon mystery has never been solved, and in all probability never will be. Whether he was a traitor or a martyr is a question of less interest, even to his descendants, than the fact that these descendants still exist. Their long family line flows like an erratic stream through the frequently uncharted fields of Cretan history, plunging underground only to re-emerge where the surface is broken by landmarks situated at intervals several centuries' long. This stream is likely to follow its course indefinitely; for, apart from the Kandanoleon who lies dead in the churchyard, there are two other relatives of the same name still living in the village; both of them are men, and both are married.

———

Before leaving London, I had been asked by the Fauna Preservation Society to see what could be done about preserving the ibex, an animal as fabulous to me as the gryphon; and, in Crete today, almost as non-existent. In ancient times the ibex used to abound on every mountain-range in the island. In the sixteenth century Belon observed whole herds of them on the north-eastern slopes of Mount Ida, and only a hundred years ago Spratt counted forty on the same slopes in a single day. Even as late as 1869 Raulin mentions them in the highlands of Lassithi. Today they inhabit only one small area of the White Mountains—the highest crags above Koustoyerako, between Mount Psilaphi and the Gorge of Samaria—and even here in such small numbers as to be virtually extinct. Their chance of survival elsewhere disappeared with the advent of the modern rifle; I wanted to know if they still had a chance in their last remaining lair.

The only people who could tell me were the very men whose activity I had been asked to curb—the poachers, chief of whom were the two Paterakis brothers, Manolis and Costis. They alone could pin-point the haunts on the Koustoyerako side of the gorge; they alone were capable of reaching them. Manolis had even crossed the so-called "Untrodden Cliffs" and brought back two animals alive: an almost incredible feat. One of these—the famous Kri-Kri—was later presented to President Truman as a token of Cretan gratitude for Marshall Aid and is now, I believe, in the Washington Zoo. But Manolis got no credit for this capture. He sold the animal to a passing policeman, not for money but for something far more precious: rifle ammunition. The policeman then gave it to a shepherd friend of his, Eftychis Protopapas; and finally Eftychis got the kudos—and a free trip to America.

I had never even seen an ibex myself, and felt that I could not tackle the problem of their preservation until I had. I therefore asked Costis to let me come with him on his next poaching expedition. At once he offered me the loan of a rifle and the chance of having the first shot; he could not imagine any other reason for my wanting to accompany him. I felt guilty about keeping him in the dark, but my conscience was clear about hunting one of the animals which I was meant to be protecting: since I had been offered the first shot, it was bound to get away unharmed.

We set off one morning while the rest of the village was still asleep, not for reasons of secrecy—poaching here is done in daylight—but so as to avoid the full heat of the sun during our ascent. With us was a friend called Vangelis, who had volunteered to act as a beater.

Day broke over us as we skirted the natural battlements above the Koutsounara spring. From here I looked back and watched the tide of night receding from the village; the darkness, like a liquid, draining from the basin until the white dregs of the houses at the bottom came to light. The sight must have reminded Costis of that same moment eight years before, when he had looked down from this spot and seen the village surrounded by Germans, with the women and children, and the few old men who still slept indoors, lined up in front of a firing-squad. Costis had fired first, killing the officer in command, and in the consequent confusion most of the hostages had escaped.

The cypress forest we were now crossing had then become a battlefield; fear had stamped each feature of it so clearly on my memory that even now I recognized at once the almost inaccessible caves—some of them little more than blind ledges in the cliffs—where we had hidden for a whole thirsty week after being split up and cut off from our nearest water-supply, the Aconisia spring, which was our present destination.

Here we filled the wine-skins which we had brought with us; there was no more water to be found further on. Disregarding the wasps which swarmed round it—a sign of a hard winter ahead, so Vangelis informed us—we buried our faces in the stream which trickled slowly through the hollowed tree-trunks serving as a trough, and drank until we felt as distended as the wine-skins actually were. When we moved on, the weight of water swirling in my stomach seemed to balance exactly the load strapped on to my back.

The path had petered out; we now walked where we could, over ground shaped like a rough sea turned to stone, hemmed in by formidable breakwaters of rock and littered with the wrecks of trees which were as brittle underfoot as cuttle-bone—a dead-sea landscape, in which sudden specks of green flashed against the dust-coloured background. These were patches of dittany which, like algae thrown up by a breaker, grew high and dry and out of reach on the smooth cliff-face.

The healing power of this herb was known even in classical times; Virgil and Aristotle both mention it as a cure for a wounded ibex. Today its tonic properties are recognized by jaded rakes and the plant is exported to foreign pharmacists. Like the mandrake, it captured the imagination of the earlier naturalists. Belon, for instance, who spent a few months in Crete in the first half of the sixteenth century, reported:

> *Entre autres plantes de Crète le Dictannum est insigne, qui à peine peut croistre sur terre: aussi vient-il tousiours es entredeux et fentes des rochers, et non autre part, et n'est trouvé ailleurs qu'en Crète.*

I have no idea whether dittany remains exclusively indigenous to the island, but I do know that it still commands a high price locally—so high, indeed, that some of the villagers risk their necks every season, lowering themselves over precipices on homemade ropes in pursuit of this vegetable gold, which has probably cost as many lives in Crete as edelweiss in Switzerland or samphire in Cornwall.

On the edge of one of these precipices Costis called a halt and outlined his plan. We were on a narrow crenellated spur, from which the whole cliff was visible, curving round for nearly a quarter of a mile like the inside wall of some gigantic amphitheatre. "Here's a perfect position for you," he told me, "I know there's at least one of the cuckolds hiding here. Vangelis will go over to the far side and try to drive it out. I'll be further down the cliff to cut it off from there. So it should make straight for you. Don't shoot till it's right on top of you. If you don't kill it outright, it'll be lost for good—a wound won't slow it up. Don't move or make a sound till you hear from Vangelis."

I was left alone to consider my position, which I found far from perfect. Balanced on this knife-edge of rock, with a sheer drop on either side, I had no intention of letting a charging ibex get anywhere near me. After waiting for over an hour without a cigarette—the wind was in the right direction but Costis had advised me not to smoke—I began to feel that discomfort was the penalty that I had to pay for being here under false pretences. Then, suddenly, something happened.

Down the far side of the cliff an avalanche of boulders was released, which I could trace from the dust-storm raised in its wake. Like the lightning-flash which silently heralds a clap of thunder, it forewarned me of the deafening crack to come; but when this did come I was not prepared for such a sustained onslaught of sound. The din of the first stones pitching into the ravine was prolonged as the rest of the landslide followed, and immediately prolonged again by the echo in full pursuit. Then a yell from Vangelis: "Look out! Here he comes!"

Something had appeared on the face of the cliff, like an object projected on to a blank screen, diminished at first by distance to the size of a fly, but in a few seconds magnified and brought into focus by the speed of its approach. Though I could not be certain of its colour—it seemed only slightly darker than the background of rock—the two growths arching over its neck, like inverted tusks, showed as plainly as scaffolding on a skyline. With no apparent means of propulsion (for its legs were invisible in motion) and with its shoulders flattened by perspective and half-concealed in dust, it came hurtling horizontally across the cliff—a disembodied head hanging on to the air by its horns.

I fired at it without taking aim. Its course altered, not its speed. The head switched into profile, and left my field of vision in a diagonal dun-coloured streak. Two shots rang out below me, then Costis's voice: "He's away! We've lost him!"

Less than a minute had passed since Vangelis had launched the landslide.

The descent into the ravine, where we had agreed to meet, would have been an anticlimax had I not found it so difficult and dangerous. I thought that it would be impossible to get lost on that slope, yet I managed to achieve the impossible. My direction I knew: downhill. But between me and the foot of the cliff stretched a vertical maze hedged in by solid rock; again and again blank walls which I could not scale forced me to scramble back the way that I had come; unwalled drops of several hundred feet had the same effect; and for twenty minutes I was marooned in a shallow basin near the top of what looked like a petrified waterfall. The sound of my hobnails shrieking over the slithery stone intensified the fear of heights that I now experienced for the first time in my life. At last I reached a scree, as long and steep as a ski-jump, which led down to the river-bed where Costis and Vangelis were waiting.

It was too late to get back to Koustoyerako by daylight, and impossible to do so in the dark. So we settled down for the night on the smoothest piece of ground that we could find. Costis was tactful enough not to mention my marksmanship; I refrained from bringing up the subject of preservation. In any case, I was now fairly confident that the ibex would never become quite extinct; not many people would want to hunt it in its present habitat.

Like those of Souyia, the charms of Koustoyerako soon began to pall; and here there was no beach to which to escape, no sea in which to spend the day. Most of the shepherds were with their flocks in the summer pastures on the slopes of Mount Psilaphi, yet every evening the two village coffee-shops, each with its own wireless set, did a brisk trade; especially during the broadcast of the daily news bulletin, which led invariably to a long and dreary political discussion.

"What do you think about the situation?" they would ask me.

I replied that I never thought about it.

"But you must know," they persisted. "You see more of the world than we do. What are the Russians up to?"

I told them that I had no idea.

They were too well-mannered to voice their disbelief beyond remarking: "Now that you're back, you can count on us again. But you'll let us know in time, won't you?"

Gradually I understood the presence of the reception committee on my arrival at Souyia, the motive behind the question: "What

news?" and the anxiety to know my opinion on "the situation."
These men were still in the state of exception in which the last war
had left them, in a state of expectancy for the next war to come; and
they refused to believe that I was not. And so when they spoke, it
was not as citizens of a peace-time village community, but as members of the original guerilla gang with which, in their minds, I had
never ceased to be associated. They were so convinced themselves
that I had come back to Crete for other purposes than to write a
book, that by the time I left Koustoyerako they had almost convinced me as well.

3

GAVDOS

FROM THE TOP of the White Mountains Gavdos looks more like a cloud than an island, floating twenty miles out to sea on an horizon which, when visible through the heat-haze, appears unnaturally high. It was probably this unsubstantial quality about it that attracted me when I first saw it, for I could not otherwise explain my immediate impatience to visit it.

Certainly, it was romantically associated in my mind with the Odyssey, but I knew this association to be false, based as it was on an old local legend which represents Gavdos as the island of Calypso, a supposition supported by the more recent but equally absurd assertion that a certain cave near Souyia was the home of the Cyclops.[1] It was also associated—romantically again, I admit—with pirates: during the Middle Ages it had been a regular port of call for Levantine corsairs and Maltese cruisers; later it was used as a base for raids on the Selino coast. But neither its false association with Odysseus, nor its true one with Khair-ed-Din, was a reasonable explanation for my urge.

The feeling that I had for this isolated triangle of land had clearly never been shared by other travellers, most of whom had carefully

1. I sheltered in this cave for a few days shortly after landing in 1942. It was then that a peasant told me its history and, as though to prove it, pointed out two rocks in the sea below: "Those are the stones the monster threw." What, then, of the rocks in the sea off Catania? Sicily will have to look to her laurels!

48

avoided it. As far as I could discover, no more than three foreigners had visited it for over a hundred years: Captain Spratt dropped anchor there while engaged on the Mediterranean survey which he had undertaken for the Admiralty in 1851; a few years later the conscientious French professor, Raulin, spent three days on the island, marooned by an October gale, and Professor Dawkins reconnoitred its coast during the first World War. Gavdos, then, represents almost virgin territory for the tourist-explorer of today: new ground to be broken. For me it represented more: a never-never land which, as I looked at it, seemed to dissolve in the air like the cloud that it appeared to be.

The only way of getting there was by caique from Palaeochora; so once again I found myself walking down that dismal single street, this time with Daphne Bath who had just flown out from England to take photographs of Crete. After running the gauntlet of staring eyes on either side of us—for although all the houses on the isthmus face the sea, their occupants prefer to sit outside in the dusty road—we turned into one of many coffee-shops grouped round a plane-tree and started our enquiries about transport.

We were in luck. A ten-ton caique, chartered by two merchants from Canea, was due to leave for Gavdos in the morning; the captain was willing to take us as well. We gratefully accepted the offer for, as far as we knew, this might have been the last link with the island until the following spring; communications, irregular at the best of times, are completely suspended in the winter owing to the white squalls of a typhonic gale, known today as the *meltem*, and referred to by St. Luke as the "tempestuous wind, called the Euroclydon."

No one could understand why we should voluntarily go to Gavdos (the two city-slickers were travelling on business; they were hoping to salvage a wreck) for no one, apparently, ever went there of his own accord. Such was the unpopularity of the place that the islanders themselves were gradually abandoning it; during the last generation alone its previous population of about five hundred had been decreased by over half.

For the present-day peasant of Gavdos, the stone-and-concrete ulcer of Palaeochora has the same attraction that the dockyards and factories of Liverpool and Glasgow once had for the Irish workman. Up to the beginning of this century, when the island still belonged to the Sphakians, and the inhabitants, being only their tenants, were certainly as poor as they are today, there was none of this wholesale emigration. It is only since the eruption of the new houses round the old Venetian fort that the islanders have started flocking over to what, for them, is the equivalent of a mainland capital. Here they have settled, and are still settling, preferring the suburban squalor of a trading-centre to the stone and sand of their native island, which, in another generation perhaps, will be uninhabited desert.

This desert island in the making intrigued me more than ever.

At four in the morning we were all on board and ready to leave, when a dog's bark, a man's voice and the rattle of fire-arms sounded on the quayside. Out of the moonless dark a human face materialised six feet above the ground; a pair of animal eyes glinted green at ground level. The village priest, Father Stylianos, dressed in black, accompanied by a black hound, and armed with a shot-gun had decided to come with us. He joined us in the boat and we set off.

Until daybreak the outline of the receding mountains was clearer than the profiles of my companions sitting next to me, the serrated silhouette of the peaks familiar from my clandestine landings. But when the sun rose I saw them, literally, in a new light; it was my first day-time view of them from this distance and direction. It was only then that I realised how admirably suitable their name is. The southern summits of these mountains really are white, so white indeed that from Alphonse de Lamartine they provoked the following remark, as inaccurate as it is fanciful:

> *Voici les sommets lointains de l'île de Crète, qui s'élèvent à notre droite, voici l'Ida, couvert de neiges qui paraît d'ici comme les hautes voiles d'un vaisseau sur la mer.*

The unmistakable cone of Mount Ida could never, even with the broadest stretch of the imagination, be likened to the sails of a ship; and no mountain in Crete is covered in snow during the month of August, when the poet was sailing past the island. Clearly, then, what he saw was the White Mountain range lying naked in the sunlight.

The sunlight through which we were now sailing affected us in different ways. Daphne and I basked in it gratefully. The two townees and the caique captain avoided it, the former by scuttling into the shadow of the sail, the latter by burying his head below the hatch-

The last flock on the Omalo before the first snowfall

"The Gates," narrowest passage in the Gorge of Samaria

way of the engine-room. The boatman, a barefoot, bearded Ancient Mariner, stared into it unblinkingly as he rested his weight on the tiller. The deck-hand, a grease-coated lad of fifteen, disregarded it completely. And Father Stylianos prepared to meet it like a High Priest, chanting hymns in its praise as he peeled off his thick black *rasso*, but switching to the latest Athenian dance tune as soon as he revealed the Fair-isle sweater which he wore underneath.

The deck-hand brought us breakfast: a demi-john of *tsikoudia*, and with it a basket full of purple grapes, which we dipped in the sea to cool. The blending of salt-water with sweet fruit was a subtle revelation to the palate, a happy marriage on the tongue between the two respective extracts of earth and ocean. Father Stylianos drank with us, nibbled, and went on with his song:

Oh, let your hair down,
Let it hang in tangled skeins . . .

To suit his actions to the words, he took off his *kalamavki* and unpinned his bun, letting his hair uncoil and fall, a black velvet curtain, over his shoulders.

There are some priests in Greece who break the rules of the Church by trimming their hair, and so incidentally deprive themselves of their androgynous attraction; for without the bun as a visible sexual counterbalance, the beard seems a pointless masculine appendage, a redundant and even suspect indication of virility. Besides, on a cropped head the *kalamavki* ceases to be ecclesiastical headgear and, disassociated, looks no more than what it is: an absurd cylinder of black felt shaped like a section of stove-pipe.

But Father Stylianos's tresses were as long as a full-grown Sikh's, and as carefully tended. He began to comb them now with great deliberation, squinting into a pocket-mirror which he asked the deck-hand to hold for him; then he looked up at me and grinned:

"Oh, what a beautiful boy I am! Aren't you jealous? I bet there's not a priest in England with hair like mine. Tell me about the priests in your country."

I told him. He was not impressed.

"But they must look just like ordinary men!" he objected.

"What a chance for me if I went to England! Do you think I'd be a success—oh, not in the Church, of course, but for breeding purposes? My stud-fee's as low as you like—I'd do it for nothing!

Not yet forty, Father Stylianos was already a widower, forbidden by ecclesiastical law to remarry, and thus condemned to many more years of celibacy than he could possibly have foreseen before his wife's sudden death. For him, then, sex was not a closed book but something far more frustrating: a book that had been confiscated when he was less than halfway through it. Gaily, he went on:

"You're not married, are you? Well, watch your step when we get to Gavdos. There's a tree there called the *kedros*—if you eat its fruit, you'll want to have as many wives as a Turk!"

Off Gavdopoulos, the tiny uninhabited island which offers winter pasture to the Sphakian herds, and serves, so to speak, as a lodge to the mansion of Gavdos, we closed a passing fishing-vessel as well stocked as a fishmonger's on land. The captain of our caique ordered a large *phagri*, a kind of salt-water carp, which was weighed in the boat before being slung across to us. "I'll pay you when I get back," he shouted, then pressed the fish into my hands: "Here, it's for you. You won't find much to eat where you're going. My boatman will cook it for you. He's going ashore anyway, to visit his family. You can have him as a guide."

Still standing at the tiller, old Sinbad smiled happily. "I'll show you all over the island," he said, "you'll like it." He was the first person I had met who had a good word to say for it.

When Spratt came to Gavdos he was shocked by the behavior of the inhabitants: "So inconsiderate was their curiosity, on the first arrival of my ship, that several swam off to her soon after anchoring, and surprised us by boarding her from the gangways and bows in a state of nudity, just like the uncivilised natives of the Pacific islands." The islanders at that time must have been very different from the modern Cretans, who avoid the sea as much as they can and would never dream of appearing naked in public.

But there was no one, naked or otherwise, to meet us when we dropped anchor in a sandy cove on the north coast. The beach was deserted and looked as if it always had been. Daphne and I were the first ashore. We undressed at once and waited in the water for Father Stylianos and the boatman to land, while the two townees sailed off in the caique to the scene of their wreck further east.

We were not allowed to bathe for long, for Sinbad was anxious to show us "Calypso's palace." As we skirted the shore, I began almost to believe that the nymph might indeed have lived here; if this was not a Homeric landscape, it was at least the sort of country that a film-producer would choose for a screen version of the Odyssey. Half-buried in the blown sands out of which they grew were the famous *kedros* trees, a species of stunted juniper, which looked like a regiment of corpses: some standing upright, like pagan prophets struck dead while uttering a blasphemy, each limb a pointed threat; others cramped and contorted, as though they had succumbed to an agonizing poison, their bodies arched like a suicide's backbone. But the *rigor mortis* of this sparse maritime forest was an illusion; these gesticulating, attitudinising trees were not only alive but in fruit, bursting with brick-coloured berries. I disregarded the priest's advice and sampled them. They tasted as dehydrated as they looked.

Further inland, where the sand was less thick and the earth showed through as though through a threadbare carpet, the scented breath of wild thyme distilled itself over porcupine-humps of scrub and candelabra-shaped skeletons of asphodel—all very different from Homer's description of the site of Calypso's "vaulted cavern." Here there was no "verdant copse of alders, aspens and fragrant cypresses," no "garden vine with great bunches of ripe grapes," and, of the "four separate but neighboring springs," not a sign of even one. Yet it was here, so Sinbad insisted, that the nymph once lived. "Look," he said, "you can still see part of the ancient buildings"; and pointed out some Hellenic remains emerging from a sand-dune.

We ate our fish in an isolated farm-house on the edge of a barren plain named after St. George, though no church dedicated to this, or any other, saint was visible in the treeless wilderness. The flat ground here, composed more of soft rock than of hard earth, reminded me in some way of the battlefields of Verdun, which I had once visited long ago in much the same mood and for the same reason, or rather lack of it, that I was now visiting Gavdos.

The owners of the house, two women, were the first islanders that we saw. According to Spratt, the people of Gavdos "are primitive in their habits and ideas, and moreover are without enterprise and energy, a mixed and degenerate race." We must have been more fortunate in our encounter than he was.

Certainly, the existence of these two peasants could hardly fail to be primitive. The walls of their house were built without mortar;

its floor was of stamped earth; its roof, of dried mud held together
by branches and supported on a single stout juniper pillar. The few
sticks of furniture inside were dwarfed by a domed oven, which
looked like a miniature hangar, and by a massive stone barley-
grinder, which might have been the prototype of an early Norman
font. There was no kitchen-stove: our fish had to be taken outside to
be cooked, over an open fire.

Yet this poverty, if anything, dignified its owners; there was
no false modesty nor pride of penury in their welcome. Although
Daphne must have been the first English woman on whom they
had ever set eyes, they did not gape and stare at her as the supposedly more sophisticated provincials of Palaeochora had done; and
when we left, they accepted our thanks as calmly as though they
had two foreign guests and a strange priest to luncheon every day
of the week.

Sleepily after so much food—for the fish had been supplemented
by gifts of eggs and cheese and, miraculously in this vineless district, wine—we crossed the plain and climbed the slope leading to
Ambelos, where Sinbad's family lived. As we approached the top, we
were met by a combination of smells which I could not at once identify: the sugary-sweetness of wild fig masking the sickly-sweetness
of carob, like cheap perfume on unwashed flesh—and there at last
were the trees, the only productive trees on the island, for the olive
cannot flourish on these storm-bitten hills.

At first glance the whole hamlet seemed to be in ruins, the dry-
walling of the abandoned houses indistinguishable from the walls of
those that were still inhabited. None of the buildings looked solid
enough to provide adequate shelter for its occupants; and once again
I had the impression of being on a film-set, in two-dimensional surroundings hastily erected to represent, say, a Foreign Legion outpost
in a scene from *Beau Geste*.

Sinbad's house was almost identical to the farmhouse in which we
had lunched: the same bare floor, the same wooden shutters, and the
same roof supported by a central wooden pillar which looked and
felt as hard as concrete; and the palaeolithic barley-grinder standing
in one corner was the largest piece of furniture in the room. With
his wife and family swarming round him, Sinbad seemed out-of-
place in his own home and even the children did not look as if they
could possibly be his; the eldest of the seven was under ten years old,
while he himself was well over sixty. Father Stylianos also noticed

this and whispered in my ear: "Now you can see what the fruit of the *kedros* does to a man!"

We started off again almost at once, for Sinbad was anxious to show us the rest of the island before nightfall. On the outskirts of the village he pointed out a recent excavation in the sunbaked soil: the shaft of a proposed well, sunk to such a shallow depth that it could not even be described as half-finished. It had been less than half-begun before being abandoned, like so many other constructions all over Greece. A small placard decorated with the Stars and Stripes and bearing the inscription *"Schedion Marsal"* indicated that this pathetic little hole in the ground was part of the grandiose reconstruction scheme financed by the United States. But in Gavdos the money had run out long before the water, for which it was intended, had even started to run in.

"To think of all those dollars going down the drain," was Sinbad's comment; "why dig so deep just to bury them?"

Water-shortage, we knew, was the island's main problem, but we did not fully realise its effect on the individual inhabitant until we came across a ragged old crone carrying an empty pitcher. Barefoot, she had walked two miles from one of the outlying hamlets to fetch water from the nearest available well. Unable to afford a donkey and a cask, she was her own beast of burden—a worn-out, decrepit one, capable of carrying no more than a two-bottle load at a time. This was her third journey to the well that day.

After a further climb through fields which looked like territory recently evacuated by an army with a scorched-earth policy, we reached the top of the cliffs on the opposite coast. The lighthouse here, which was once a familiar landmark for shipping between Egypt and Europe, had been destroyed by the R.A.F. in a war-time raid and was now nothing more than a useless stump—an accidental architectural "folly." But it delighted me no less than if it had still been in working order; it was its site that mattered, not its curtailed function.

There are some people who cannot look at a mountain without wanting to climb to the top of it. I have the same feeling about capes and promontories; to stand on the furthest edge of a piece of land gives me a far greater sense of achievement than reaching its highest point. (Did Byron share this feeling, I wonder? Was it only the Temple of Poseidon that attracted him to the "Cape of the Columns," Sunium?) Here, at the foot of this lighthouse, I stood at the very end not only of a small island but of a whole continent—this was the southernmost tip of Europe—and with unaccountable pleasure I realised that Africa was closer than Athens.

Inland, the vegetation grew less sparse: partridge-country. For a mile or more Father Stylianos kept us ducking as he whirled round every few yards, pointing his gun in all directions. But he never fired a shot; there was nothing to fire at. The only thing that we ever saw moving in the bushes was the priest's black dog, which more than once was accidentally stalked by its owner. Empty-handed, we finally reached Kastri, the capital.

Here, as in the other hamlets which we had passed on the way, not more than half-a-dozen houses were inhabited. The remainder stood scalped and blinded, with roofs capsized; the supporting pillars, as well as all the doors and windows, had been immediately purloined on the previous occupants' departure. But Kastri had two features to distinguish it as the capital—a police-station, which was the only properly constructed building that I had so far seen, and a coffee-shop, to which we were at once invited.

Here we met the police-sergeant, who described himself as "the loneliest man in the world." He had been serving in Gavdos for over a year, with only these few impoverished peasants for company; there was no doctor on the island, since the climate was so healthy; no schoolmaster, for there was no school; no priest—no one, in fact, to relieve his monotony by conversation of the slightly higher level to which he was evidently accustomed. There was not even any crime to keep him busy; his present responsibilities were limited to looking after a solitary "bandit" exiled for Communist activity. He was so lonely indeed that he wanted us to stay the night with him in the police-station, but was honest enough to admit that we would find better accommodation in the retired lighthouse-keeper's house on the other side of the island. As this was another hour's walk away, we took to the path again.

It was dark by the time we reached what, for Gavdos, was a fine modern house on the top of an inland cliff. By then we were so tired that all we wanted was somewhere to sleep, but the lighthouse-keeper insisted that we first have dinner. Since he had not been expecting us there was no food ready; we had to wait for a couple of chickens to be killed, plucked, cooked and eaten before we could, at last, settle down for the night.

This must have been the first time in her life that Daphne had shared a bedroom with a barefoot boatman and an Orthodox priest.

We were woken early next morning by the deck-hand; somehow the boy had tracked us down to this house on the cliff, with news that the caique was waiting for us further down the coast. We wanted to leave at once, but our host would not let us go until we had first drunk some goat's milk and then admired the view from his terrace. From this height the plain below looked like a plasticine model crudely moulded with a minimum of effort and imagination; features such as hillocks and furrows were indicated only in rough outline, and the few scattered trees and bushes that were visible were more like a cartographer's conventional signs than genuine living growths. This was the country which we had to cross before going down to the sea.

We found the caique lying at anchor in a shallow indentation known as Ship's Bay, which must once have been the pirates' main harbour—the *Porto Sarachinico* of *Il Regno di Candia*, Boschini's seventeenth-century map. More than half the population of the island had collected here on this narrow strip of shingle to witness the event of the day, the ship's departure; and the owner of the solitary shack on the beach was doing a brisk trade in fizzy lemonade, wine, *tsikoudia* and coffee. This unexpected early-morning gathering was imbued with its own brand of seaside holiday spirit—*panegyric*[2] in the Greek, not the English, sense of the word.

The two townees were the only skeletons at this particular feast. They had found that their wreck was unfit for salvage; their journey had been fruitless. Sulky and unshaven, they were now anxious to get away as soon as possible. We were prepared to humour them—after all, it was they who had chartered the caique—and no doubt we would have left immediately after our first farewell drink, had it not been for the impulsiveness of Father Stylianos. Without any warning he loaded his gun and fired it into the air.

"I brought it all the way here in order to use it," he explained. "I couldn't very well leave without at least one shot."

"But you still haven't hit anything," I objected.

He accepted this remark as a challenge; the *pallikari* in him had been roused. "We'll soon settle that," he replied, "let's have a target."

2. This word may be literally translated "a general circling round," i.e. the mood and movement of a crowd at a public holiday; hence its present-day meaning in Greece of festival or feast-day.

I set up an empty cigarette-box for him on a rock a few yards away. His shot tore it to shreds. Delighted, he handed me the gun: "Now you have a go." I perforated what was left of the largest bit of cardboard: "Too easy; let's have a longer range." The shooting soon developed into a competition, which became more lively when the police-sergeant presently joined us with his tommy-gun. Targets of every kind were selected and then shattered—empty bottles, old tins, bits of driftwood—and the crowd yelled with pleasure and plied us with wine while the glass and stone shrapnel burst all round us and bullets bounced off the rocks. We stopped only when the ammunition was exhausted.

Meanwhile the two townees had cautiously taken cover in the caique and, with fear as a spur to their impatience, were more than ever anxious to leave; but the captain and the crew, who had abandoned ship to enjoy the shooting at closer quarters, were now on shore to enjoy their share of the drinking that was bound to follow. It was almost noon before we eventually weighed anchor.

A few minutes later we were sailing past the pierced rocks of Tripiti which, like the central Faraglioni off Capri, form a gigantic maritime arch; and then along the cliffs under the lighthouse which, again like those of Capri, are pitted with sea-level grottoes. Drowsily I wondered whether I could do for Gavdos what the German painter Kopisch did for the Italian island in "discovering" a local Blue Grotto; but my imagination was incapable of contaminating this parched Greek purity with an infection of vulgar or voluptuous tourists; and my last impression of the coast before I fell asleep on deck was of hunched stone formations which reminded me of prehistoric animals—dinosaurs and pterodactyls trapped and enveloped in a flood of lava.

When I woke up we were off the Cretan coast and opposite another Tripiti, a needle-narrow opening in the littoral ramparts, which travellers until recently believed to be inaccessible except by sea. It almost is, but not quite. The gorge behind it, which marks the boundary between the provinces of Selino and Sphakia, is paved with the dry river-bed into which I had descended, admittedly with great difficulty, after the ibex-hunt; and the narrow beach in front of it had served throughout the occupation as a clandestine landing-point for the whole of the area—an impossible fulfillment, had it not been accessible also by land.

Now that I studied this coastline for the first time by daylight, I noticed how dangerously close Tripiti must have been to the German coastguards who were then stationed at Souyia. From the caique the beach looked within strolling distance of the village; on a calm night it would certainly have been within earshot; and the sound of the motor-vessels, which we had had to use for landing stores and agents once our submarines were no longer available for these duties, must have been clearly audible to the enemy outpost. It was on such nights that, warned in advance by me, a local violinist used to entertain the German guards with an impromptu concert in the hope that the shrill notes of his instrument would drown the deeper ones of the motor-boat's engine.

Evening encircled us shortly before we reached Palaeochora. The sun went down like a theatre-light going out, gradually but patently, silhouetting for a few blazing seconds a cloud which, riding low on the intervening horizon, looked as much like an island as Gavdos, from the top of the White Mountains, had looked like a cloud.

When we landed I asked the caique captain how much Daphne and I owed him for the fish that he had bought us and for our fares. "Nothing," he replied and nodded towards the disgruntled townees. "I've made quite enough out of those two cuckolds. Besides, you and the lady are strangers; it's we who should be giving you something— here, take these." And he presented us each with a large soft sponge.

4

SAMARIA

THE RAVINE BEHIND TRIPITI which we passed on our way
back from Gavdos is one of several deep fissures which split the
mountains at regular intervals along the south coast, like parallel cracks in the graining of a block of wood. Geographically, it is
the least important, for it leads nowhere—as one of our stray soldiers found to his cost after the fall of Crete in 1941. Attempting to
escape into the interior, he followed the river-bed to where it ends,
abruptly against a sheer inland cliff, which he must have then tried
to scale. Years later his skeleton was recovered by Costis during an
ibex-hunt in the waterless wilderness of the Rotten Crags.

More famous is the Gorge of Samaria, which cleaves the range a
few miles further east. Some early writers, anxious to romanticise
their travels, have called Samaria the "back door" or the "secret entrance" to Sphakia (the "front door" presumably being the broader
valley of Askyphou at the other end of the province). In point of
fact, Sphakia can be penetrated at several points; and Samaria has
never been an entrance to anywhere. The chasm contains only one
small village, a convenient bolt-hole which is completely cut off
from the rest of Crete for at least four months of the year; the snows
of winter isolate the gorge from the northern plains and Canea,
while a spring-time torrent blocks its only other exit, southwards to
the coast.

The utter isolation of Samaria has furnished pseudo-historians
and gullible travellers with an excuse for regarding it as a sort of

inverted Shangri-la, a forbidden area metaphorically signposted "*noli me tangere*" and protected by ethereal cohorts. For centuries, it is true, no foreign invader ever set foot in the village—there seems no reason for his ever wanting to do so, since it is of no strategic importance to an occupying force—so that throughout its history the gorge has served as a safe revolutionary asylum. Under the Venetians, in 1319, the rebellious Skordylis family used it as a refuge, and the later unsuccessful raids against it, by Turkish punitive expeditions, are too numerous to mention individually. But the legendary theory of its inviolability was exploded during the German occupation when a handful of Bavarian soldiers entered Samaria, not to exact reprisals but simply, out of a feeling of *heimweh*, to indulge in their native sport of mountain-climbing. The invisible guardians of the gorge, however, were not slow in punishing such hubris: two of the climbers, who were considered, presumably, to have violated the local taboo, slipped over a precipice and fell to their death within a few hours.

The present-day conception of Samaria as a seething hot-bed of banditry is just as romantically false as the older legends and superstitions. During the German occupation the gorge was, admittedly, a safe base for sheep-thieves and a secure, though somewhat stony, pasture for stolen flocks; and in the civil war that followed it was used as a last line of defence by the so-called Communist guerillas. Fourteen of these "bandits," being still unaccounted for, were believed to be in hiding somewhere in the neighbourhood, and the people of Samaria were suspected of sheltering them. Some of these people were old friends of mine; the suspicion thrown on them seemed to me so unjust and unreasonable that I determined to probe it at once by visiting the gorge myself before it was again sealed off by the weather.

———

Si haute et si infranchissable est du côté de Selino la barrière qui couvre les vallées sfakiotes que le plus court chemin pour pénétrer à Sfakia est encore de repasser par La Canée.

This remark of Georges Perrot, a Frenchman who visited Crete less than a hundred years ago, is typical of the exaggerated fear in which most foreign travellers seem to have held the Sphakian hinterland. It is nonsense to talk of the long detour via Canea as the shortest

route to Sphakia. The paved Roman path from the main Selino valley to the Omalo plateau must have been as good, if not better, in
Perrot's day as it is now; and there is an even shorter cut, straight up
the mountains from Koustoyerako. This was the way that Daphne
and I went, accompanied by Vardis, the youngest of the Paterakis brothers.

I found it heavy going; it must have been heavier still for Daphne
who was fresh from England, and for Vardis whose war wounds
have caused him a permanent limp. But after a steep climb all
morning through a burnt-out forest, in which no track was visible,
we reached the paved path at the Selino entrance to the Omalo.

The entrance is guarded by the isolated church of St. Theodore,
an insignificant building which I would scarcely have noticed, had
I not seen outside it the graves of two friends of mine, both members of the Pendaris family, who had been killed in a feud with the
equally well-known Selino clan of Sartjetis.[1] I no longer remember
the cause of the trouble—it was robbery, no doubt, or rape—but the
sight of these graves reminded me of the day on which it began, in
1943, and of the course that it followed for the rest of the occupation when these two famous families, which would otherwise have
been united in a common purpose, were split into rival factions and
thrown into opposing political camps. Since then more than eighty
men have been killed. The Greek Church, it seems, has lost the
power which it once had of reconciling, at a moment of national crisis, two communities at war.

Entering the Omalo was as satisfying as reaching an oasis in
the desert, and more surprising. This saucer of fertile land half-
submerged in a mountainous ocean of limestone floated suddenly
into sight, with nothing to forewarn us of its concealed presence
round the corner. Though the earth was hard and dry underfoot,
it seemed, compared to the encircling rocks, almost lush. But the
whole plain was deserted; the flocks which had spent the summer
here had already been removed to pasture beneath the winter snow-
line; and of the shepherds' huts built around the rim of the saucer,
all but one were abandoned. Its owner, a cheese-maker called Christos, the last man on the Omalo that year, was glad of our unexpected company and asked us to stay the night.

1. Euphemistically called *oikoyeniaka*, or "family matters," these feuds are still as
common in Crete as the vendetta once was in Corsica.

The Omalo "season" lasts from early May until the end of September. During these months the surrounding villages are almost totally evacuated and the plateau is transformed, as some market-towns in England are transformed overnight, into a pastoral fairground. Whole families leave their houses in the valleys and come here to settle with their herds in the summer-huts round the plateau's edge; the inhabitants of the south in what is known as the "Selino Ring," those from the northern village of Lakkoi in a "Ring" of their own on the opposite circumference.

Out of season, the plain looked like the auditorium of a disused concert-hall; the hills, which rose like tiers of stalls round it, seemed to be enveloped in dust-covers; and the sound of our voices, as we sat chatting outside Christos's hut, was distorted by the unusual acoustics. Christos was describing the difficulty of preparing the hard ground for the potato-crop, for which the Omalo is justly famous though only a small fraction of its area is sown.

I remembered that during the occupation the Germans had organised forced-labour gangs from Lakkoi to transport a steamroller and a couple of heavy tractors for the construction of a small satellite air-field on the plateau. I wondered whether these machines, which had been man-handled up the rough mule tracks with such appalling effort, were now at last being used as they should, for agricultural purposes. There was a self-conscious, though not unsatisfied, smile on Christos's face as he replied:

"As soon as the cuckolds left, we smashed them up as completely as we could. You see, they were enemy machines."

There were potatoes of course, for supper. Christos apologised for having no other food to offer us—his cheeses had already been sent down to the village—and no proper china or cutlery. With spoons roughly carved from slivers of pear-wood we ate out of a single central bowl on the floor, using large stones to sit on in the absence of chairs. It was one of the most satisfying meals that I ever ate in Crete. The food, coming straight off the fire, was hot instead of being tepid, as it usually is when served in village houses; and the hut itself was warm although its thick walls, plastered on the inside with mud, were made, like those on Gavdos, of loose stones without mortar.

The sleeping accommodation was equally primitive, but far more comfortable than any village bed. We lay down on stone shelves spread with resilient thorn-bushes and covered with goat's wool rugs: a perfect mattress. Our bedclothes were a borrowed shepherd's cloak. Even so, I did not fall asleep at once. I was kept awake—and I realised even at the time how unreasonably—by a problem connected with that dreariest of sciences, geology. The problem was still unsolved in the morning, but by then it seemed unimportant and unworthy of solution. During the night, however, this one question kept recurring to me: had the Omalo once been a lake or not?

Many travellers describe the plain as "lacustrine"; and the way in which the encircling hills converge to form a hollow, inverted cone certainly suggests a sheet of water at their base. The earth itself, moreover, if properly tilled, would be of the same colour and consistency as the reclaimed soil of the Italian *Maremma*.

Michael Dephner, a Greek-speaking German, whose father had joined the suite of Prince Otto of Bavaria on the latter's election as King of Greece in 1832, had lost none of his Teuton thoroughness when, at the age of seventy-five, he visited the Omalo shortly after the first World War. He claimed that the plain had once been a lake (an opinion shared by the Austrian botanist, Franz Sieber) but based his observation only on the fact that in Venetian maps it was marked *Lago di Omalo*. To my mind, this proves nothing. During the winter the Omalo is, in fact, under water and remains so every year until early spring, when the melted snow escapes through a *katavothron*, or cavern, at its northern entrance. This seasonally marshy area could, I suppose, have been mistaken for a permanent lake by a mediaeval cartographer.

Professor Raulin, whose opinion I would value more than any other, has nothing to say on the subject; and even the conscientious Captain Spratt, who made a series of meteorological observations with barometer, self-registering thermometer and hygrometer, who established the height of the plain as about four thousand feet above sea-level and recorded that its minimum temperature on a mid-summer night fell as low as 38½° Fahrenheit,[2] refused to tackle the problem.

If it really had been a lake, how could it have avoided being drained, as it is now, by the *katavothron* into which the melted snow pours underground only to re-appear miles away in the northern

2. The corresponding night temperature on the coast was as high as 76° Fahr., two degrees less than the highest *daytime* temperature on the Omalo.

plains at Ayia, the present water-supply for Canea? And if the *kat-avothron* had at one time not existed, and the water been permanently retained in the basin, then why is Kournas, in the plain of Apokoronas, reputed to be the only lake that has ever existed in Crete? Finally, if such a large expanse of water had existed in these mountains, separating the valley of Selino from the northern plains, what purpose would have been served by the paved path leading to it? The Romans are unlikely to have accomplished this feat of engineering simply to enjoy the lake-land scenery.

As far as I know, these questions have never been answered. The problem still exists, and its solution will no doubt yield some surprising revelations. As far as I am concerned, the only surprise is that I should have bothered my head about it for so long.

Vardis woke me up with the announcement: "Winter!" I put my head outside and saw that the Lakkoi Ring directly opposite was hidden in a fine drizzle, which looked as if it would last all day. Christos was closing his hut up for the season that morning, so we had to push on.

We were soaked with sweat and rain by the time we reached the entrance to the gorge a little further along the circumference of the plain. A narrow pass—one of the three outlets of the Omalo—took us to the very edge of the chasm, like a radial aisle leading to the topmost tier of seats in an amphitheatre, whose outer wall we now began to descend. The path here, said to have been built by the Turks, and known as the Xyloskala, or Wooden Ladder, zigzags down the almost perpendicular face of the cliff direct from the lip of the ravine into the river-bed three thousand feet below, the drop being so abrupt that even on a large-scale map the contour lines in this area give way to conventional hatching.

Normally the view from here is the most splendid in Crete; today we appeared to be looking into, and climbing into, the crater of a steaming volcano. I began to understand the awe in which some of the earlier travellers had held this route. Spratt, for instance, who was dissuaded by his guides from entering the gorge, seems to have fallen victim to the usual superstitions about it. "I do not recommend a traveller to try it against the native prejudice," he remarks, "as there is evidently some jealousy about it amongst them." The "jealousy" to which he refers, was probably nothing more than local fear of the Sphakians.

Sieber also experienced some difficulty when travelling in Sphakia in 1817, but this was largely due to his being issued with an incomplete *firman* by the Turkish authorities. A botanist with an invalid passport, he accomplished the journey by posing as a doctor. He, however, realised that the dangers of this area were of a practical rather than mystical nature, and so warned his successors: "Any European travelling there should not have a Turkish guide for fear of creating an incident."

Pashley, a quarter of a century later, disregarded this advice. Fortunately the Turk whom he took with him when he started his journey had only recently arrived from Anatolia, and so was completely ignorant of the Cretan countryside and language; he was therefore dismissed almost at once in favour of the famous Captain Manias, who subsequently acted also as Spratt's travelling-companion and later died in his service.

More recently still, in the summer of 1893, Sir John Myres took as his guide through the northern provinces of the island a Cretan Moslem *zaptieh*. When Sir John announced his intention of entering Sphakia (in which at that time there were no more than four Turkish inhabitants—and of these, one was illiterate[3]) the guide, quite reasonably, refused to risk his neck in such a fanatically anti-Moslem area. At the same time he had been ordered by the British Consul in Canea not to desert his charge. Sir John solved the problem by making out a written receipt for himself—"one Englishman, safe and sound"—and then entered the Gorge of Samaria, escorted by two heavily-armed Christians from Selino and by an Orthodox priest who spent his time killing snakes by jumping on them. On his return a few days later he was rejoined by the *zaptieh*, who, now that he was once more in charge of his Englishman, punctiliously returned the receipt which he had been given: a unique document if ever there was one.

With Vardis as our guide, Daphne and I were in no danger, even from the so-called bandits, all of whom were known to him, and many known to me. Limping confidently a few yards ahead of us

---

3. The information in brackets is drawn from contemporary statistics; for the rest of the paragraph I am indebted to Sir John himself.

and singing as he went, sometimes in a high falsetto, he led us down through the mist which, when static, seemed to cling to the branches of the giant cypresses and pine-trees lining the path. More often, however, it was blown up in gusts from the bottom of the ravine, like smoke through an engine's funnel; and when we thought that we had at last passed through it after reaching the river-bed, a change of wind sent it whisking back overhead, so that the rain never stopped for a second. At this lower level we came across plane-trees sprouting miraculously between boulders worn smooth by the weather, and on their leaves the rattle of the rain blanketed every other sound; so that the turbulent waters of the Neroutsiko, which we reached a little farther on, seemed to be cascading inaudibly.

On the way down we had passed several overhangs in the cliff blackened with smoke and littered with the sort of trash that is jettisoned by an army in retreat: boot-soles, rusty tins, old bones, bits of clothing—the property of the Communist forces who had controlled the gorge for three years in the civil war that followed the German occupation. Under one of these deep ledges we sheltered and tackled the food which we had brought with us: cheese, raw onions and *paximadia*—home-baked rusks with a satisfying nutty flavour, but so hard that they have to be soaked in water before being eaten. As we sat there, shouting to make ourselves heard above the noise of the storm, the low-hanging network of cloud was from time to time torn apart, offering a tantalising glimpse of the Rotten Crags rising above us, only to mend itself invisibly again before Daphne could focus her camera.

We had to abandon our plans for photography, even when we came to the chapel of St. Nicholas which, in good weather, would have been a perfect subject, a visual symbol of the gorge's seclusion. Architecturally it has no merits, even though Pashley (who never visited it) exalts it by describing it as a monastery. It is a squat, commonplace ecclesiastical construction typical of the hundreds of other small isolated churches scattered throughout the island; at a distance it is barely distinguishable from the enormous rocks out of which it is built. Its beauty and what fame it has are due only to its site.

The cypresses surrounding it are the tallest in the island and are venerated, if not consciously worshipped, even today. That these few trees should for centuries have escaped the woodman's axe in a country where the science of forestry is unknown, is significant of the respect which they still command—a legacy, no doubt, from those ancient times when the Graces, whom the Cretans in particular adored, were identified with the horizontal Cypress, *sempervirens*.[4]

A theory exists that this grove was once sacred to the goddess Britomartis, whose identity imposes a problem; for it is still not clear whether her name is a Cretan synonym for Artemis or whether Britomartis was only one of the Huntress's protegées. When Dephner visited St. Nicholas, he was so moved by its associations with the goddess that he enlarged on the theory, claiming that not only was the cypress sacred to her, but also the Cretan ibex. To support his contention he called to witness the remains of an ancient tympanum which he had seen in Gonia monastery, on which Britomartis is portrayed accompanied by Aphrodite, followed by two hounds and flanked by an ibex.[5]

His suggestion is reasonable; for the animal also figures on ancient Cretan coins in the same way that the owl, Athena's sacred bird, appears on the coins of Athens.

Only three miles separate St. Nicholas from Samaria, but we took over an hour to cover them. The path here exists only where it is allowed to exist by the swirling waters. These encroach on the narrow ribbon of dry land and send it serpentining from one side of the gorge to the other, so that we were constantly crossing the stream and re-crossing it by a series of slippery stepping-stones. As we approached the village Vardis's singing grew louder and shriller, to warn the inhabitants of our arrival. For the last year or so the men

4. Cypress-worship is not yet dead in Crete; in modern Cretan folksongs the girl who is "worshipped" by her lover is still compared to the cypress, and her gestures are likened to the graceful motions of that tree. In practice, however—if we are to believe Pashley—a girl's gait is more admired if it closely resembles the waddle of a goose.

5. To verify Dephner's contention, I visited Gonia monastery myself. The antiquity he describes had disappeared. The abbot and the monks remembered it well; it used to stand outside the church door. I asked when it had been removed and where it was now to he found. No one knew, no one cared. This attitude to ancient remains obtains throughout Western Crete, which has not yet developed the sense of responsibility that the eastern half of the island has acquired thanks to the discovery of Knossos.

of Samaria have been suspicious of strangers coming unannounced down the gorge from the north, a direction in which they have had to keep a sharp look-out ever since their feud with the villagers of Lakkoi. From the conflicting accounts of this feud which I heard from both sides concerned, I tried to piece together an accurate history of the events leading up to it.

The inhabitants of Samaria, who belong almost exclusively to a single family, the Viglis, have for generations been notorious as the most successful sheep-thieves in the whole of Crete. Members of this arduous profession require strong legs as well as stout hearts. I can imagine no other form of dishonesty which pays such small dividends in proportion to the effort put into it. I used to pity more than admire the thieves whom I sometimes came across at midnight on the mountains—weary footsloggers who moved in the dark but still kept awake by day to guard their wandering loot.

When I first knew the Viglis during the occupation, the head of the family was a certain Theodore, an impulsive creature breathing fire and slaughter and garlic through an outsize moustache. He was then engaged, so his enemies assured me, in a feud with all the saints; and he had, I heard, committed a number of unspecified sacrilegious acts in almost every church in the neighbourhood. Clearly a man of advanced ideas. "I never steal from the poor," he once told me, "I only punish the rich." He believed quite genuinely in his vocation; had he heard of Robin Hood, he would have modelled himself on him.

His vocation did not include participation in the resistance movement. He used to visit my headquarters in Selino, but only to tell me that he was willing to take orders from the Russians. Meanwhile he entertained the Germans, including the German general commanding *Festung Kreta*, whenever they passed through his village on shooting expeditions—not out of a spirit of collaboration, I am sure, but only for reasons of hospitality. With his good looks and personal charm he was a perfect host; and he knew it. And with all that stolen meat to draw on, he could have entertained an army.

Which is what he was finally accused of doing. When the post-war Communists made their last stand in the gorge, Samaria naturally became their base. Willingly or not, the Viglis family offered them the usual hospitality—they could scarcely have done otherwise. For this they were proscribed and hounded by the local gendarmerie, though what the handful of men in the hamlet could have done to resist "bandits" in battalion strength is a question which no Cretan policeman has ever attempted to answer.

This official action, unpleasantly reminiscent of the methods adopted by the Germans during the occupation, could only have been prompted by a sense of frustration. In the final stages of the civil war Government troops advanced on Samaria from both directions, confident—and with reason—of capturing all the "bandits" who were concentrated in the gorge, since the Omalo entrance in the mountains and the exit to the sea at Ayia Roumeli had both been sealed. The two forces eventually converged on the village, but the "bandits" had vanished—presumably up the sides of the gorge and over the Untrodden Cliffs, which are reputed to be inaccessible to all but the ibex. The miracle of the exodus has yet to be explained. And the lips of the Viglis are sealed.

Shortly afterwards, on the Omalo, Theodore ran into a police patrol reinforced by a section of the Home Guard recruited from the village of Lakkoi. He was called upon to surrender. "A Viglis never surrenders," he shouted and, single-handed, opened fire. He was shot dead at once.

In the Home Guard section which took part in this action was a certain Matthew Skoulas, once a wealthy shepherd, who had beggared himself in the Allied cause. But his ineffaceable smile gave no hint of the sacrifices which he had made; each time that he sheltered me in his hut on the Lakkoi Ring, within sight and sound of the Germans on the plateau, I was always impressed by his cheerful generosity. A modest, fearless man and—what in Crete is a *rara avis*— a disinterested supporter of law and order; hence his membership of the Home Guard.

It was clearly impossible to tell whether his was one of the many bullets that had struck Theodore dead; his mere presence at the killing was sufficient to condemn him in the eyes of the remaining Viglis clan. A few days later he in turn was murdered by some relations of Theodore's, who have so far remained unidentified. The feud had started, not in this case between two families—the political motive behind both crimes had raised the quarrel to the level of a small-scale civil war—but between two whole villages. And the Omalo became a sort of no-man's land for the inhabitants of Lakkoi and Samaria. Since then the former have confined themselves to the area round their own Ring, while the latter never venture further north than the Xyloskala.

As we now approached Samaria from this direction, we found three young men on guard at the criss-cross of subsidiary ravines which intersect at the entrance to the village. Men of the Viglis brood, unmistakeably, and all three dressed in the same sort of uniform: black top-boots, khaki breeches converted from battle-dress trousers, battle-dress blouses left intact, and fringed head-kerchiefs of black silk, their ends loosely knotted so as to hang down behind like pigtails. From their headgear alone the trio would have been distinguishable in a crowd as Samarians—each village in these mountains has its own individual way of tying and wearing the *sariki*.

Vardis was known to them; but they regarded Daphne and me with suspicion, even after we had been introduced. I tried to return their glance of appraisal—that uninhibited stare which is typical of the inquisitive, critical Cretan—and our visual duel lasted a full minute before their spokesman, whose name was Vangelis, allowed a smile to efface his expression of mistrust. "Let's go indoors," he said—a welcome suggestion since the rain had increased during our protracted encounter.

We crossed the torrent over a rough wooden bridge slung between anchoring boulders, and entered one of the half-dozen houses: square blocks of stone which stood like miniature forts between the mulberry and olive trees. Appropriate to the landscape, the buildings were austere and featureless, as though they were not yet fully developed: embryonic dwellings slumbering in a long-forgotten terrestrial womb-pocket.

The house consisted of a single room, as rudimentary as its exterior. On a bed in one corner lay a young man, fully dressed except for his boots, his bare feet protruding from the army greatcoat thrown over him as a blanket. He was shivering and groaning alternately. "I'm afraid he's ill," Vangelis superfluously explained, "he's been ill for some days."

It was a clear case of influenza, an endemic disease in the gorge, where even the midsummer sun can penetrate no more than three hours a day. This lack of sunlight accounted for the characteristic sallow complexion of the inhabitants, all of whom looked as pale as if they had only just come out of prison; several of them probably had. But there was no doctor nor was there any priest or policeman. No wonder these forsaken people have become inured to the wild justice of revenge—they have never had a government to attend to their needs, nor a police force to protect their interests.

It was an uncongenial afternoon, with the sick man lying beside us and the storm raging outside. We sat there in our wet clothes—there was no fireplace in the house, a deficiency unnoticed by the owners who would no doubt feel uncomfortable in comfort—nor was there any means of warming ourselves internally with wine or *tsikoudia* since the vine cannot grow in this all but sunless shaft in the mountains. Even our conversation was unusually restricted, for out of deference to my hosts I avoided any topic which might conceivably touch on the two subjects which I felt to be taboo: feuds and sheep-thieving.

Though sheep-thieving is now less prevalent than it used to be a few years ago, it still occupies more of the Cretan gendarmerie's time and energy than any other criminal activity. Apologists point out that this scourge—for it is a scourge, not only in itself but in its consequence—is a legacy from the Turkish occupation, when the outlaws who kept the banner of independence flying in the mountains lived on the land—in other words, on the flocks of their less intrepid brethren—to such an extent that "patriot" and "thief" became synonymous, the one word "*klepht*" being used for both. The klepht: how many songs (usually, of course, composed by himself) have been sung in his praise!

But it is all too easy to trace and attribute every modern evil to the so-called hereditary foe. Sheep-thieving was known in Crete at least two hundred years before the Turks invaded the island; an agreement exists, dated 26 October 1435 and signed respectively by the heads of the Skordylis and Valerianos family, whereby the former gives his daughter in marriage to the latter's son in order to end a feud caused by the theft of some sheep in the region of Kalo Lakko. Sheep-thieving, after all, is merely a form of dry-land piracy; and the Cretans, particularly the Sphakians, were renowned as pirates from Roman times right up to the beginning of the nineteenth century. Would it, then, be a wild deduction to state that the crime became more common in the island when Crete ceased to be a maritime nation and her criminals were consequently forced to switch their activity from the high seas to the higher mountains?

With the dark came a break in the rain, and supper: dried broad beans with rice—an obtrusively vegetarian dish for such a notoriously carnivorous household. Despite the sick-room atmosphere which persisted even though no notice was taken of the man on the bed, Vangelis had insisted on entertaining us in his own home. But to sleep, we had to go elsewhere.

An elderly couple took us into their house: a larger building but consisting again of a single, unpartitioned room. The only bed was allotted to Vardis and me; Daphne was given a couch; and the owners prepared to doss down under some blankets on the floor. It seemed most unreasonable that we should occupy their bed—Vardis and I would have felt the discomfort of the bare boards far less—but they would not hear of any other arrangement. "You are our guests," they explained. Nevertheless I felt selfish and guilty when I heard the creaking of their bones as they bent and stretched in their undressing; and like an erratic clockwork motor in the corner of the room, the cracking continued all night, though there was no visible movement from the shadows in which the two old bodies lay.

Further proof of their hospitality was furnished in the morning. They produced for us a bottle of *tsikoudia*—not a demi-john, admittedly; not a litre-bottle nor even a half-litre; but a small medicine-bottle, barely sufficient for one drink each. But this was the only spirit of any sort in the village and had been set aside for medicinal purposes; for besides being taken to good effect internally, it can also be used as an embrocation and in a dozen other different ways. This old couple, I imagine, had kept it for the winter, to rub into their rusty joints; it seemed criminal to be drinking it, instead, as an aperitif before breakfast.

Vangelis came in shortly afterwards and sat down with us to eat: large slabs of cheese and platefuls of honey—better here than anywhere else in Crete; for the bees in the gorge feed on *malotyra*, a sage-like herb which is used instead of tea and tastes far better than any product of India, Ceylon or China. Then we left, to make our way down to the sea.

I saw Vangelis again a few weeks later: in prison. He had sent his younger brother with an urgent message for me to come at once to Canea and see him in his cell. I found him locked up with three other men from his village, in the detention-room of the central police-station. None of them had come up for trial, but all seemed in high spirits and greeted me as though the iron bars between us were not there. I asked Vangelis why they had been arrested.

"I still don't know," he replied. "They say it's because of the theft of some sheep in the hills on the Selino border. But I don't know a thing about it, I promise you. I've often been up to that game before—you know that as well as I do—but this time, I swear, I had nothing to do with it. They've just picked on us because we're the most likely. Now they're going to make an example of us, that's what they say. Exile in Gavdos, they're threatening us with that. I couldn't stand it. Prison's bad enough, but exile—please see what you can do for us. Go to the Chief of Police, he might listen to you."

I had no wish to become involved in the harlequinade of the Greek legal system which, with its corrupt judges, ambitious lawyers and semi-professional false-witnesses, is a sinister parody of civilised judicial procedure. But Vangelis had sounded sincere; and his horror of exile was genuine.

A term in prison to the average Greek means as much as a term at school to an English schoolboy; sometimes it means far more, for the leisure of a long sentence has given many illiterates their only chance of learning to read and write. Prison, for them, is a seat of learning of which they are frequently as proud as an Old Etonian is of Eton; and membership of their *alma mater* is indicated not by an old school tie but by something more permanent: a design tattooed on their skin, which will endure the rest of their lives.[6] But exile, though far less arduous, is considered an intolerable disgrace. Can the sense of shame which it imposes, I wonder, be traced back to the ancient Athenian practice of ostracism?

The Chief of Police was one of my war-time colleagues, whose appearance may be divined from the *nom-de-guerre* I gave him during the occupation: "Butch." He was amused—and so, I admit, was I—by my coming directly from the one friend, who was in prison, to the other, who had put him there; but his little pig's eyes lost their twinkle when I asked him what his plans were for the prisoner.

6. Although my comments on Greek justice cannot in all honesty be anything but unflattering, I do not wish to create a false impression of the Greek prison-system which, since the war, has improved out of all recognition thanks to the progressive spirit of the British Police Mission (unfortunately withdrawn from the country at the end of 1951). I must explain, therefore, that a Greek prisoner is not forcibly tattooed by the prison officials; he is not even beaten up nor put through the "third degree," as he used to be up to 1945. Tattooing in Greek prisons is simply a traditional pastime, and a tattoo-mark is a sure sign of a former prison sentence—which explains why those of our troops in Crete who affected this form of personal decoration, were invariably mistaken for ex-jailbirds.

"Exile," he replied, "I can't do anything else. I daresay he didn't commit the crime but he certainly knows who did. You can tell him from me that he'll make things easier for himself if he helps us with a bit more information."

I had always liked and admired Butch, and so was unprepared for such an appalling statement. His answer proved that not only was he sentencing a man on suspicion, but that he knew the suspicion to be false. I went back to Vangelis and told him what Butch had said. His reply convinced me all the more of his innocence. He made no show of selfless nobility in shielding somebody else, no pretence of shocked surprise at being asked to betray a friend. "It doesn't make sense," he said. "Does the Chief really think I'd willingly take the rap for someone else's crime? If I knew who'd done it, of course I'd tell him, so long as I got off. But I can't just think of a name out of the blue. Why doesn't *he* suggest one?"

Butch, of course, made no suggestion, and Vangelis was sentenced to six months on Gavdos.

The day that we left Samaria was the last warm day of the year. The sky—what we could see of it—had been scrubbed clean by the storm; the narrow belt of blue which followed the parallel edges of the crags sparkled distantly above us, like tubular lighting in the roof of a lofty tunnel. Beyond Samaria the gorge contracts still further, and the torrent, augmented now by other waters—those of the Kephalovrysis, or Head Stream—lashed savagely at our feet as we negotiated the series of stepping-stones: the only bits of dry land between the almost perpendicular cliffs which enclosed us on either side like the walls of a lock.

No wonder the Turks thought twice about attacking Samaria, and failed to reach their objective at each attempt. This narrow gap, called "Turk's Pass" in memory of a Moslem killed at the head of an invading column in 1770, was the limit of any Turkish approach from the direction of the sea, while from the Omalo each advance was checked by the "Night Fighters of Sphakia" before it ever reached St. Nicholas's.

But Turk's Pass is not the narrowest part of the gorge. A mile or so further along, the chasm contracts again, unbelievably, into an opening aptly named "The Gates," through which the torrent tumbled, as though through a sluice; fortunately for us at low level. The foot of each cliff is scoured and polished by the stream up to a height of six feet; when the water reaches this level the Gates are closed.

Measurements, I know, are usually unevocative, but only the yardstick can adequately describe this quite extraordinary rift: the cliffs on either side, with less than ten feet between them at their base, soar upwards fifteen hundred feet in the air, their edges at that height no more than forty feet apart. In Franz Sieber this pass inspired the sort of romantic awe that is expected from a Central European; but he must have been a creature of simian proportions or exalted imagination, for he claims that when he went through The Gates he could touch each side with the tips of his outstretched fingers.

A curious man, that Sieber, whom I have often tried to visualise. What sort of a traveller was he? He records that during his journey through Sphakia he was once made to pay for the food which he had eaten in a peasant's private house. This mercenary action, as described by him, seems so completely out of character that I am tempted to doubt his veracity. If a traveller in Crete was ever asked to pay for his board and lodging—and I have yet to hear of this demand being made on anyone but this strange Bohemian botanist—then he must have made himself, in some exceptional way, objectionable. How else explain such improbable behaviour on the part of the Cretan villager who, for all his faults, could never be accused of lack of hospitality?

Foreigners who dislike Crete, or fail to get on with the Cretans, usually have only themselves to blame. Take William Lithgow, for instance, known in his native Lanark as "Lugless Will."[7] During the "painfulle peregrinations" on which this unhappy Scotsman embarked at the beginning of the seventeenth century, he seems to have laid himself open to every form of persecution, hardship and humiliation; it is only the fortitude with which he endured his torments, and the quaint style in which he describes them, that incite his readers' sympathy. In Crete he complained about almost everything, including the "deepe draughts of Malvasey I received hourely, and oftentimes against my will." (To do him justice, I must confess that I frequently felt the same aversion to compulsory drinking myself.)

7. "Foure blood-shedding wolves," brothers of a certain Miss Lockhart, had cut off Lithgow's ears when they found him in a compromising position with their sister. This was the first of many indignities which his "martyrd anatomy" sustained.

Another, more recent, example: Ralph Brewster, the author of a scandalous work about Mount Athos, who wandered through the island shortly before the last World War. Accompanied by a saucy German catamite in *Lederhosen*, and extolling, as was his custom, the virtue of the Italians, he was surprised to find himself unpopular in Crete—at a time when Axis designs on the Balkans were only too apparent. The Cretans, who might have stomached the Fascist propaganda, were choked by those cute little leather shorts.

As we passed through The Gates and entered the glen of Ayia Roumeli, I felt as though we were being exhaled. The landscape, which had seemed to be holding its breath in the constant half-twilight of the gorge, now sighed, as it were, with relief and relaxed again in the sun.

A stranger landing on the coast beyond would no doubt consider this village a dull, decaying sort of place; to one who has just left the scoured rocks of Samaria, it seems a shady summerhouse set in meadow-land. Oleanders fringe the many streams into which the torrent is here canalised, the water coursing between houses sheltered by plane-trees and dwarfed by cypresses. There are fig-trees, too, and pomegranates and Japanese medlars, which create a false impression of plenty; but, as in Samaria, not a single vine. And so, for the third day running, no wine.

Vardis took us to the house of one of his friends, Yiannis Tzatzimas, who proved to be a relation of mine; he was the cousin of the wife of my Koustoyerako godbrother and therefore, though many times removed, godbrother also to me. Like most of his fellow-villagers, Yiannis had the blue-grey eyes and red-blonde hair that are common in this part of Sphakia; he could easily have been mistaken for an Englishman, an Elizabethan type of buccaneer.

It was he who introduced us to the *spécialité de la région*: cream-cheese pancakes soaked in honey, which he produced for us as soon as we arrived. Honey is the pride of this village, whose inhabitants a few years ago made an unusual sacrifice in order to preserve its high quality. When offered the chance of ridding their houses and fields of lice by allowing them to be sprayed with D.D.T. from the air— an offer which was gladly accepted by every other village in Crete— the people of Ayia Roumeli chose to continue being plagued by their vermin rather than risk their bees in the insecticide.

The influenza epidemic had struck here also, and again there was no doctor to attend to the sick. I distributed the few tablets of aspirin which Daphne had in her bag, although I knew that they would be of little use; aspirin in Crete has lost the magic properties which it was once considered to have. A few years ago, when it was still a novelty in the more sequestered villages, it was in constant demand as a cure for almost every imaginable ill. A blistered heel? A cut finger?—take an aspirin! Alas, the popularity of the wonder-tablet vanished overnight with the advent of penicillin. The new drug, since it is still comparatively rare, is now looked upon as the only satisfactory *vis medicatrix*. When, if ever, it is made easily available in these remote districts, the peasants will no doubt immediately lose faith in it as they already have in aspirin. For the moment, however, they were shocked to discover that two English travellers should wander so far afield without the latest thing in analgesics.

We left them to ponder on our lack of foresight and hurried down to the coast, for Daphne and I wanted to bathe before taking the caique which we had ordered back to Palaeochora. The village, invisible from the sea—and therefore invisible to any lurking pirate—is purposely separated from the beach by a mile of sandy soil and rock overlooked by two protective cliffs: ground which could easily be defended against a potential enemy landing. If Barbarossa ever reconnoitred this particular bit of coast, he must have been discouraged by its wild, unfruitful aspect and so sailed past it, unaware of the spoils secluded only a mile inland; for at that time there was not a single building on the beach to give a hint of the village behind it.

The beach today, with its three fishermen's shacks and coffeeshop planted in the shingle, gave us some idea of how Souyia must have looked about eighty years ago; and the memory of Souyia made us visualise how this beach will probably look in eighty years' time. There will always be one difference between them, however: no motor road will ever reach Ayia Roumeli; no motor road could ever be constructed through that gorge—not in eighty years' time, nor eight hundred.

5

AZOYIRES

OUR SHORT SALLY through the Gorge of Samaria reminded me how much these mountain regions vary, although separated from each other by distances which, in flatter country, would be negligible. The Paterakis family, for instance, seems to differ fundamentally from the brooding, abstemious Viglis clan, though their respective districts are divided only by a narrow chasm, a geographical boundary which gives no indication of the barrier it really represents. Selino and Sphakia are worlds, not miles, apart.

In those six Paterakis brothers, alike in looks but different in character, every feature of their district is embodied: the physical courage, the mental sobriety, the moral pride and dignity. They will always appear to me as a microcosm of Selino. Vasilis, whose gentle manner conceals the sense of purpose and responsibility that made him a successful leader; Manolis, combining the virtue of the sophisticated gentleman with that of an unspoilt shepherd, better known perhaps than the other brothers through the part he played in the kidnapping of General Kreipe; Costis, highly-strung but deadly cool in a crisis, a fine shot with a loyalty as steady and unswerving as his aim; Antonis, whose film-star features and high spirits remain unaffected after years of adolescence spent in mowing down the enemy with a machine-gun; Vardis, the youngest, wounded and crippled at the age of sixteen, whose singing is only slightly less permanent than his limp. . . .

. . . and George, even wilder than the rest of the family, a sentimental roisterer who literally does not know his own strength. The kiss with which he welcomed me on my return to Crete developed into a passionate bite which scarred my cheek for several days; and the playful taps that are sometimes part of the traditional Cretan greeting, when administered by George almost felled me. We had met again in Koustoyerako, though he no longer lived there; since the war he had married and settled in his wife's village, Azoyires. It was here that he invited Daphne and me to attend the christening of his son, which was to take place on the Feast of the Holy Fathers.

The path from Palaeochora to Azoyires is normally an easy one to follow; but on the day that Daphne and I set off along it, whole stretches had been wiped out by an unusually early storm which had flooded the lowland areas overnight; the fresh mud which now coated and disguised the nearby slopes had the same slippery stickiness, and almost the same colour, as hot caramel sauce. We should never have found our way through that pudding of a landscape had we not been accompanied by George's father-in-law, who was returning to the village with a mule-load of provisions for the party.

I have often wondered who was responsible for the myth that mules are sure-footed animals, capable of going anywhere that a man can go. All the mules that I have known seem to have been as restless as the most hysterical racehorse, and even more unreliable. Uncle Theodore's was no exception. The brute kept stumbling in the trenches newly-carved by the rain, mistook every furrow for the path and—to judge from its vicious insistence—gloried in the mistake. During one of these erratic circuits it floundered more heavily than usual and, after a short struggle, succeeded in dislodging its saddle; the saddle-bags burst open and a load of *koulouria* and *xerotygana*—the shortbread and biscuits that are specially prepared for feast days—cascaded into the mud. As we packed them on to its back again, the beast struck out at Uncle Theodore with its hind legs, crushed Daphne against a rock and stamped on her feet, and bared its teeth and tried to bite my hand. In its owner's presence I could not do to it what I felt like doing, but managed, by pretending to hold the reins, to twist its jaw—I hope, really painfully. In certain circumstances kindness to animals, like tolerance to humans, is an equivocal virtue.

After three exhausting hours we reached Azoyires. The size of the village is not at first apparent; the main part of it, in a horse-shoe

ABOVE: *The old harbour of Canea*

LEFT: *A Turkish house on the quay*

ABOVE: *Michalis, landlord of "The Seal," with an assistant*

RIGHT: *Antonis Vandoulas of Vaphes with his grandson*

bend of the valley, is invisible from George's house; and its outlying farms, on the summit of the surrounding crags a mile or so away, are concealed by intervening olive groves which blanket the carefully terraced slopes. This was the richest land that I had seen since my return to Crete.

George's house, too, looked more prosperous than any other which I had so far visited; his wife, the only girl in the family, must have had a handsome dowry. The large brass bedstead was hung with an embroidered canopy; there were also curtains—a rarity in Cretan villages where wooden shutters usually take the place of glass window-panes—and these were of lace; blankets and rugs of many colours hung from a long horizontal pole and screened the whole of one wall; and in the place of honour, on top of a chest of drawers, stood that symbol of peasant affluence: a wireless-set.[1]

Everything in the room was spotless. I wondered how long it would remain so. Most Cretan homes degenerate unnecessarily quickly after their owners' marriage. The animals, which at first are carefully restricted to the courtyard outside, gradually encroach so that the house soon becomes a mixture of chicken-run and pig-sty, its furniture reduced to a minimum, its maintenance and decoration abandoned. Long before she becomes middle-aged the wife has forgotten what it is to be house-proud since her husband has probably invested all their money in additions to his flocks or his fields. But George's wife, Angeliko, had not yet reached that stage.

When we arrived we found her busily preparing for the party: temporarily a Cinderella figure in wooden clogs and ragged clothes, crouching outside her kitchen over a fire on which the head of a freshly slaughtered goat was being singed. At the sight and smell of it, I prepared myself for the worst. George was also busy, so his father-in-law entertained us with his memories of the village in the time of the Turks.

Uncle Theodore was old enough to have taken part in the anti-Moslem struggles at the end of the last century. His family, the Kriaris, was originally from Koustoyerako, but in 1854 moved to

---

1. In spite of the absence of electricity in Cretan villages, the first thing that a wealthy Cretan villager will buy is one of these superfluous products of so-called civilisation—and two car batteries on which to run it. I can only suppose that to him it is as much a symbol of social security as a television-set seems to be to the suburban Englishman.

this richer village of Azoyires which was then almost entirely in Turkish hands; olive-groves as productive as these could not long remain the property of Christians.

I had always imagined that the later anti-Turkish revolts were genuine bids for freedom and national independence, as widespread as the general rebellions of 1821 and 1866. Uncle Theodore's description of them disabused me. Those battles on the heights above Azoyires were little more than parochial brawls, squabbles over the imposition of an extra tax or the confiscation of some property. The truth was a caricature of the heroic picture which I had painted.

The Christian call-to-arms was merely one way of airing a grievance, a formal protest against the traditional enemy, the "Turks," few of whom were Turkish and all of whom were fellow-citizens. Superficially, then, the fighting resembled a small-scale civil war, between Cretan Christians and Cretan Moslems; actually, it was little more than a display of mutual defiance, in which insults more than bullets were used as ammunition. After a few days spent in stalking and shouting at each other, both sides would get bored and call a truce.

Even during the more serious rebellions the battles seem to have been conducted in a way which, compared to modern methods, can only be described as homely. Hilary Skinner, an independent English observer, gives this account of an engagement which he witnessed on the 18th of May 1867:

> There was again a brisk skirmish between Cretans—Christian and Moslem—who fought each other, in their own fashion, with no little skill, defying the opposite side with sarcastic shouts, and even calling to one another by name.
>
> "Demetri, you old rascal, you have escaped me many times; but I shall kill you today!"
>
> "Accursed Fazil, I have a bullet ready for you! Come a little nearer, if you dare!"
>
> "Hold your hand above the rocks," says one, "and I will hit it."
>
> "Hold up your finger," replies his foe, "and it is a lost finger."

Shades of Hector and Achilles!

The four prospective godbrothers, who had been travelling all day from their village near Canea, arrived in the late afternoon, and with them we set off for the christening. George and Angeliko remained at home. According to the traditions of the Greek Church, parents never attend their child's baptism; they do not even know what name it is to be given but leave the choice to the god-parents, who inform them on their return from the ceremony.

Leading the procession was old Uncle Theodore, splendidly dressed in Cretan costume: *tsalvaria*, baggy breeches of royal blue face-cloth, with a double-breasted waistcoat of the same material embroidered with black arabesques, and a scarlet-lined cloak to match; his shirt and top-boots were black; a dark red fez perched jauntily on his head and his waist was encircled by a mulberry-coloured cummerbund of heavy silk which supported an ivory-hilted yatagan in a sheath of hand-worked silver. His grandson, a boy of eighteen months, sat astride his shoulders. The village midwife (invariably an old maid, whose role at a baptism is as important as at a birth) followed behind with the ceremonial impedimenta: a bottle of oil (for anointing the child's body), a pair of scissors (for snipping off a lock of its hair) and the christening robes (which are provided by the god-parents).

The storm of the previous night had caused a landslide across the steep path leading up to the church, and our progress was further impeded by crowds of pilgrims who had come in from the surrounding villages to celebrate the feast-day. Large parties of them were preparing to settle down for the night in the churchyard; others had already done so, although rain threatened and there was no cover apart from the church itself which was already filled to capacity. Not one of them seemed to care; all were in the same holiday mood, which kept them moving to and fro between the iconostasis and the nearest supply of wine. Lips which, a few seconds before, had been in contact with the image of the Virgin were now applied to the bottle; kisses planted reverently on the faces of the saints were accompanied by vinous exhalations. Anyone with doubts about the pagan source of peasant Christianity should attend an Orthodox feast.

I had planned to make detailed notes of the christening, but found the task impossible. Within a few seconds I was hemmed in by the congregation which pressed into the church, a happy mob: happy for the additional diversion of this unexpected ceremony, happy too for being so numerous—there is nothing that a Cretan seems to enjoy more than being part of a mass of humanity seething about in a confined space.

The officiating priest, Father Theophanis, had not long been ordained. During the occupation he was a member of the Selino guerilla gang—not a popular one since he was suspected of being a thief. The full black beard and ecclesiastical robes that he now wore lent his face a certain dignity but did nothing to dispel the original suspicion. In spite of this I could not help liking him—he had always been so ready to debunk himself—and I was glad that he had managed to become a priest; priesthood had been his early ambition.

It was so many years since I had stood as godfather to a Greek child that I had forgotten most of the procedure. I remembered only the sort of *pas de deux* that the priest and I had danced round the font. There was also one point in the service at which I had been required to spit out the Devil. But the various responses, the precise moment of immersion, the stage at which the symbolic anointing and hair-cutting are performed—all these I had forgotten. I had hoped to refresh my memory by studying the present ceremony; but there was little of it that I could see or hear. At intervals the sweat-stained face of Father Theophanis would rise out of the moving sea of other faces, and occasionally his voice appeared more audible as he interrupted the litany in mid-sentence to shout: "Make room there! If you don't make room, I'll burst!" During most of the service, however, the congregation had the upper hand.

Daphne had luckily been offered one of the stalls lining both sides of the church; she could therefore lean back against the wall in moderate comfort. I was in a worse position. I had apparently found my way into the female part of the congregation—the men, I noticed, were cracking jokes and discussing politics by themselves in another corner—so the various conversations being conducted round me were mostly concerned with household matters or the usual village gossip. From time to time a woman would detach herself from one of the chattering groups and elbow her way through to the large icon of the Holy Fathers propped up against the wall. There she prostrated herself for as long as it took to deliver a short prayer and a kiss; then, with a Sign of the Cross, she rose to her feet and resumed her interrupted discussion.

For a moment I was almost convinced that this iconolatry had produced a miracle; I suddenly noticed that the faces of the saints seemed to be streaked with tears. Yes, there was no doubt about it; the icons were actually weeping. And it was not even as if they were old or were known to be invested with thaumaturgic powers, like the icon of—which saint was it, now?—that swam all by itself to Mount Athos. These tears, streaming from recently-painted pseudo-Byzantine monstrosities, were all the more impressive. I could not imagine why no one else was surprised by the phenomenon. Surely the moisture that beaded the magenta cheeks of that postcard Virgin Mary, and indecently coursed down the technicolour thighs of this punctured St. Sebastian, was not an everyday occurrence? Then I looked at the plastered walls and the wood of the iconostasis. They too were soaking wet, coated, I regret to say, with a condensation that could be only too easily explained. The church was simply sweating in the damp and the heat, sweating in sympathy with the multitude under its roof.

––––––––

Back in George's house, we found ourselves again in the centre of a crowd. For an hour or more the villagers kept dropping in to congratulate the hosts on the baptism and to wish their child long life. Christening favours were distributed—small metal crosses with a bow of blue ribbon, which we pinned on to our lapels—while George and Angeliko went round with trays of *tsikoudia* and we drank to the toast: "May he live for you! May he live to be a hundred!"

Father Theophanis had also dragged himself away from the church for a few minutes. I knew that he would; during the service I had more than once caught his eye which, if it had not exactly winked, had certainly fluttered its lid. It winked unashamedly now, as he buttonholed me and said:

"You never expected to see me dressed like this, did you? No, no, of course you didn't—me of all people in the robes of a priest! I was once the biggest liar in the world—remember? Well, now I'm just the biggest rogue!"

He drained his glass, then continued *sotto voce*:

"Look out for those strange godbrothers; they're just a bunch of Communists!"

His remark culminated in an almost audible exclamation mark, but he made no attempt to explain it. Instead, he took my hand:

"Well, I must be going. It's a busy day for me—people praying all night, you know!"

And he left.

The feast that followed was identical to the many that had been forced upon me during the Paterakis wedding at Koustoyerako;

only the guests were different. Remembering Father Theophanis's warning, I studied the four godbrothers at the opposite end of the table. They were certainly far from handsome: typical products of the plain, undersized and overdressed, each one "sporting"—there was no other word for it—the sort of pencil-thin Hollywood-hero moustache that is still known in Crete as a "Douglas," after Douglas Fairbanks *père*. But Daphne and I quickly discovered how unfair it would have been to judge them by their appearance alone; as soon as the wine began to circulate they were as friendly as any peasant from the remotest mountain village.

Daphne, as usual, was the only woman at the table though not the only woman in the room. The family's female friends and relations were also there, but in the background: onlookers, not participants. Occasionally one of them would be offered a glass of wine and a piece of goat-gut on a fork—crumbs from the men's table, accepted with gratitude and consumed in the shadows.

Foreigners today tend to regard this Cretan attitude to women as yet another legacy from the Turkish occupation. Superficially, it does indeed resemble the Moslem view of woman's place in a man's world; but the Cretans had put this system of exclusion into practice long before the Turks invaded the island. Classical authors have alluded to it, and even if it was abandoned under the more enlightened rule of Byzantium, it came into force again as soon as Crete fell to Venice; the French botanist Belon remarked upon it in the sixteenth century and so, at a later date, did the *proveditor* Foscarini. Besides, whereas the Moslem makes a point of keeping his wife or wives at home, the Christian peasant sends his out to work—olive-gathering and harvesting, for instance, are exclusively, and compulsorily, female occupations. Women in Crete, then, have the worst of both worlds. Oddly enough, they appear not to mind; those in George's house showed not the slightest trace of envy at the sight of Daphne swigging away with the men.

Soon the inevitable singing started. George, who had been busily serving us, stopped circling round the table and broke into a wonderfully tuneless dirge in honour of his guests and his godbrothers. The sweat trickled down his cheeks, his eyes and the veins in his neck bulged, his mouth gaped and his shoulders heaved as he stood there and shrieked. But for the wine-jar which he still held, it might have seemed that he was shrieking in agony.

This solo performance was followed by a chorus from the god-brothers, an amplified version of the same song. Sitting in this enclosed space under such a shrill bombardment was like lying under a bush full of cicadas in action. Out of loyalty to my host I could not bring myself to echo the opinion of the eighteenth-century traveller, Sonnini: "*Leur ton nazillard est fort déplaisant.*" But I had to admit there was something in what he said. Whenever I heard a Cretan sing I instantly found myself speculating on the condition of his adenoids.

There was worse to come, however. As though to punish us for our silent criticism, the other guests asked Daphne and me to sing something in English. Direct and instantaneous retribution! It was almost as if they had known, just by looking at us, that we were both, to say the least, unmusical. Fortunately George had been generous with the wine; our rendering of *There's a Tavern in the Town*—the only song we could think of—was uninhibited, if not melodious.

I was wondering when the usual festive shooting would begin; had this been Koustoyerako, every rifle and machine-gun in the place would have long ago been blazing away. But in Azoyires I had not yet seen as much as a pistol, though I felt certain that somebody would eventually produce one. Somebody eventually did—the most unlikely person in the room: a young man with a Buster Keaton face and a Salvador Dali moustache.

Since the singing, this expressionless figure had relieved George of the wine-jar and ensured that no glass was left empty for a second. Silently he kept circling round the table, stopping only to pour out more wine, performing this duty with the smooth efficiency of a perfect machine: a *de luxe* model automatic dumbwaiter. Halfway through one of his rounds he hesitated, as though some mechanical hitch had occurred inside him, but his face showed no sign of an internal breakdown. The waxwork features were unaltered as he quietly laid down the wine-jar, and remained unaltered as he drew a Colt 45 and fired six shots out of the window. They were still unaltered as he put his pistol back, picked the wine up again and resumed his rounds. The ritual was over.

George's child, which had been put to bed as soon as the party started, slept soundly through the noise. It went on sleeping, even when overlaid by one of the guests who had passed out on the big brass bedstead—for there was nowhere else in the room to lie down. Such a display of weakness by one of their compatriots—and in front of two foreigners—could not be tolerated by the godbrothers, who at once set out to drink us under the table. They were full of confidence: Daphne, after all, was only a woman and naturally could not be expected to have a strong head; as for me, they had noticed that I drank each glass of wine without taking a mouthful of meat "to cover it."

All Cretans pride themselves on their capacity for drink, which they attribute to their sensible habit of always having solid food, even with a single glass of wine. I can drink large quantities only if I eat next to nothing; Daphne can do likewise, whether she eats or not. The godbrothers were therefore astonished to find that our heads remained as clear, or as unclear, as their own. It is always alarming, I suppose, to see a pet theory easily exploded.

In desperation they asked George for *tsikoudia* to be served as well—a rare request for a Cretan to make in the middle of a meal, since he looks upon a mixture of wine and spirits as fatal. It *was* fatal, but only to the godbrothers; drinking in defiance of their own superstition had an immediate and adverse psychological effect on them. This was only to be expected. After all, they had never practised *le trou normand*; Daphne and I had.

None of us had noticed how long we had spent over the feast until we were reminded of the time by the sunshine outside filtering through the curtains. We had sat down to eat and drink at eight o'clock in the evening; it was now a few minutes past eight in the morning.

The godbrothers were anxious to revive themselves with coffee; we struggled up the path to the village shop, which had been open since dawn to deal with the communal hangover. Elsewhere we would have appeared disreputable, with our bloodshot eyes, unshaven chins, wine-and-sweat-soaked shirts and husky voices; here we were indistinguishable from the crowd in a similar condition.

The approach to the church was blocked by a mass of dazed and drunken worshippers; the service which had started in the night had not yet come to an end; the second day of the feast was about to begin. Daphne and I decided that one day was enough for us; we went back to George's house to say goodbye. He and Angeliko were already preparing food for the next twenty-four hours. In vain he did his best to make us stay.

"But you can't go now," he objected, "I'm just going to get some more wine in. And we'll always find something to eat."

That, exactly, was what I feared.

"How much wine have we drunk already?" I asked him.

"Seventy okes."

Seventy okes is equivalent to twelve dozen bottles; there had been less than a dozen of us drinking. No wonder our footsteps faltered on the slippery path. But Daphne and I were glad that it was so slippery; it served as an excuse for the number of times that we fell as we wove our way downhill to the coast.

PART TWO

Autumn–Winter

Huge, frenzied pillars of stone, scarred by wind and lightning, greyed to the colour of fright, trembling, top-heavy, balanced like macrocosmic fiends, abut the road. The earth grows wan and weird, defertilised, dehumanised, neither brown nor grey nor beige nor taupe nor ecru, the no colour of death reflecting light, sponging up light with its hard, parched shag and shooting it back at us in blinding, rock-flaked splinters that bore into the tenderest tissues of the brain and set it whimpering like a maniac.

Henry Miller

6

ASI GONIA

My original intention was to travel slowly through the mountains from east to west, calling on old friends in the villages that I already knew, making new ones in those that I had not yet visited; in this way I hoped to traverse in a single journey the whole semi-circle covered by the White Mountain range. But in making these plans, I had not accounted for the weather. An early winter had struck the island; daily showers of rain were drenching the foothills; snow had already fallen on the highest peaks; the more remote villages would soon be inaccessible until the following spring. I was forced to abandon my neat itinerary and timetable.

So instead of climbing straight into the highlands of Sphakia from Selino, I accepted an invitation to a wedding in a village at the very opposite end of the range. That was why, on a threatening afternoon in early October, Daphne and I found ourselves in a bus bound for Asi Gonia. Our host, Petros Petrakas, was travelling with us.

Petros was one of the founders of the Cretan resistance movement, one of the handful of leaders who, a few days after the fall of the island, were busy making plans for its liberation. Our first, and for many months our only, clandestine wireless transmitter had been operated from various hide-outs based on his village; Petros had been personally responsible for its safety. Even during the occupation, when he was dressed like any other mountaineer in breeches and boots, with a fringed *sariki* protecting his bald pink head, he had never presented the conventional picture of the dashing guerilla chieftain. There was nothing aquiline or sinewy about him; he had none of the Paterakis litheness. But then he was much older—exactly how old, he himself was uncertain: at the time that he was born, birth certificates were unknown in Crete.

The city clothes which he now wore—for since the occupation he had moved to Canea, where he was working in a bank—were more suited to his bulky frame and slow, deliberate movements; a grey homberg shaded the pale blue eyes and rubicund cheeks which, when his face was in repose, gave him the benign appearance of a teddy-bear—a muscle-bound teddy-bear in a pearl grey suit. But the most surprising feature was his voice, soft and high-pitched, out of keeping with his all-in-wrestler's body. In that measured tone of his—so measured that it almost seemed a mannerism—he pointed out the familiar landmarks on either side of the road, prefixing his allusions to each with the words: "Do you remember?"

Certainly, I remembered. There is a pass in the mountains above Asi Gonia, from which Petros and I had frequently studied this section of the northern coast. The whole of the Apokoronas plain would be unrolled like a map at our feet, enviably flat country stretching from Souda Bay to the promontory in which the small market-town of Rethymnon taunted us with its promise of urban comforts. I used to envy the Germans in those apparently contented villages which could be reached by motor-car, and I longed for the day when I, instead of them, would be able to drive along that main road which I then had to avoid except when an emergency forced me to use it. The thought of wandering freely through those flat fields under my own identity, instead of shuffling past them in shabby disguise, had obsessed me each time that I had looked at them from the trackless mountains above.

———

As soon as the bus had circled the Malaxa ridge—that dark-green rocky zareba which seems to bisect the White Mountains horizontally and, from Canea, conceals the northern foothills—the main range shifted more clearly into focus; there was no obtrusive feature in the foreground to distract the eye. The greyness of the stone, almost the same shade as that of the sky, had the quality of a Russell Flint water-colour; the uniformly pale area above it was painted in with the same meticulous, unimaginative brush, so that the saw-toothed edge of the range was barely discernible; not because the two tones fused, but because they fitted into position as neatly as the pieces of a jig-saw puzzle. The limitless, distant sky and the flat sheet of stone seemed to be on a single plane; even the villages visible through the olive-groves in the foothills appeared in two dimensions only: scattered squares of white painted on a grey and grey-green background.

The bus stopped for a few minutes at Vrysses, where the road divides, the right-hand fork leading inland through the mountains to the village of Sphakia—the only motorable highway in the whole of Sphakia province and that only in the summer months; a few weeks more and it would end halfway, blocked by an impenetrable snow-drift.

After crossing the root of Cape Drepanon—a natural breakwater, seven miles long, which protects Souda Bay from the east—we emerged into the plain that Petros and I used to study in such nostalgic detail. Here the wall of mountain on our right pressed down upon us almost palpably, less high in fact, but in appearance higher for being so close and so bare. I could hardly imagine those lank slopes forested, as by all accounts they once must have been; travellers in Venetian times described them as "all wood." Since then this *pays de cocagne* has been transformed, by the appetite of goats and by human negligence, into a *pays de loup*, softened only by the arcadian waters of Lake Kournas.

This lake, which I had only seen from above, was invisible now from where I sat in the bus; but the sight of the familiar landscape surrounding it reminded me of the legends and superstitions it had evoked. Fish, it is said, are unable to keep alive in its depths, which are bottomless (although Buondelmonte, a mediaeval priest with a more scientific turn of mind than the modern peasant, remarked upon the number of eels which he saw thriving there); and no rifle-bullet fired across it is expected to reach the opposite shore, less than a thousand yards away.

The very formation of this unique basin of fresh water is shrouded in mystery. It is supposed to have once been the site of a village—no traces of which have been found, presumably because deep-sea divers have never been employed to locate it. One summer day, according to the legend, a villager and his daughter were going out to work in the fields. On the way the girl sat down on a rock to comb her hair, which was so radiantly fair that, in the father's eyes, it rivalled the most brilliant sunbeam. "Shine on me," it seemed to be saying to the sun, "and in me see your brilliance reflected." The old peasant was seized with such desire for his daughter that he raped her then and there. As the outrage was committed the girl cried out: "May the ground cave in beneath me; I will haunt the lake that takes its place."

As far as I know, her ghost has never been seen.

As we passed through the village of Dramia on the north coast of the plain, I noticed a group of men who looked utterly unlike the inhabitants of any other village in the neighbourhood. All were in heavy boots and mountain breeches, and each wore his fringed *sariki* tied with studied negligence, the ends hanging gracefully loose. This headgear, even more than their height and their swaggering walk, betrayed their origin; no one but a Sphakian shepherd dresses and moves with such proud abandon. Every autumn these mountaineers migrate here with their flocks, perennial exiles in a seasonal shepherd colony. Their early appearance this year was ominous; the black and bearded harbingers of winter had arrived.

At the far end of the plain we left the main road and turned inland, following a route roughly parallel to the circumference of the mountains which, along this eastern arc, slope less steeply down to form a broad ascending valley: the border between Apokoronas and Rethymnon. A quarter of an hour later we reached Argyroupolis, where the road ends.

The bus drive had confirmed my original view of the White Mountains as a semi-circular stronghold, a walled city rising from plains that fringe its circumference, with the sea as a moat along its diameter. The walls are pierced at irregular intervals with entrances and, at certain weak points, can even be scaled. I had already been through two of those main gates—the passage from the Selino valley to the Omalo and the sea gate of Ayia Roumeli. I was now about to negotiate a third—the inlet at Asi Gonia. I had made a note of the remainder, and planned to use them all in turn before leaving Crete for good.

At the bus-stop we were met by Petros's eldest son, George—the only member of the family, apart from a married daughter, who had stayed in the village since his parents' move to Canea; the other children were all at school in the capital. George, who had refused any education, preferred to look after the family flocks and the house—a sensible arrangement which suited his father as much as it suited himself.

He had brought two mules for us to ride—mercifully only two—so one of us would have to walk. I made up my mind in advance which of us that would be. Daphne, being a woman, naturally had to ride; being intrepid, she mounted her mule at once. I, as the other guest was offered the second beast; not being intrepid, I did not mount at all. With a great show of self-sacrifice I declined in favour of Petros and tried to persuade him that I needed some exercise; yes, exercise on *foot*, in spite of all the mud. To my relief, he accepted. He too, I think, was relieved; since the war he had developed an exaggeratedly dignified walk, holding himself so upright that he almost leaned over backwards—a position which would have been hard to hold on a slippery mountain path.

The ravine leading from Argyroupolis to Asi Gonia is too narrow to be called a valley, not deep enough to be termed a gorge; it is simply the indented bed of a torrent which divides the two prefectures of Canea and Rethymnon. Efforts had been made to transform the path along it into a motor-road—and had immediately, it seemed, been abandoned. The hard earth had been broken up with pick and shovel; boulders weighing several tons had been dislodged, and these, with a number of uprooted trees, now lay along the path as additional obstacles. What man had begun, the weather had completed: with the recent rain the ravine had turned to mire. Fortunately it took us less than two hours to ascend. Then, after a yet steeper climb straight up from the river-bed, the olive-groves came into sight.

The olive trees of Asi Gonia are less abundant, less attractive, less fruitful even than those of many other districts in Crete; but in the twilight of that afternoon, with the rain that comes in the dark beginning to fall, they seemed to be a decorative feature essential to the otherwise denuded landscape. Entering the first cluster of them was like being welcomed by a group of friends. Some stood like silver pillars, their bark as smooth as skin; others crouched like hunchbacks, with crippled shoulders twisted by the wind. Some, in pairs, had coupled like snakes and intertwined into a single barley-sugar column; others had grown old in solitude, hollowed out by the centuries and pierced as though by shrapnel, the wooden filigree miraculously alive and enduring.

The villagers regard these trees through eyes which are sensibly less fanciful; but even the dullest clod stands in awe of them, if only for what they represent in terms of productivity. Nothing of their

fruit goes to waste. Apart from the solid food it furnishes, it yields
also the oil which provides both a basic material for cooking and
the only available source of artificial light; and the crushed residue,
after the juice is squeezed out, can be used as fuel for heating—
but not before being put to even further use: mixed with chemi-
cals it is transformed into soap by a secret process divulged some
time after the Turkish invasion by a gentleman from Provence, who
thereby earned the gratitude of the Cretan peasants and the wrath
of the Marseilles soap-manufacturers whose trade he had in consequence impaired.

The wedding at Asi Gonia was a tame affair compared to the Koustoyerako orgy; rain kept almost everyone indoors. But since the
bride-to-be was Petros's niece, we called on her soon after our arrival.
Her house was packed and, to my relief, there was not a gobbet of
goat's meat in sight—the feasting was over; dancing had already
begun. On a raised platform two musicians were making fiendish
noises with a lute and a lyre, though I dare say they could have given
a better performance if their movements had been less restricted by
the guests surging round them. A small space had been cleared in
the middle of the floor, round which a few young men were circling
with more deliberation than grace. Given more room, they too perhaps could have produced a prettier effect. But I doubt it; the average Cretan dances no better than he sings.

The *pentozali*, which is supposedly based on the ancient Pyrrhic
dance, is Cretan *par excellence*; yet nowadays it is scarcely ever performed—why, I cannot imagine, for its lively tune and swinging
steps (in which the whole circle of dancers takes part and not only
the leader) are far more suited to the full-blooded, independent Cretan character than the mincing measures of the *syrto* which seems
to have acquired an undeserved popularity. I admit that I am preju-
diced against the *syrto*, but only because have yet to see it adequately
presented. As performed that night at Asi Gonia, it was the same
dull routine that I had witnessed a dozen times before: the leader,
with a scowl of concentration, hopped, skipped, jumped and occasionally slapped his heel; while his supporters, linked together by
handkerchiefs in their hands, shuffled listlessly after him, as though
embarrassed by the part they had to play.

We watched them for a few minutes and drank some *tsikoudia*; then Petros suggested going home to bed. He had never been a *glentzis*, the life and soul of a party; and by tradition this party would be going on all night.

It was still raining when we woke up in the morning. "Typical Asi Gonia weather," said Petros, "if God had only one shower left, He wouldn't let it fall elsewhere. Let's hope it will clear up for the ceremony."

It did not clear up. We reached the church in a downpour, to find that the service had already begun; in fact it was almost over. As usual, no one had known exactly when it was meant to take place. We were just in time to catch a glimpse of the bridal pair standing side by side in front of the priest. Each wore a coronet of artificial orange-blossom symbolically linked by a length of white cord; both looked quite wretched with embarrassment. But they had not long to wait for the ordeal to end. There was an explosion of fireworks just behind them—the work of some urchins on the fringe of the crowd—and presently a queue had formed to kiss and congratulate them. Everything happened at bewildering speed: a fusillade of rifle-shots greeted them as they came out of the church, and a minute later the bride had been placed on a mule and was being dragged off into the mountains in the direction of her husband's home—a splendidly primitive departure, far more significant than driving off in a motor-car with an old boot in tow.

The wedding had provided me with an opportunity to meet many of my old friends. One of them, George Psychoundakis, came back to Petros's house with us. George was the first guide that I ever had in Crete. In the ten years that I had known him he appeared to have changed hardly at all—until he whipped off the old army beret he was wearing.

He was now completely bald, though still in his twenties. The shining, sun-burnt pate crowning the dark-eyed, unlined face was infinitely comic; and he knew it. It suited him far better than the straight black hair, of which he had once been so proud, and was somehow more in keeping with the nickname that the villagers had given him: Bertodoulos, the jester. But to Paddy Leigh Fermor and me, he will always be known by another name, a *nom-de-guerre* of Paddy's inspiration. In the summer of 1942, when I went to Cairo on leave, Paddy took over my area; he also took over George—my own particular Sancho Panza—whom he consequently christened "Changeling," and subsequently "Changebug."

During the years that he was with us Changebug had learnt a number of English songs. I asked him if he still remembered them. Without a moment's hesitation he started to sing:

> Hitler has only got one mpall;
> Goering's got two, mput very small;
> Himmler's got something sim'lar;
> Mput Doctor Goempells' got no mpalls at all![1]

Asi Gonia is encircled by tall mountains which seem constantly stretched to their full height, as though anxious not to miss the smallest shower. Once the rain is in their grasp they hold on to it, until they have squeezed out the last drop of moisture over the village. The present downpour clearly had several days' life left in it. Through the watery curtain, which at times appeared almost solid, I tried to make out the sites of the many hide-outs which we had established in the surrounding hills; but the only one that I recognized was the Cave of the Khainides, a small black dot as conspicuous in the shadowless cliffs as a lighthouse in the dark.

It had not always been so easy to pick out. In its heroic heyday— for every cave of any size in Crete is associated with some patriotic exploit which has since imbued it with legend—it was invisible in the thick woods which once used to cloak these hills, and had served as a long-term *limeri*, or hide-out, for that original anti-Turkish organisation after which the cave was named. It was here that the *khainides* established their clandestine printing-press, and it was over the cliff beneath that they hurled themselves to death rather

---

1. I have made no attempt to reproduce a phonetic rendering of Changebug's English accent, apart from substituting *mp* for the *b* sound, which is unknown in Greek (a conventional transliteration: thirsty foreigners, even in westernised Athens, still look for the sign "Mpar" if they want a drink). But the song would be incomplete without a description of the appropriate gestures that accompany each line—a single finger raised to indicate Hitler's singular defect; forefinger and thumb joined to form a circle, representing a magnifying-glass through which to view Goering's minute appendages; a negligent wave of the hand to dismiss any claim to superiority on Himmler's part (or parts); and an affirmative thump of the closed fist to stress the final demonstrative negative.

than surrender when a Turkish raiding force had set fire to the surrounding forest in an attempt to smoke them out of their lair. That, at least, is the legend current in Asi Gonia today; and if it conflicts with the local claim that no Turk ever set foot in this remote bowl in the mountains, it serves none the less to perpetuate the memory of those seventeenth-century heroes whose relatively short career might otherwise have been eclipsed by the more widely-publicised exploits of later generations.

For the activity of the *khainides* lasted no more than half a century; and the clandestine nature of their operations—in so far as clandestinity can ever be achieved among such chatterboxes as the Cretans—precluded the spread of their fame. They were equivalent, then, to the *insaisissables* of Nazi-occupied France, those anonymous agents for whom security was more important than notoriety since they operated in and among the enemy garrisons. If this rough comparison between Crete at that time and France during the last World War may be taken a stage further, the *khainides* would represent the "sedentary" element of the resistance movement, the inhabitants of the urban and industrial centres, who led their normal lives by day but at night crept out in secret to sabotage and assassinate; while the Sphakians in the freedom of their mountains were the counterpart (and prototype) of the armed *maquis* groups. The parallel between Crete under the Turks and France under the Germans suggests itself again in the attendant circumstance common to both countries: neither territory was at first completely overrun by the invaders. During the first fifty years or so of the Turkish occupation three outposts of Christianity (equivalent to the "free" zone of France) were maintained on the northern coast of Crete, in the Venetian fortresses of Grabousa, Souda and Spinalonga.

It is difficult to understand why the Turks allowed these three thorns to remain so long in their flesh. They had taken almost a quarter of a century to subdue the island—the siege of Herakleion alone had lasted over twenty years—yet they made no immediate attempt to neutralise these three lesser strongholds before extending their administration throughout the rest of the newly conquered territory. These pockets of Christianity, so long as they remained intact, not only stood as a religious symbol—a sort of geographical Holy Trinity—for Venetians and Cretans alike, but also served as secure bases for the subversive activities of both. Into them the *khainides* could retire at dawn after raiding the countryside all night, and for fifty years no aga or jannissary could have slept very soundly if his house was within striking distance of them.

But by the end of the seventeenth century the days of the *khainides* were numbered. In 1692 Grabousa was betrayed to the Turks, following an unsuccessful Venetian attempt to recover the land that had been lost[2]; and seventeen years later Spinalonga and Souda were also abandoned. The Venetians had never been popular in Crete; as taskmasters, they had been harsh and as allies, half-hearted. Yet their final departure was deplored by the islanders, if only because it was recognised as the death-blow to anti-Turkish activity. Deprived of their bases, the *khainides* were forced to disappear, either as fugitives into the mountains or as crypto-Christians into the ranks of the new converts to Islam. Almost overnight the entire Cretan resistance movement ended in flight and apostasy.

The half-century that followed was the darkest period of the Turkish occupation. With the collapse of the *khainides*, there was nothing to prevent the occupying forces from indulging, officially and unofficially, in an orgy of persecution; and the history of this period, as taught in Cretan schools today, is almost exclusively an account of excesses and atrocities committed by sultan, pasha, bey, aga and jannissary. But this teaching should be taken with a grain of salt. The list of crimes is based not on circumstantial records but on contemporary folk-songs of an inevitably chauvinistic nature; even though the modern Cretan historian prefers the role of prosecuting counsel to that of objective reporter, the evidence available against the accused is, to say the least, unreliable.

A major crime, for instance, with which the Turks are charged, is the attempt to convert the conquered islanders by compulsion. But the policy of the Sublime Porte was, on the contrary, to maintain a large class of *rayahs*, or Christian subjects, who, being of inferior status to the Moslems in accordance with Moslem law, bore much heavier fiscal burdens than the Moslem ruling caste. Admittedly, the indirect result of this policy was to turn large areas of the island into an unproductive wilderness—for the Christian cultivators preferred to let their land go to waste rather than lose most of its produce in taxation—but this agricultural catastrophe was not the Turks' intention.

2. According to Tournefort, the Venetians themselves handed the fortress over to a vizier of the Sultan's in exchange for a barrel of sequins.

Some descriptions of the individual barbarities that occurred read like an extract from the verbatim report on the Nuremberg trials. Rape and murder seem to have been daily events; and a favourite sport of the Moslem *herrenvolk* was to make young girls and old hags dance naked on a floor strewn with dried chick-peas, until they inevitably tripped and fell—a compulsorily immodest performance calculated, I suppose, to satisfy the onlooker's quaint sense of fun in addition to stimulating his jaded sexual appetite.

The Turkish treatment of women is the most popular Aunt Sally for the coconuts of our modern Cretan critic, the inference being that no Christian virgin ever succumbed voluntarily to the demands of the insatiable Moslem. But a very different picture is painted by a disinterested French observer, who spent a few days on the island in 1710 and lodged one night with a Turk who had taken a Christian as his wife. This is what their guest, La Motraye, has to say:

> *Ce couple vivoit fort bien ensemble: Ali-oglou alloit à la mosquée, et sa femme à l'église. Pour les enfans, ils étoient élevez dans le Mahometisme. Il ne faisoit point de scrupule d'allumer pour elle la lampe les samedis, devant l'image de la Panagia.*

And in case this couple should be considered exceptional, other instances could be cited of successful mixed unions of this sort. Olivier, another French traveller, lays special emphasis on the Turkish custom of marrying Greek girls *"au capin"*—a temporary arrangement whereby the husband was required to pay for his wife and support any child she might bear him—and claims that far from feeling ashamed, the women were flattered, *"tant il est vrai qu'ici, comme ailleurs, l'autorité séduit et la vanité entraîne."*

But in underlining this method of tailoring the events of two hundred years ago to suit the patriotic sensibilities of today, I do not wish either to exonerate the Turks or to disparage the Cretans. The Cretan women in particular, especially those of outstanding beauty, showed a correspondingly outstanding courage. Many of them chose to suffer death by their own hand rather than dishonour at the hands of an aga. Others managed to avoid either fate, but only at enormous self-sacrifice, by leaving their homes for ever and taking refuge with the outlaws in the mountains. Thus, involuntarily, was repeated the eugenic experiment of the ancient Cretan magistrates, who reserved the fairest of the daughters for the most valiant of the youth.

A new period of resistance began—the frustrated resistance of the passive fugitive—and the *zeitgeist* is reflected in the songs which made their first appearance about this time, in the klephtic ballads composed and mournfully intoned by brigand-poets on the look-out and on the run. Superficially, these dirges resemble the negro spirituals of America, though they lack both the melodic virtue and poetic imagination of those early cotton-field compositions. What has kept them alive, even up to the present day, is their patriotic fervour. The fate of the country as a whole is lamented more than the circumstances of any particular individual; the hero-victim is always the community, never the man. It is this sense of mass persecution, of brotherhood in adversity, which prompted the best of the allegorical ballads. When the klepht sang of the eagle waiting for the sun to melt the snow from its frozen wings, the bird represented not only the singer himself but the whole Cretan people ice-bound in slavery and longing for the thaw of liberation.

The sun and summer-time are used again and again in these ballads as symbols of freedom and independence, and in the specifically Cretan versions the note of despair is accompanied by the threat of revenge. One of the best-known of these *rizitika* begins:

When will the weather break, ah when will spring be here? . . .

and the singer goes on to describe exactly what he proposes to do when the weather does break:

I shall make mothers childless,
Make widows of the women
And orphans of the babes in arms,
Who'll cry all day for mother
And cry all night for water
And at sunrise cry for mother's milk.

But this dream of a "night of the long knives," when every Turk would be slaughtered in his bed, was postponed for two generations. Revenge was the subject of the songs; it was not in fact the policy of the singers—not, that is, until the rebellion of 1770,[3] when the men

---

3. This rebellion, the first of a long series, is referred to on p. 202. For various reasons I have described it there in some detail; but my general intention is to avoid large slabs of undigested history, especially since Cretan history is mainly a chronicle of alternating phases of insurrection and retribution, as repetitive and indigestible as a pickled onion.

in the mountains were given their first opportunity to put into practice what they had so long preached by incantation.

———————

We made the rain an excuse for a long bout of indolence. Petros's house was one of the few in Crete suitable for this form of self-indulgence, and we took full advantage of it. In the absence of his family, there was space for Daphne and me to spread ourselves in moderate comfort. The whole of the top floor, consisting of two rooms, was put at our disposal, and for the first and only time on our travels we were enabled to unpack the rucksack which contained our personal belongings. Prisoners of the weather, we spent all day and every day upstairs, in the larger room which we gradually came to look upon as a cell. But we were both grateful for the unaccustomed privacy it afforded. In any other village-household we would have been forcibly roused from our lethargy by the duties demanded of a guest; hours would have been spent in crowded discomfort and pointless small-talk. Here, in the almost monastic atmosphere of the top floor, we could idle as we liked. At last I could open a book without being asked what was worrying me—for reading, in Crete, is regarded only as an anodyne—or could write a few notes without having them examined by half-a-dozen people peering at them without understanding. Daphne could knit without being told that she was holding the needles in the wrong way and without having her knitting unravelled by inquisitive fingers feeling the quality of the wool. And we could both help ourselves to the *tsikoudia* on the table without having to utter a conventional toast each time we downed a glass.

What a relief to be left, for once, to ourselves! Even the meals were effortless. Twice a day food was brought up from the kitchen below and, since Petros knew my aversion to goat, there was never a sign of meat. Cretans have an odd idea about English gastronomic habits. We are still known in the island as *marmaladzides* ("jam-eaters") or *avgolades* ("egg-eaters")—no doubt from the observations of those villagers who in 1941 worked in our military canteens and so, not unnaturally, came to the conclusion that those two articles of food form our staple diet. There was no jam in Asi Gonia, but we were given eggs to eat for every meal.

Every meal, that is, except for one dinner, to which we were invited by an old friend of mine, Pavlos Gyparis. Our visit to Pavlos's house, at the very top of the village, was our only expedition out of doors during our entire stay in Asi Gonia. It was unremarkable. I do not even remember what we had to eat; and I should probably have forgotten both our struggle in the dark up the torrent-bed lanes and our return down the streaming hill, had it not been for something I saw which, for me at least, made the evening memorable.

The walls of Pavlos's house were adorned with vast family photographs, the only form of pictorial decoration to be found in Crete. These enlargements, from out-of-focus snapshots or postcard-size provincial studio portraits, are invariably "blown up" to such dimensions that the features of the subject are blurred out of all recognition. Pavlos's collection was better than most; there was still a faintly wraith-like quality about the pictures of these relations of his—each bearded *pallikari*, frozen in a stiffly conventional pose, glared angrily from his frame as though emerging from an ocean of ectoplasm—but they could at least be identified as members of the Gyparis clan. There was, however, one exception: a slightly clearer print representing some gross lout who was clearly not one of the family; his coarse flabby face had nothing in common with the finely-chiselled traits discernible in the other portraits or with Pavlos's own darkly-noble countenance. I asked who it was.

"Don't you really know?" Pavlos replied, "Look at it again."

I examined it more closely, studying each individual feature: the hydrocephalic skull unevenly covered with a scabrous growth resembling moss more than human hair; the shifty, boot-button eyes leering beneath brows arched in a frown of artificial ferocity; the arrogant tilt of the nose and the affected sneer; the weak mouth pulled down at each corner in an attempt to achieve an effect of strength; the jowls, planted with pitiful tufts of beard, drooping into an outsize muffler worn with over-emphasized careless abandon, the general impression of studied toughness—all these stamped the man as a charlatan. Even the photograph itself looked a fake, like the picture of an alleged materialisation—the sort of thing a bogus medium might produce as evidence of his spiritualistic powers.

Yet there was something disturbingly familiar about it. In this unpleasant portrait of an unpleasant person I seemed to recognize someone whom I had known years before. But it was the muffler, not the face, that finally provided a clue to the subect's identity. I had worn one like it myself during the occupation; and suddenly I remembered the photographs which Pavlos and I had taken of each other in the winter of 1943, just after our encounter with a German patrol on the Hill of the Holy Ghost. He smiled now at my gasp of recognition:

"You see? I knew you'd remember."

I held a lamp up to the photograph for Daphne to examine it more closely. Loyally, she at first refused to believe that I could ever have looked like that.

"It's a good thing you've changed since then," was her comment once I had finally convinced her. But Pavlos, an initiate of the Cretan virility cult, looked sadly at my face which was now half as large and a quarter as hirsute as the face portrayed on the wall.

"You've certainly deteriorated," he said.

———

Throughout the occupation our upper room in Asi Gonia had been used as a clandestine meeting-place; no one had ever come near it without Petros's permission. From force of habit the rest of the village seemed to regard it still as "out of bounds"—hence our present privacy. But, apart from Daphne and myself, there was another guest in the house—a young man with a beard so blond that it looked quite false, like part of a disguise.

"Unfortunately it's not a good enough disguise," said Petros, when I questioned him about this stranger, "otherwise he wouldn't have to spend his life in hiding."

"Why, what has he done?"

"Oh, nothing much. Just a little trouble. But now he's on the run."

Petros's reply was not purposely evasive; nor was the word "trouble" intended as a misleading understatement. However euphemistic it sounded, it was the word which any Cretan would quite naturally use to denote a crime of violence. It was equally natural for the culprit to be still at large; the pursuit and apprehension of a single criminal in these mountains would demand the mobilisation of the island's entire gendarmerie. In any case, a man who has committed a strictly personal crime—even the crime of murder—is not necessarily regarded as a criminal; and a fugitive from justice is simply looked upon as a citizen who has been forced to change his status.[4]

---

4. Greek is the only language that I know which has a single word for "to be on the run," and this verb is commonly used to denote the fugitive's profession, almost in the same way that "to farm" denotes the occupation of the farmer.

As such, he can always find refuge with the hospitable villagers—even with such a law-abiding one as Petros—until he is granted the inevitable amnesty.

The only other guests who called on us regularly were Pavlos and Changebug; especially Changebug. He came in one morning, more drenched than usual and covered in mud. His roof, he explained, had collapsed in the night and poured down on to his bed—a great joke! He described the scene in every comic detail. But Changebug was not only Bertodoulos the Jester; he was also Psychoundakis the Poet. In a more serious mood, he would spend hours reciting his own compositions—not the doggerel *mantinades*, which any peasant is capable of making up on the spot, but surprisingly sophisticated verses.

My favourite was his *Ode to an Inkspot on a Schoolmistress's Skirt*. But the one which he had most enjoyed writing, he said, was an anti-feminist poem satirising the women who, during the previous particularly bitter winter, had worn men's trousers to protect themselves from the cold when engaged on olive-picking in the fields. The whole village had been shocked by such wanton behaviour; and more shocked still to find next day, pinned to the floor of the coffee-shop for all to read, a sheet of verses commemorating this shameful breach of modesty. Changebug had been careful to sign them, not with his own name but with that of the village cobbler. The cobbler was promptly beaten up.

Changebug's talent was, in the true sense of the word, natural. His education—three years' erratic attendance at the village school—had been, to say the least, rudimentary. His poetic facility, then, must have been inherited. His father, one of the poorest shepherds in the area, had had no education at all; he had never learnt to write but had taught himself to read in order to enjoy, visually as well as orally, the traditional peasant poems which he had often heard in his youth. He had learnt them all by heart and now, at the age of eighty, could still recite the whole of the *Erotokritos*, a composition of over ten thousand lines.

Changebug also knew large parts of this Cretan epic and would intone them in a conventional sing-song voice which invariably put me to sleep. During one of these recitals I was roused from my stupor by a break in the rhythm and a burst of sound as unexpected as a trumpet blast in the middle of a violin concerto: "Dang! Dang! Dang! Dang! Dang!" I opened my eyes to see Changebug stamping about the room, firing an imaginary pistol. He had come to one of the passages describing a battle.

I must confess that I have never read the *Erotokritos* from beginning to end; only a philologist or a serious historian would have the patience to plough through so many pages of jog-trot verse interspersed with tedious repetitions and disfigured by redundant words introduced simply for the sake of rhyme and metre. And the story itself, a chivalaresque tale set in Hellenic times, is fairly commonplace. The poem has never been popularly acclaimed anywhere outside Crete, although it has been admired by leading Greek poets like Solomos, Palamas and Seferis, whose professional opinions I trust. My own judgment, therefore, must be at fault, for I still consider the poem a crashing bore, a typical "provincial" effort. To my mind its only value lies in the picture which it provides of life in Crete under Venetian rule, a period of social history which is almost a complete blank; even now more is known about the everyday habits of the common man in Homer's time than about living conditions in the time of the author of the *Erotokritos*.

The poem was written, as far as we can make out, about 1645. Of the author we know nothing save his name: Vincent Kornaros, and his birthplace: Sitia, in the eastern prefecture of Lassithi. His manuscript must have been taken out of Crete a few years later by refugees fleeing from the Turkish invasion, for it was first published in Venice in 1713. Apart from a popular edition issued from Patras in 1818 (which could not have been easily available in Crete), it was not reprinted until 1915. Yet it was well known in the island throughout the nineteenth century. It must therefore have been handed down all those years either by word of mouth or in manuscript form— proof enough of the regard in which it was held.

No doubt its popularity was, and still is, due to the language in which it is written. The few Greek poems composed after the fall of Byzantium are in a stilted "literary" jargon incomprehensible to ninety percent of the Greek population. The early fourteenth-century *Chronicle of the Morea*, for instance, is so full of pompous gallicisms that it sounds more like the work of a civil servant than of a poet—the author's profession may be conjectured from his lack of imagination, insistence on political details and familiarity with feudal law and custom; he was probably an attorney or a clerk in the chancellery of the Frankish Principality of Achaia. The *Machairas Chronicle* of Cyprus, written a century later, suffers from the same faults. As the chronicler himself remarks, so long as Cyprus was part of the Byzantine Empire the inhabitants had been obliged to know "standard" Greek, but after the Lusiguans took the island the language was reduced to a barbarous jargon, "so much so that today no one in the world can say what language we talk."

But the *Erotokritos* was written in the living, demotic tongue unmixed with the foreign words peculiar to *katharevousa*, the so-called "pure" language of the urban communities.[5] It was therefore understandable to every Cretan shepherd, and loved by him all the more for being composed in the characteristic Cretan metre: the dekapentesyllabic line.

This preservation of their mother tongue is yet another example of Cretan tenacity, and not an isolated one. Proof of it is furnished in a number of other contemporary works: in the *Sacrifice of Abraham*, a mystery play written as a church performance by an unknown author; in the *Erophile*, a sort of musical comedy with rustic songs composed by George Hortatzis of Rethymnon; in the *Fair Shepherdess*, another rustic idyll by yet another anonymous writer; and in the *Account of the Cretan War*, an historical poem about the siege of Herakleion, by Bounialis who also came from Rethymnon. All these works retain the pure Cretan idiom, although they were composed when the island had been dominated by the Venetians for about four hundred years; (whereas in Cyprus and in the Morea less than a hundred years of foreign occupation were needed to reduce the language to a hybrid jargon).

How are we to account for this inspired renaissance? We can only assume that during those four centuries the Venetians in Crete had, to a certain degree, lost their Italian character and language (and sometimes, through mixed marriages, even their Roman Catholic faith). Linguistically at least, the conquerors had been defeated by the conquered. Crete, then, although politically oppressed, remained spiritually free: the only Greek-in-feeling remnant of the former Byzantine Empire. Elsewhere all intellectual and artistic development had been arrested by the Turkish invasion; in Crete alone a native literature survived and, fostered by the many refugees from

---

5. A parallel may be drawn with modern Greek as spoken and written today: the language spoken in Athenian drawing-rooms or used as the medium of Athenian journalism is full of gallicisms which are wholly absent from the really "pure" speech of the provinces and countryside.

Constantinople,[6] reached its height during the sixteenth and seventeenth centuries, in Venetian-influenced dramatic form.

That influence cannot be denied, even by the most chauvinistic modern critic. Though the language of these Cretan masterpieces is pure unsullied Greek, most of their themes are emphatically foreign. The *Erotokritos*, for instance, is based on *Paris et Vienne*, written by Pierre de la Cypède and printed in Antwerp in 1478; the *Sacrifice of Abraham* can be traced to a late sixteenth-century Venetian tragedy; the *Erophile* has its parallel in Giraldi's *Orbeche*; and scenes from an earlier Italian idyll are repeated in the *Fair Shepherdess*.

Champions of Cretan literature should not find cause to defend their heroes against a charge of plagiarism; they need only refer to the ancient Athenian dramatists in order to assure themselves that the treatment of a story is no less important than that story's originality.

I was determined to leave Asi Gonia as soon as the weather broke. I wanted to push deeper into the mountains before the snow settled in for the winter; and so I proposed a short visit to Alones, a village further south, which had been a refuge for us during the occupation. Changebug also wanted to visit it again and volunteered to come with us.

"We'll move off when we see the women going out to pick the olives," he said, "then we'll know the weather will hold long enough for our journey."

Two days later the rain stopped. The village, which for a week had been as dead as a submerged city, suddenly came to life; its inhabitants emerged as though from a deluge, their clothes still wringing wet since almost every house had sprung a leak during the long downpour. I was grateful for the tiles which had protected us when I saw the condition of the mud roofs of the neighbouring houses. It would require weeks of sun or wind to drain the puddles from their uneven surface. Meanwhile their owners were doing what

---

6. A similar, and equally beneficial, influx of Greeks from Turkey occurred more recently. In 1921 large numbers of the refugees from Smyrna were allotted to Crete. These settlers, with their higher standards of living, introduced comforts of civilisation which the islanders had never even imagined; in some villages beds were unknown commodities until they were imported by the new residents from Asia Minor.

they could to plug the leaks by stamping down the slush, then rolling it with a heavy cylindrical stone which is always kept on the roof for that purpose. I felt that there must be some more effective and permanent means of repair, but could think of none; after the next storm this depressing and slightly ludicrous performance would have to be repeated.

Alones was only about five miles away; the walk was, for this area, a fairly easy one; and we had given ourselves ample time to arrive before nightfall. But we did not reach the village that evening, nor even the following day. It was my fault, I suppose; I should never have made a definite plan; or, having made one, should have stuck to it. But I had reckoned without an unexpected visitor.

He turned up at Petros's house just as we were leaving. Changebug had opened the door to let us out and, instead, let in a gesticulating, bawling, grey-bearded giant who, within a few seconds, had embraced me, shaken hands with Daphne, patted Changebug on the cheek, taken the rucksack off my back and poured out a round of *tsikoudia*. All this he accomplished without an interruption in his monologue, which could have been heard from the furthest end of the village.

"At last, at last! And after so many years—how are you? Who's this? Long life to her! Where do you think you're going? You're not going anywhere. Here, sit down! Take this! Your health! Another? Your health! There now, you see, mountains don't meet, men do. How long have you been here? Why haven't you been to see me? Frightened of the walk? Or of the rain? Look at me, an old man; but I've come all the way here to see you—and with this foot. Here, look at my foot! Nasty, isn't it? A burn. Hot metal, red-hot . . ."

It was only then that I remembered who he was: Stelios Gavalas, the blacksmith of Arolithi. His face was familiar, indeed unforgettable, but as usual I had failed to identify him, until his mention of hot metal had provided the clue. While he rolled his sock back over the open sore on his shin, he continued without drawing breath:

"You were just going off somewhere, weren't you? Where were you going? Alones? You're not going to Alones. No, don't argue, you're coming with me. Never been to my village, have you? Well, then! You can go to Alones later, Arolithi's only just off your road—and it's nearer. Stay with me tonight, then go tomorrow. What's wrong with that? Tell me, what's wrong with that?"

There was nothing wrong, as far as I could see.

7

ALONES

THE AROLITHI PATH leads straight up from the river: the steepest ascent of all from Asi Gonia. Unlike the bare rocky walls to the south and west, this eastern slope is cloaked in arbutus-bushes, which added to the labour of climbing; the soil in which they grow was now a cataract of mud and, as we struggled through the barrier of branches, each leaf, bent back into a miniature catapult, bombarded us with its charge of raindrops. In spite of these obstacles, and disregarding his sore foot, Stelios plunged uphill with Changebug close on his heels. Daphne and I made the arbutus an excuse for loitering. The bushes were in fruit and we rested every few yards, ostensibly to pick the berries. These were the colour of blood-oranges and the size of gooseberries, but tasted like a blend of strawberry and mango.

There is a popular superstition that this fruit is intoxicating—nonsense, of course; one might as well say the same of the grape—but it does provide an intoxicating drink: a particularly potent *tsikoudia*, too potent, it seems, for some people. Pashley, for instance, says of the arbutus: "The fruit . . . is pleasant to taste; which is certainly more than can be said of the spirit extracted from it." But then he was hard to please; even the delicious *tsikoudia* distilled from mulberries he condemns as "perhaps the most execrable of all the preparations that bear the name."

It is delightful to meet comments of this nature in the account of any traveller; they afford a rare clue to the author's personality. A Fellow of Trinity College, Cambridge, Pashley was a typically donnish traveller, more interested in places than in people. Ancient topography was his main pursuit, but the spell of Crete almost induced him to enlarge his activities; in addition to his *Travels* he had planned to write a history of the island. He was well equipped for the task and, had he carried it out, would have done me, for one, a great favour; I have yet to find a reliable history of Crete in any language.

Pashley, perhaps, was one of those adventurous people who, as soon as they return to a university atmosphere, simply run to seed in the Common Room. So many academic travellers, once their travelling is over, affect to be positively ashamed of it, as though it had been a youthful indiscretion which had better be tactfully ignored. When questioned, they will do no more than smile in a gently deprecatory sort of way, or else firmly hold their tongue. This attitude[1] is more commendable, I suppose, than that of the garrulous bore; but neither is really necessary. After all, there is nothing so very shameful in being on good terms with a peasant. Pashley understood the Cretans as well as any foreigner can, but he refused to share their way of life and preferred to keep them at a distance, so much so that at times he seems even to dislike them in a quiet, gentlemanly way. I wonder what he would have made of Stelios.

———————

The mist that enveloped us at the top of the hill seemed to accelerate the dusk; it was almost dark when we reached Arolithi. A score of houses loomed up at our approach: squat rectangular silhouettes, from one of which a smaller rectangle of yellow light gleamed suddenly as the door was opened to let us in. The gleam was accompanied by a babble of voices, which our entry cut short: there were about a dozen children in the room, the mouths hanging open in amazement and in mid-sentence. They stared at us until Stelios broke the silence:

"What are you gazing at, you little cuckolds? Go and fetch your mother!"

His voice boomed round the room and, before the echo of it died, above the hollow sound made by the children's retreating feet, another voice boomed back from down below: "Coming!" Presently, from the hole in the floor through which the children had disappeared, a head popped out and a pair of shoulders emerged, fol-

---

1. Professor Dawkins tells me that even today this attitude prevails.

lowed by the rest of the body, which, when no more than a yard and a half above ground level, ended abruptly in two tiny feet: that was all there was of Stelios's wife, Styliane. But her lack of inches was compensated by the strength of her vocal chords. Her greeting echoed round the room as loudly as her husband's words of command. This shouting puzzled me, until I heard my own voice in reply; it provoked an even deeper thunder from the walls. The house was a huge sounding-board.

These odd acoustics seemed to make us all slightly hysterical—or was it only the *tsikoudia*? The bottle was produced, and our glasses filled, without the normal inhibitory ceremony; instead of serving us and then retiring into the darkest corner, Styliane joined us at the table and drank her share like a man. This unusually sophisticated behaviour was a welcome surprise for Daphne, who had hitherto always been the solitary woman in an otherwise exclusively male company—a position which she might have enjoyed in any other country but Crete, where the barrier of language and local custom reinforced her social isolation. How often had she been forced to sit in silence while I exchanged conventional platitudes with the men? And how often had I failed her as an interpreter? With Styliane, she needed none. Instead of listening to my translation of a feeble joke at which I might have laughed out of politeness, she could now share in the general hilarity; Styliane's vivid pantomime did away with the need for words.

The little woman was a comedian; she was also a cook. Food suddenly appeared on the table: dozens of hard-boiled eggs and *dolmades*, vine-leaves stuffed with minced meat, rice and herbs. The *tsikoudia* bottle was removed; a beaker of wine took its place. All this, again with a minimum of fuss and ceremony. We simply ate and drank and laughed and shouted, trying to make ourselves heard above the amplified voice of the house. The noise seemed to increase our thirst.

I have to rely on Daphne's account of our activities after dinner; my own recollection of them is hazy. I have a mental snapshot of Styliane coughing over a cigarette, the first that she had smoked in her life; she was wearing Daphne's belt slung over her shoulder like a bandolier since it was too small to go round her waist; she had also, I believe, daubed herself with some of Daphne's lipstick; anyway she looked more like a jolly cosmopolitan lesbian than a Cretan peasant-woman.

Daphne tells me that later we paid a visit to the coffee-shop. I was not aware of it. The last thing that I remember was going to sleep in a bed made up on the floor. From somewhere below my head came the sound of dripping water, each splash painfully magnified, as though my ear was connected by a stethescope to the pulsations of an underground pool. So this was why the whole house echoed; I was sleeping on top of a cistern.

———

The mist was still there in the morning: unsuitable weather for photography. But Styliane had noticed Daphne's camera and insisted on being taken. She let down her Red Indian hair, soaked it in olive oil and replaited it; apart from its new metallic sheen it looked much the same as before. She swabbed her legs with water and scrubbed off the dirt—which would not have shown in any case, since her skirt came down to her ankles. When this ritual was over she summoned Stelios outside and, with him, struck the conventional Cretan attitude, standing stiffly to attention, staring straight into the lens. Together, they looked almost freakish—a circus giant with a female clown—and their appearance was rendered more comic by the gravity of their expressions. But of this they were unconscious: in these villages, posing for a photograph is always a serious business.

The Cretans have a passion for snapshots. Although a camera was a rare thing in the mountains, almost every villager I met had his pocket-book stuffed with photographs of his friends and relations, which were displayed at the first opportunity. Stelios went one better: in his pocket he carried a dozen studio portraits of himself, one of which he now presented to us as a parting gift. "But first I must have it inscribed," he said and, since he could not write, dictated his message to the owner of the coffee-shop, who copied it out on the back of the print.

Just as we were leaving, Styliane rushed up with another present which she pressed into Daphne's hands: "Something to remind you of Arolithi." Daphne found herself holding a small piebald rabbit.[2]

Luckily we only had a short walk in front of us, so the transport of this pet was no problem. Since our path led through Villandredo,

---

2. It was lost, alas, a few days later; and the loss reported to Styliane. To put us at our ease about it, she sent a message back to us at once: "Tell Daphne her rabbit came home quite safely."

a village where Changebug and I both had friends, we decided to
spend one night there before going on to Alones. We were now just
outside the White Mountain area, in the relatively flat province of
Rethymnon. Asi Gonia was out of sight, but the crags surmount-
ing it were visible on our right—an entrance to the acropolis of the
main range beyond. On our left the nearest peak was that of Ida,
separated from us by an almost uninterrupted expanse of fertility
which, compared to the landscape behind Canea, seemed as gentle
as the Sussex downs.

The countryside of each of the four prefectures of Crete has bred
its own individual type of man, and a popular jingle exists which
describes their respective qualities. Reading from west to east, then:

Men of Canea love to fight.
Men of Rethymnon love to write.
Men of Herakleion love their wine.
Men of Lassithi—simply swine!

This generalisation is not entirely accurate. The men of Lassithi
are not so much swine as sheep. Everyone in Crete, excepting them,
loves to fight; everyone, including them, loves his wine. Hardly anyone in the island loves to write, but the few that do almost all come
from Rethymnon. The people of this prefecture are altogether more
sensitive than the mentally hirsute highlanders. Their aesthetic faculty is immediately apparent from the lay-out of their villages; their
appreciation of comfort is noticeable in the design of their individual houses.

As the crow flies, Villandredo is no more than five miles from Asi
Gonia; architecturally, it is in another world. As soon as we entered
the village we found ourselves walking along a well-drained cobbled lane flanked by white-washed walls which gave the place a self-
contained, almost urban atmosphere. Through a door at the end of
the lane we entered a cobbled courtyard which in summer would be
shaded by a hanging vine. One side of it was open to the valley and
Mount Ida; another formed the front of a house; opposite, a flight
of stairs led to a broad terrace and a second floor; the remaining side
was occupied by outbuildings. This was the house of Stathis Louka-
kis, another godbrother of mine.

Anglia, Elevtheria, Nike were the names that Paddy Leigh Fermor and I had bestowed on his youngest daughter when we chris-

tened her in 1942. And Stathis had not turned a hair; in fact he had thought that these names sounded rather pretty in Greek, prettier than when translated into English as "England, Freedom, Victory." For the rest of the occupation Stathis had shouted for his daughter as loudly as he could whenever any German was within ear-shot.

Anglia had now developed into a shy, silent girl with thought-ful eyes; her father had scarcely altered at all. A little heavier per-haps, a little greyer under the *sariki* and above the upper lip, but as forceful and energetic as ever. Within five minutes of our arrival he had produced the usual drink, sentenced two chickens to death and launched into a torrent of reminiscences. The mist outside had dis-solved into a steady drizzle; we spent the rest of the day at table.

I suppose the uniformity of these impromptu celebrations was in-evitable. Although the people we stayed with were all distinct indi-viduals, their mode of life was identical; so that there was nothing to choose between here and Arolithi or any one of a dozen other vil-lages. Everywhere the same social rules were applied: aggressive hos-pitality on the part of the host, to be repaid by the guest in the form of conversation, the same conversation in each successive house. I could never make up my mind whether my perception was dulled or sharpened by this routine. At times I felt that I was talking not to a man but to a type; his house was no longer a house but a simple conventional background. Even my own sensations became stylized and conformed to a recognizably repeated pattern: the initial plea-sure of seeing an old friend would gradually be stifled by an increas-ing burden of *ennui*; just when this was reaching its climacteric, it would be swept away on a wave of nausea induced by over-eating; the wine-bred euphoria at bed-time terminated the cycle. But the symmetry and order of these emotions were sometimes disturbed; an unimportant factor would obtrude to distinguish one evening from another—nothing vital of course, for no vital distinction was possible—all that was needed was a minor anomaly, the sort of thing which in less standardized circumstances would pass almost unnoticed. At Arolithi, for instance, it had been the cistern under-neath Stelios's house; here, in Stathis's room, it was the telephone.

That a telephone, even an old army receiver such as this, existed in a peasant's private house was surprising enough; the way in which Stathis exploited it was more so. As soon as the wine was brought on to the table, he began ringing up every exchange in the neighbour-hood. We clinked our glasses together at the mouth-piece and made appreciative gurgling noises; from the ear-piece came an immediate response: the sound of liquid being poured out of a bottle, followed by a toast: "Your health and many years to you!" The words came crackling across the distances. But we soon tired of this game; to avoid the persistent bell we unhooked the receiver, which filled the room with Donald Duck noises until we replaced it and went to bed.

More photographs were taken in the morning while Stathis showed us round the village and took us to visit his younger brother, Stavros. Once again a sort of purification ceremony was performed because of Daphne's camera. Stavros's three-year-old child had recently been extremely ill; the parents had made a vow to the Virgin that they would keep it dressed in nothing but black for a whole year, if only She would spare its life. The child had recovered. It was still dressed in black when we first saw it: a tiny penitent in sackcloth and ashes. But, for its photograph, it was at once scrubbed clean and put into a brand-new sky-blue coat—which was removed with guilty haste as soon as the snapshot was taken.

"What will the Virgin say about your broken promise?" I asked.

Stavros grinned uneasily: "It was only for a split-second, you know. She'll understand. After all, we don't come across a camera every day of our lives."

It was typical of Stathis to provide us with mules for the last lap of our journey. After a more than usually alcoholic luncheon I was, for once, grateful for my animal. Daphne and I rode off singing, she with her rabbit balanced on the pommel of her wooden-slatted saddle; Changebug loped along behind us.

For the first half-hour we picked our way through fields bristling with blades of early wheat; but as we slowly ascended into the foothills, stone and rock began to encroach on the diminishing fertile areas, until the only green feature in sight was an ilex-covered hump in the distance straight ahead. The horizon beyond was formed by a long ridge of mountain as sheer and even as a sea-wall; we were approaching the last natural barrier before the south coast. One of the beaches where we used to land during the occupation lay hidden on the further side, less than a mile away, but the intervening country gave no hint of the sea's proximity: an embryonic landscape as empty as an unlined face. Somewhere on this side lay Alones, also hidden; it was only when we were almost on top of it that we were able to identify the conglomeration of bush and rubble at the base of the ridge as the houses and plantations of a village.

Alones is one of the poorest hamlets in Crete. The buildings here are huddled together, as though in mutual sympathy for their wretchedness, the walls and roofs tumbling untidily into courtyards and muddy lanes. The general impression is that of a burst suitcase whose contents have been dropped in a puddle. The very sight of this mountain slum would have depressed me, had I not already known its virtue. Throughout the occupation it had served as one of our hide-outs and headquarters; for four years every man, woman and child had taken an active part in the hazards and discomforts of resistance. Other villages, it is true, had played an equally honourable role; but none so wholeheartedly as Alones. In Asi Gonia we had relied on one man, Petros Petrakas, rather than on the community; even in Koustoyerako, where the entire population knew the exact site of each successive *limeri*, the village was divided into rival political factions. Only in Alones had there been perfect unity of sentiment and purpose, and for this we had one man to thank: the priest.

When the Germans came, Father John Alevizakis had made a declaration: "I'm an old man without worldly goods and my own life is valueless; I can contribute little to the struggle. But I have three sons old enough to be soldiers. All three will be sacrificed, if necessary, in the common cause of victory and freedom." A high-sounding speech, perhaps, but Father John had meant every word of it. And when his vow turned out to be partly a prophecy, he had not complained. Siphis, his eldest son, who had been acting as our courier, was caught by a German patrol early in 1943. Incriminating documents were found on him; for six months he was tortured, then shot. Father John had been compromised by his son's arrest and forced to take to the hills himself. He had joined us in a cave a few days afterwards. He knew as well as we did what Siphis's fate would be. "It's God's will," he had said, and refused to discuss the subject any further.

Faith in his God and tobacco in his pouch were all that Father John needed to be perfectly happy; as far as I know, he was never short of either. A cloud of smoke greeted us as we entered his house, but it came not only from his pipe. A fire of damp wood was burning in one corner of the room; forewarned of our arrival, the priest's wife was already preparing a meal.

Before the meal was over about twenty or thirty visitors—almost the entire male population of Alones—had joined us round the table. This was the sort of gathering that Father John most enjoyed; it brought out the patriarch in him. He made a point of addressing even his sixty-five-year-old brother as "my child," a phrase which he repeated each time he called for a toast. Behind the steel-rimmed spectacles his eyes streamed, either with emotion or from the smoke, but he winked away the tears as we raised our glasses together. He held his cupped in his hands, there was no answering clink when it met mine—"so that the priest can't hear us drinking, my child," he explained.

It was an old joke of ours, and one which proved that Father John was in an unusually gay mood. I felt that in a few minutes he would start to sing. I was right. "In honour of our foreign guests I'll give you my French song," he announced; then, stroking the twin silver prongs of his beard, he prepared for the hurdles of unusual consonants and nasal sounds:

L'arbre du mal, ton fruit est infecté . . .

I wish I could have discovered the rest of the words, but there was no way of identifying the strange noises that followed this first line of the song. Father John had learnt his French years ago in Egypt, where he had also acquired a smattering of Arabic. Perhaps the two languages had become confused in his mind ever since.

As soon as darkness fell the visitors started to leave. It was raining again; as each man stepped out into the night, he pulled forward the pointed hood of his thick white shepherd's cloak. But for their hairy faces, these departing figures could have been taken for a group of Cistercian monks filing out of their chapel after vespers: yet another example of the unconscious ritual so often found in Crete.

There was no bed in Father John's house. Two raised platforms accessible by ladder from the barn-like main room, were where his wife and he spent the night. Daphne and I were given the loft above, which we reached by an outside staircase. A small area of bare boards, cleared of the apples, nuts and carob beans which now filled the remaining floor-space, had been spread with bedclothes and pillows: sleeping accommodation for two. No luxury here, but wine and weariness are twin guarantees of deep sleep under any condition; and we had had plenty of both.

It was still raining in the morning. We struggled into our clothes, which in one night of this larder-like atmosphere had become as damp as the sheets in which we had slept; and went downstairs to join Father John for breakfast. We had scarcely finished the sage-tea and rusks before our first visitor of the day turned up.

Though the front door was not particularly narrow, the early caller had to turn sideways to get through it. In his white cloak he looked as thick and cumbersome as a polar bear. As he lowered himself into one of the small kitchen chairs, his thighs, inflated by the pressure of the wooden seat, expanded visibly inside his thick hairy breeches, then subsided and, with a final shudder, settled over the tops of his knee-high boots. For several second those freakish limbs, which seemed to lead a life of their own independent of the corresponding mass of flesh above them, diverted my attention from the man's face. Then I glanced up. In the smooth bald globe from which every line had dissolved into the core of fat underneath— the few wrinkles visible above the naked-looking eyes seemed to be painted on rather than etched in—I recognised the features of Manolis, known locally as "The Beardless One." In a harsh *castrato* voice, which made up for its lack of depth by the volume of sound it produced, he asked Daphne and me to come over to his house and have something to eat at midday.

I accepted with pleasure.

"Then what are we waiting for?" he screamed, heaving himself upright bit by bit. "Come on, we're late."

By my watch it was just after nine o'clock; to Manolis, who had been up since dawn, it was already high noon.

He led the way outside, taking a short cut over the roofs of the adjacent houses built into the side of the hill. His own house was a detached building on a relatively flat piece of ground a hundred yards further down the slope. As we entered the courtyard in front of it, my heart sank. There, framed in the front door, hanging from a large meat-hook attached to the lintel, was the carcase of a freshly-slaughtered ram. We brushed past this nauseating arras and sat down at a table laid for three.

Gobbets of grey and yellow meat, fused by cooling into a single glutinous whole, lay flabbily on a large central platter, flanked by dishes of equally lukewarm *khorta*. Segments of a loaf the size of a cartwheel were distributed round each of the plates. We started to eat before the food got completely cold.

I shall never get used to Cretan village cooking. It could, I suppose, be tolerable if the food were served hot; but it never is. Yet it is not without its refinements. Although the peasants have no sense of temperature or texture, they insist on such delicacies as lemon juice squeezed over almost every dish. Lemons were rare in Alones, so the Beardless One had gone to the trouble and expense of buying on the black market a tin of synthetic American lemonade-powder, which he sprinkled over every mouthful. This certainly sharpened his appetite; he seized piece after piece of meat, gnawing the lean and the fat and the gristle off the bones, which he then threw out of the open doorway, one after the other.

His last tit-bit was a triangular block of flesh, which he wrenched at with his teeth until he finally uncovered its central core: a ram's shoulder-blade. This he cleaned so meticulously that I thought that he was going to use it as an oracle and foretell the future from the marks on its translucent surface—a form of necromancy that is commonly practised in these parts. But the Beardless One was no seer; picked clean, the shoulder-blade followed the other bones out into the courtyard.

The meal had put our host into a benign, expansive mood. He settled his great eunuch's thighs more comfortably on his outsize chair, leant back and started to sing in a raucous pseudo-treble.

"Come on!" he screamed at us; and embarked once more on the only song he knew:

When will the weather break, ah when will spring be here . . .

But Daphne and I felt too ill to join in.

There is no reason to suppose that the Beardless One's food could have caused our influenza, but I do know that as soon as we left his house Daphne and I started to shiver and sweat. Our bones began to ache as much as our heads and we both longed for the comfort of a sick-bed—a mad aspiration in Alones, where there was no bed of any kind. It was too cold to spend all day stretched out on the blankets in the loft, so we sat instead in the downstairs room where clouds of smoke and a gleam of heat made us conscious of the fire.

There were other casualties in the village besides ourselves. The Beardless One was suffering from ear-ache. Whenever he came to see us, he would pour the glass of *tsikoudia* he was offered over his head, then rub the liquid into his scalp. I asked him how effective he found this cure.

"Better than nothing," he replied. "If only I had some penicillin. I suppose you haven't got any on you?"

We had another request for penicillin from a young man who had got something in his eye. I located the foreign body—it was a chip of wood—but I could not dislodge it; probing with the corner of a handkerchief was too painful. So I told the patient to try washing his eye out with warm olive-oil.

"Do you mean that stuff we cook in and eat?" he exclaimed. He was not trying to be funny; he thought that I was. How could olive-oil be a medicine, when it cost next to nothing? Naturally he scorned my suggestion. But his eye grew worse and worse. He put up with the pain stubbornly for two days. On the third day he came in, looking both pleased and ashamed. His eye was still sore, but was now at last free of the chip of wood. He had washed it in warm olive-oil the night before.

Daphne and I were not so quickly cured. We could not face our food which, since a pig had recently been killed, consisted almost entirely of boiled blubber. Father John and his wife grew daily more anxious; a Cretan only stops eating if he is going to die. They tried to tempt us with an invalid diet of *khondros*, a sun-dried compound of green wheat and sour milk. Cooked as a porridge, it might have been palatable. Boiled in the blubber-juice, it was horrid.

But it was not only the food that affected us. Confined by the rain, we were at the mercy of every caller, and this lack of privacy exaggerated the normal discomforts and irritations. The smoke from the fire seemed to blind us more than ever; the bedclothes seemed damper than they actually were, and the fleas more numerous and active. A spider that scuttled across the floor looked larger than a land-crab. Changebug lunged at it with his stick and broke off one of its legs. "There goes a crippled pensioner!" he chortled; and picked up the abandoned limb. It was hairless, and as brittle as a lobster's claw.

Father John was aware of our impatience. Whenever he caught me staring angrily out of the window, he would ask the same old question:

"Who is raining, my child?"

I always gave him the answer he expected, which would bring a "there-you-are-then" smile to his lips:

"It's God, Father John. God is raining."

The rain stopped overnight. There had been a storm; we were kept awake by the lightning which seemed to hurtle right through the loft; at every flash the cracks in the wall pierced the darkness like beams from a miniature searchlight; the room seemed alive with an almost audible electric charge; the walls rustled as though a million candles were being blown out all at once—a sound far more nerve-shattering than the thunder-clap that followed. But we woke up to sunshine, with the paths and the plantations outside steaming in the heat like a jungle.

We spent that morning wandering round the village. Many of the existing springs were now blocked by landslides and sudden ablation, but Father John pointed out several fresh ones which the storm had excavated: "God is good to us, my child; He always compensates." Certainly, there was no water shortage here; and all the streams flowed loyally in the direction of the vegetable-plots and potato-patches.

As though he intended us to give thanks for this dispensation of nature, Father John showed us into the church, indistinguishable from a thousand other churches on the island: the same companionable dirt and dust: the same crude icons, with their small silver plaques strung below them—votive offerings to this or that particular saint. The designs embossed on these *tassima*, as they are called, are the Christian equivalent of the witches' effigy in wax: philacterics to remind the saints of the object which requires their care. The Beardless One, for instance, might have invested his favourite icon with the representation of an ear; the young man who had cured himself with olive-oil, with a silver facsimile of an eye.

In the church of Alones almost every part of the human anatomy was represented, including an obscene, distended belly—no doubt the offering of an expectant mother. There was also a mannikin in uniform, like an illustration in a children's picture book, placed there perhaps by a relative of a soldier serving in Korea. A ship, too: the practical prayer for a fisherman or merchant seaman. There was even a donkey, probably the donation of a farmer anxious not to lose his only beast of burden. And a fox—but why should the saints be asked to look after a fox? In this case, the request was in reverse; the donor was praying to be spared the depredations of that animal.

Although Father John's parish church was Alones, he officiated as well in Argyroupolis, the large village at the road-head down the

valley. He had to walk there and back—a distance of twelve miles—
at least once a week, for Sunday service; and some weeks, when he
was needed at a baptism or a wedding, more than once. He was now
over seventy, but still content to perform these double duties.

On Saturday afternoon, then, he left us. Had there been a bus
from Argyroupolis on Sunday we should have gone with him; for
we wanted to get to Canea as soon as possible, since Daphne was
due to fly back to England. But there was no point in hanging about
the main road for twenty-four hours; we decided to stay the extra
day in Alones. Father John arranged to meet us on Sunday evening in Argyroupolis, which we would leave by the early morning
bus. Meanwhile he entrusted us to the care of his younger brother,
Christos.

Christos had been mayor of the village when his nephew, Father
John's son, was captured by the Germans; and had therefore been
held personally responsible for the attitude of the whole community.
It was due to his boldness and cunning in the face of incriminating
evidence, that so few houses in Alones were burnt in reprisal and
so few hostages shot. Since the war he had married—at the age of
sixty-five—and was now the father of twins. A sturdy lot, the Alevizakis family, and long-living, too: the grandmother of the twins
was still fairly active about the house. She told me that she had married late in life, like her second son. So she must have been well
over a hundred. To me she just looked very old and in no other way
unusual; but it made me feel like a time-traveller to be talking to a
human being of such antiquity who could measure her age, not in
years, but by the century.

Our last day in Alones was devoted to a series of farewell parties. Christos had slaughtered a couple of hens in our honour, but I
was still too ill to enjoy them served as a stew at ten o'clock in the
morning. My squeamishness must have looked like base ingratitude.
Christos pleaded with tears in his eyes: "Please eat, please, please. It
isn't every day we have chicken, you know." I did my best, but my
efforts were poor payment in return for such extravagant hospitality.

There were still the other houses to visit—just a glass of *tsikoudia*
in each. But every glass was accompanied by a full-scale dessert:
mountains of walnuts, cascades of pomegranates, chains of dried
figs. What we could not eat on the spot was stuffed into Daphne's
bag, into the pockets of the rucksack and the pockets of my coat. As

a final gesture, mules were provided for us. We found it difficult to mount them, with the unaccustomed burden which bulged, shifted, thumped and rattled in every part of our clothing; but at last we were off, shedding our extra weight on the way, leaving behind us a long trail of discarded shells and skins.

8

CANEA

AFTER DAPHNE'S DEPARTURE I decided to stay on in Canea. I wanted to revise my plans. I had intended to spend the whole winter travelling through whatever villages in the mountains were still accessible, but Alones had taught me how uncomfortable that might be.

During the occupation I had scarcely ever slept indoors, and so had never personally experienced the day-to-day existence of the average peasant household; on the rare occasions when I had spent any length of time in a village, I had been too occupied to envisage the dreary routine of the place. Or perhaps there had then been no dreariness. The German invasion had certainly modified, if not completely altered, the normal daily round; and possibly my visits used to be made an excuse for intensifying the atmosphere of exception. Anyway, I had always enjoyed them at the time and, after weeks and months of living like a troglodyte, had looked upon them as luxurious rest-cures.

But, in retrospect, the caves in which I spent those war-time winters now seemed infinitely more desirable than any village house. I remembered the great trunks of pine that we used to burn, which gave out no more smoke than the fire at Alones, and far more heat; I remembered, too, the couches of thorn spread with a shepherd's cloak, softer and more springy than any bed; and the meals, eaten only when we felt like food, not forced on us at all hours of the day. In spite of the hazards of war, this life had been ideal. Or so it seemed to me now. I wondered if I would still find it so. After all,

I was ten years older; creature comforts mean more to a man in his early thirties than to one barely out of his teens.

But more intolerable than the shortage of comfort was the lack of independence. There was no way of dealing with the villagers' aggressive friendship, except to submit to it; completely in their hands, I sometimes felt that I was their prisoner. Nor was there any way of returning their hospitality, no chance of standing them a second round—money could buy nothing where there was nothing for sale. Companionship was all that one had to offer; and they could never have enough of it. But I found it impossible to be companionable for hours and hours on end, to spend whole days in a crowded room cheek-by-jowl with people whose only recreation was eternal talk, talk confined to political discussions, war-time reminiscences and peasant humour, talk at any price. In the rare intervals they would turn on me: "Say something. Anything. Anything you like, but something." Silence was never golden; not a moment for reading or reflection.

This was more than I could stand indefinitely; I had to have some asylum to which I could retire by myself. No village could provide this, but only Canea. So I decided to make the capital my base, anyway for the winter. From here I would be able to complete my itinerary, not in one unbroken journey, but as a series of visits.

I found what I wanted on the top floor of a ruined Venetian palace: a large, lofty room with a view in three directions. To the south, over roofs that stretched like fields to the fields themselves, were the White Mountains, looking less white where they were still untouched by the purer white of the first falls of snow. To the east, more roofs, or bits of roof, or ruins. Westwards, the best view of all, the only view in the whole town with nothing ugly in sight: the harbour.

The house, so my landlord told me, had once belonged to Damolino, the villain of the Kandanoleon episode. Quite likely: for this part of the town, which may once have been the acropolis of the ancient city of Kydonia and has since come to be known as "The Castle," in 1610 contained, so Lithgow tells us, "ninety seaven Pallaces, in which the Rector and other Venetian Gentlemen dwell." Under the Turks it was turned into the Pasha's seraglio, part of which was burnt to the ground in the 1897 rebellion. In May 1941 German bombers finished off most of what was left.

Fortunately the bomb-sites here had not yet been rebuilt; the uncleared rubble—segments of arches, broken pillars and bisected doorways, all overgrown with weeds and shrouded in morning-glory—looked more attractive than other areas under so-called reconstruction. For the Cretans have no sense of architecture; whatever is ugly in Canea today dates from the liberation: the eye-sores are all Christian-built. Worse still, they have no feeling for antiquity. The age of a building seals its fate; it is either destroyed, or defaced to make room for something new.

In some towns the cathedral looks like a warehouse. In Canea it *was* a warehouse; the interior of the spacious building dedicated to St. Mark was now used as a dump for surplus army stores. Even the much-maligned Turks had never reduced it to this state of decay and indignity; the "debasement" of which they are always accused was confined to converting it into a mosque—a process which, apart from the addition of a minaret (and even this had the charm of a "folly"), did nothing to harm the structure of the building.

Far from destroying, the Turks tried to improve and enlarge— not always with happy results, it is true. But they did build a number of solid, well-designed houses, which conformed as far as possible to the original Venetian plan. They even built houses based on the contemporary equivalent of existing Venetian blueprints. To the untrained eye these would be indistinguishable from the genuine article if it were not for one important feature—with typical Moslem megalomania the Turks made all the doorways, which were faithfully copied in every other respect, just a little larger than the original, and so ruined the proportions of every façade. Still, it was an attempt; and a sign of appreciation.

But to the Cretans, the historic charm of their town seems antipathetic. They would pull down rather than preserve. When Italy declared war on Greece in 1940, they were restrained, only with great difficulty, from demolishing the Morosini Fountain in Herakleion—it was an "enemy monument," you see. Such bursts of misplaced patriotism, combined with fifty years of civic inefficiency, negligence and corruption, are responsible almost as much as the war-time air-raids for the desolate appearance of the town today.

There are two schools of thought about the site of the ancient city of Kydonia, which gave its name to the modern province. One claims that it lay inland, at Vrysses; the other, that it stood on the present site of Canea. There can be no doubt that a city did exist here on the coast: its stones were used for the walls and battlements of the town which the Venetians built in 1252. The purpose of this foundation is recorded in an official chronicle:

> The Greeks of the island of Candia have always been badly disposed towards the Venetian Government, not content to dwell under it. With this knowledge, the Venetian Government planned to found a city between Candia and Retimo,[1] and in this way the site of Canea was made a city, and many men of noble birth were sent to dwell there on the terms on which the rest of the men of noble birth were sent to Candia.

For a description of the town in its hey-day we must rely again on Lithgow:

> Canea is the second Citie of Creete, called aunciently Cydon, being exceeding populous, well walled, and fortified with Bulwarkes. . . . There lye continually in it seaven Companies of Souldiers who keepe Centinell on the walles, guarde the gates and Market places of the Citie: Neither in this Towne nor Candia, may any Countrey Peasant enter with weapons (especially Harquebuzes) for that conceived feare they have of Treason. Truely this City may equall in strength, either Zara in Dalmatia, or Luka, or Ligorne, both in Tuscana, or match-lesse Palmo in Friuly: for these five Cities are so strong, that in all my Travells I never saw them matched. They are all well provided with abundance of Artilery, and all necessary things for their defence. . . .

Quite a tough nut to crack, then, for the Turks who attacked the town thirty-five years later. But in spite of its defences it fell in fifty-seven days, thanks partly to the number of Cretans who deserted to the Moslem lines; the "conceived feare" which the Venetians had of treason was not groundless. For this reason, perhaps, most Cretan historians dismiss the siege of Canea in a few lines, while devoting whole chapters to the subsequent siege of Herakleion. This ostrich-like attitude cannot be excused on the grounds of lack of material; the campaign has been described in detail by an eye-witness, who took part himself in the storming of the walls.

Mohammed Zilli Ibn Darvish, better known as Evliya Effendi, was chief *muezzin* to the Turkish commander, Yussuf Pasha, when

---

1. A strange topographical error on the part of the chronicler: Canea is, of course, on the opposite side of Rethymnon from Candia (Herakleion).

the attack on Crete was launched. Whether he had had any military training is not recorded, but his account of the march on Canea shows an acquaintance with the art of siege warfare.

After securing a preliminary base on St. Theodore, the small island a few miles west of the town, the Turks advanced with artillery to within striking distance of the walls. For twenty days seven batteries pounded the fortifications, and this softening-up process was immediately followed by mining, a method of attack which was extensively used in the subsequent siege of Herakleion. One mine was blown up on the west side of the wall "and with it seventy yards of the wall, with all the Infidels upon it, who were sent through the sky to hell."

This must have lowered the morale of the mixed garrison; though the Venetian troops continued to defend this sector stubbornly, the Cretans were observed to be weakening, and one of their number presently descended the walls by a rope-ladder and entered the Turkish camp. Here, after undertaking to embrace the faith of Islam, he came to terms with the Moslem general on behalf of his fellow countrymen, and proposed that the Turkish attack be intensified against the Venetian sector, while arrows bearing a flattering offer to surrender should be launched into the Cretan lines.

The plan was completely successful. Ten more Cretans came over to the enemy at once; mass desertions followed; the defence collapsed; the town fell; "and the Infidels embarked for their accursed country,"[2] their general blinding himself in order not to see "the crosses upset and the green banner of Mohammed waving on the spires."

The Turks then acted with incredible speed. On the following Friday prayers were said in the Church of San Nicolo, which had already been converted into a mosque and renamed after Sultan Ibrahim. "The clarions sounded after the prayer was performed, the shouts of Allah! pierced the skies; and a triple salute was fired, the report of which shook not only Rome and Irak, but the whole of Earth and Heaven." Then the plunder: "gold, silver, brass vessels, fine boys and pretty girls were carried in immense numbers to the Ottoman camp, where there was such an abundance that a boy or girl was sold for eighteen piastres."

2. Unlikely: they probably embarked for Rethymnon and Herakleion, which were still in Venetian control.

But what Evliya does not include in his account is the Turkish casualty list. 44,000 men lost their lives during this siege both in battle and by plague; which, with the numbers subsequently killed outside Herakleion, led to Crete being christened the "Mussulman's grave." Three centuries later it was again described as a grave: "the grave of the German paratroops."

From certain angles the harbour looks two-dimensional. The arc of tall, narrow houses flanking the quay rises like a hoarding: an immense, eye-catching poster to advertise the rest of the town behind. Like most advertisements, it exaggerates the virtue or value of the goods on show or for sale. Penetrate this frontier of masonry and there is nothing but a mediaeval maze, with a modern hotchpotch of brick, stone and tile a few streets further back. I preferred to spend most of my time on the sea side of the boundary.

Sandrivani Square, little more than an inland projection of the wharf, still retains some of the charm that it must have had in Turkish times, when it was the life-centre of the capital. The fountain— the Turkish *sandirvan*—after which the square was named, ceased to exist after 1885; and the surrounding buildings, which once housed the best barbers' shops, cafés and taverns, were destroyed in a fire during the night of the 20th of February 1930. Since then the focal point of the town has shifted to the modern market-place. But Sandrivani is still popular in the summer, especially on Saturday or Sunday evenings. The broad Venetian paving-stones have been worn slippery-smooth by centuries of twilight promenades. Here, after the heavy hour of siesta-time, while the young men are at the barber's having their weekly shave, the young girls of the town come to stroll, in their best clothes and always in groups of two or three. This regular ritual is a far more pleasant pastime than attending a church service, which was once their only opportunity for showing themselves in public. Their behaviour, however, is still very much the same as when Belon first observed it:

La coustume est que les femmes des Grecs ne se monstrent en public: et toutesfois s'il y a quelque belle femme en la ville on l'on pleure le trespassé elle se sentira moult heureuse d'avoir trouvé l'occasion de monstrer sa beauté, accompaignant les autres par la ville: attendu qu'elles vont en troupe toutes escheuelées et espoitrinées, monstrants aumoins leur belle charnure.

Nowadays, admittedly, they keep their breasts covered, and their hair is usually twisted into a common little perm; but the custom is essentially unaltered. They wander up and down together, giggling, chattering, catching the eye of the men drinking or dining at the water's edge—an *allumeuse*, every one of them.

But by the time I had taken my room in Canea, many of harbour taverns were closed; there were no more tables or chairs outside on the quay, which was now being washed with rain before being dried in the wind. Mud from the upper end of the town was swept into the harbour, dyeing the water there brick-red; then the waves would retaliate and heave their seaweed up onto the paving-stones, where it would settle in patches of bright green. This alternating battle for possession between the two colours was a constant feature of the harbour throughout the winter.

Apart from the snow, which day by day crept further down the mountains, there were other typical signs of the season. The first oranges were already on the market, miniature suns in an increasingly sunless world. And the long summer holidays were over; schoolchildren were appearing once again in uniform; the boys in patent-leather-peaked Germanic caps; the girls in short dresses, black and satiny, and so sexy-looking that I was more than once tempted to risk the penalty imposed for *détournement de mineurs*. Luckily for me, they rarely frequented the harbor.

"Don't Hurry" was the name of a tavern which still defied the blizzards and the gales. To say that it "kept open" all winter would be inaccurate; it simply *was* open. It's roof was a sheet of corrugated iron sloping from the wall of the house next door; it had no walls of its own. Sailcloth, stretched on an eccentric assembly of wooden poles, served as a sun-shade during the summer, as a wind-break in the winter; that was all there was to the place. But I enjoyed eating there more than anywhere else in Canea.

There was no menu; one only had to lift the lids of the copper cauldrons bubbling over charcoal braziers to see, quite literally, what was cooking. The food was sometimes excellent and always unpretentious: young octopus stewed with tomatoes and olives; sucking-pig cooked in the same way; cod-steaks with *skordalia*, the Cretan equivalent of Provencal *aioli*; veal-steaks grilled, or grilled red-mullet; sometimes only soup, lentil or chick-pea or bean with—when the ingredients were available—my favourite "volcanic" salad: garlic and raw onions, red and green and orange peppers and—as a cooling element—half a dozen little pear-shaped winter tomatoes.

The food was not the only attraction at the "Don't Hurry" tavern; nor was the clientele, which sometimes included melancholy merchants and their blowsy wives out on a "slumming" tour of the fishermen's quarter. The magnet which drew me there almost daily was its owner, Manolis, white-haired and working in shirt-sleeves even in mid-winter. He looked like a retired sergeant-major and, in fact, treated his favourite clients as though they were raw recruits: "Not finished yet? Eat up at once, or you'll get ten days C.B."—"Go on, it's not as tough as all that. Here, hold the knife like this!"

Occasionally he would let a note of despair creep into his bantering tone: "Christ and the Holy Virgin, but you haven't eaten a thing! How do you expect me to live? No bill for you today; I can't charge you a penny. But you must pay something. Here, order another bottle of wine; we'll drink it together." The staff would then join us—the one waiter and the kitchen-"boy," a shambling, barefoot, tattered old bear of a man with thyroid eyes and heavy tear-bags. He had never been known to smile—not that he was bad-tempered, he just never felt like smiling. Perhaps there really was some truth in the rumour that he was the natural son of Prince George of Greece, the first High Commissioner in Crete.

At each of these afternoon sessions more wine was later produced, but I was only allowed to pay for the first bottle. I never discovered how Manolis did manage to live.

Further down the arc of the harbour, where the wooden houses lurched like cripples, kept upright only by the pressure of the neighbouring buildings in stone, was another haunt of mine: "The Seal." Fastened over the front door, the desiccated corpse of one of these animals served as an inn-sign.

"The Seal" was the favourite midday meeting-place of the Canea fishermen. Sometimes their tackle lay like flotsam in every corner of this echoing, asymmetrical chamber; long bamboo poles, tridents, coils of rope, cork floats and floats made from hollow gourds; and everywhere, erupting out of outsize baskets, serpentining over tables and chairs, hanging from the gallery and draping the walls, length after length of salt-bleached, rust-coloured net.

Daylight invested "The Seal" with a deceptive atmosphere of innocence and toil. Most of the early-morning drinkers were bearded men in blue jerseys, haggard after the night at sea; some of them with hands deficient of a finger or two—the result of dynamite fishing, proscribed but still practised. These were the crews of the deep-water vessels. Others preferred to potter about the coast in rowing-boats, scraping their living off the rocks or sounding the shallows in an eternal search for sunken treasure. My friend Panayiotis belonged to the latter group.

His principal calm-weather quest was for sea-urchins and a successful morning's work would yield half a boat-load, from which he always kept back two or three dozen for me. The taste of these improbable creatures—a mixture of grit, slime and iodine: the very essence of the sea—delighted me as much as their appearance. I used to watch, fascinated, the purple-black prickles still squirming with a life of their own long after the body which they once protected had been neatly bisected and the deep orange contents scooped out on a crust of bread.

White wine was the obvious thing to drink with this mid-morning appetizer, but Michalis, the owner of "The Seal," who shared this daily urchin-orgy with me, never took anything but *ouzo*, a popular spirit on the mainland, unusual in Crete. But then Michalis was an unusual Cretan, one of the few I met with a deep-seated love of animals. He kept rabbits, not for food, but as pets; a family of black cats lived comfortably camouflaged between the piles of charcoal behind the bar; and a tame partridge, a dove-grey *bartavelle* with bright red claws and red-rimmed eyes, perched all day long on his shoulder. I always felt that this bird should have been a parrot; it would have been more in keeping with its owner's slightly old-fashioned sea-dog appearance—his day-time appearance, that is; for in the evening he was transformed.

I never quite discovered how this transformation was effected, nor exactly in what it consisted; he still looked essentially the same—the same crinkly grey hair, the same deep-blue eyes (growing progressively more bloodshot as the evening wore on), the same leathery cheeks of indeterminate colour—and he still wore the same old reefer-jacket. Yet imperceptibly, as soon as darkness fell, his nautical aspect would desert him, to be replaced by one of gentle raffishness. In the artificial light I found myself aware, as though for the first time, of the heavy gold chain stretched across his paunch and the heavy gold rings on his fingers.

In the same way the décor of the room itself seemed to alter with the dusk; the maritime objects melted away, swamped by the vespertine obtrusion of billiard-table, gramophone and exotic French prints hanging—until then unnoticed—in gilt frames from the walls. The fishermen in jerseys had vanished; in their place, the wide boys in gaberdine coats. If only "The Seal" had been as *louche* as it appeared then to be! But no, everything here was pervaded by the fundamental Cretan innocence.

Nothing, for instance, could alter the innocence of the young n'er-do-well who sat one evening at my table. He was still a shepherd at heart, though he longed to be, tried to be, depraved.

"What do you do for a living?" I asked him.

"I'm an assistant to an idler," was his reply.

This fair-haired lad with the "Greek" profile (as rare in Greece as it is in England), who looked like one of the characters in El Greco's *Massacre of the Theban Legions*, was a typical Sphakian, though born and bred in Canea. It was interesting to see how he contrasted with his two companions, one of whom was a heavy-lidded Oriental type, the other a dog-faced youth with semi-negroid lips—Cretans, all three of them, but each of a distinctly different race.

In appearance, at least, Dog-face was a singularly ugly customer. Criminal blood, I said to myself; and was delighted to have my guess confirmed when he told me where his family came from— Alikampos. In Venetian times this village in the Apokoronas plain was renowned as a hide-out for murderers, thieves and bandits; so much so that its inhabitants gradually developed a dialect of their own, a localised *argot des filous*. To this day certain phrases currently used in Alikampos cannot be understood in the neighbouring villages.

The third boy, I already knew; knew also why his eyes had that remote, weary look—we had smoked hashish together two nights before. Yet now, when his father came into the bar, he quickly discarded the perfectly innocuous cigarette which I had just offered him—it would have been an act of impiety to smoke in the patriarch's presence! As far as I knew, he was the only one in "The Seal" who regularly indulged in "the black stuff"; the rest came in simply to enjoy the *fumerie* atmosphere, to listen to the *rebetiko* records played on Michalis's gramophone and to dance, or watch others dancing, to them.

Rebetiko music is a strictly urban entertainment, unknown in the villages. The name itself is derived from the Turkish *rebet*, meaning "undisciplined" or "disorderly," and *rebetiko* has come to be essentially the music of the non-conformist (in the social sense, of course, not the religious), the favourite music of the spiritual anarchist. Some people say that these songs—invariably hymns in praise of hashish—were imported from the docks and harbours of Anatolia which served the white-slave traffic. This may be so; after the disastrous Asia Minor campaign in 1922, when tens of thousands of refugees left those coasts to settle in the mother-country, the *rebetiko* spread rapidly through every urban centre in Greece, reaching the height of its popularity among the lower classes of the capital and the wharf-rats of the Peiraeus.

It may have been known at an even earlier period, but was then confined to a comparatively small section of the community, to the *manges*[3]: men with no visible means of support, who live on their wits, on immoral earnings and petty crime. Like the *apaches* of Paris, the *manges* have developed their own particular customs, language and dress. Any one of their number can at once be distinguished by his cap worn on the back of the head to reveal a billow of well-oiled curls, by his coat usually worn loose over one shoulder, by his cummerbund and watch-chain and pointed black shoes and— more than by anything else—by his *komboloi*, the chaplet of heavy amber beads, which he incessantly flicks through his fingers.

The forces of reaction and regeneration are slowly doing away with this picturesque slice of society. These leisured gentlemen, more decorative than dangerous, are gradually being regimented off the street-corners and away from the café-tables. Soon, no doubt, they will be remembered only as an extinct sociological phenomenon. But their music still lives, and is spreading. It has spread even as far as Crete.

In "The Seal" the best *rebetiko* singers, and the best dancers, were the refugees from Asia Minor; they gloried in the *pas seul* which is performed to these tunes, a perfect dance for any exhibitionist. One man at a time would take the floor as soon as a record was put on;

---

3. An untranslatable word, the nearest English equivalent would be "spiv" or "wide boy," but neither of these does justice to the *manges*.

stand there for a moment with arms outstretched, waiting to be pos-
sessed by the music. The rhythm seemed to invade his body first
by way of his fingers, which would begin snapping impatiently as
though to summon the other limbs into motion. An answering shuf-
fle from his feet, two or three stealthy steps forward, and the dancer
was then launched into the long series of complicated movements,
flicking his ankles, stamping his feet, slapping his heels. Then came
the sinister swoops and dips, the drunken, off-balance lurches and
miraculous recoveries—all executed as though in a trance, with the
performer's head thrown back and smiling at the ceiling or else bent
forward in dreamy contemplation of his own shoes; and all the time
his fingers would be snapping, the left hand still jerking noisily even
when the right was lowered to thump the floor with the flat of the
palm, or to seize a trouser leg between finger and thumb with a gesture of exaggerated primness, or, with a more obscene gesture, to
grope further up for the crutch.

These gestures, no doubt, once had some special significance, of
which none of the present executants was aware; the twisting and
writhing, the heaving and thumping, the hissing through clenched
teeth—all these were regarded simply as the recognised phases of
each performance, as opportunities for self-expression and, occasionally, for self-advertisement. Some dancers would pick up a chair
in their teeth and whirl about with this additional burden clenched
horizontally in their jaws; others would interrupt their steps to balance upside-down on the back of a chair, which often collapsed
under their weight.

Michalis, after his eightieth *ouzo* of the day, never minded the
destruction of his furniture; nor did he object to his plates being
smashed when they were pitched in drunken jest at a dancer's
feet. But an accidental breakage would make him tremble all over
with anger.

I soon knew all the records in "The Seal" by heart, and began to tire
of the same tunes repeated every night. But just outside the town,
past the genteel villas of the Canea "aristocracy,"[4] was another so-

4. This word in Crete is used to denote what in England would be called "plu-
tocracy."

called tavern, where I could hear the latest *rebetiko* numbers sung to the accompaniment of a couple of *bouzouki*-players.

The only attraction to this squalid sea-side shack was the vocalist Sonia, a rather plain girl with dark frizzy hair, who made the worst of her bad looks by wearing a vertically striped mauve-and-scarlet jumper over her flat chest, and a perpetual frown above her pointed yet shapeless nose. But her voice was a wonder, its coarse quality perfectly suited to the words which she sang. With a player on either side of her strumming his mandolin-shaped instrument, as though in a masturbatory frenzy, Sonia would sit frigid and unconcerned, with her bad-tempered expression unaltered even when her mouth opened wide as she effortlessly hit the high notes. At these moments her air of unassailability made her provocatively, perversely desirable.

There was not much room for dancing in this crowded establishment, every cubic inch of which seemed to be awash with vibrating waves of sound. Sonia insisted always on singing into a microphone, and a loudspeaker above the door amplified her voice to a volume which, in this confined space, was equivalent to the scream of a factory-siren. But a few eccentrics occasionally took the floor.

There was one old cripple who tackled the intricate steps of the *zeibetiko*, the "quicksilver dance," also imported from Anatolia, and so named because the dancer's movements are supposed to represent the quivering motion of mercury: a difficult feat for an old man to attempt, especially an old man who is blind drunk and on crutches. But this one seemed delighted with his macabre effort. A little later a labourer came in, ordered a glass of wine, drank it down, tore off his jacket and shirt, kicked off his shoes, thumped about the floor more or less in time to the music, returned to his table, paid for his drink, picked up his clothes and marched out barefoot into the dark. The whole performance had lasted less than five minutes.

There were, of course, a few slightly more normal bars and restaurants in Canea, but I rarely visited them. I resented having to pay more for a meal or drink consumed in chromium-plated surroundings and under neon lighting—decorative features on which the richer bourgeoisie of the town seems to dote. Moreover, the semi-educated lawyers, doctors and merchants who frequent these places are, with very few exceptions, crashing, pretentious bores, whose conversation is even less entertaining than that of the completely illiterate peasant.

These gentlemen always wear smart suits, since clothes are the criterion by which they judge their fellow-men; and they grow their little finger-nails as long as a Chinese mandarin's, to show the world that they are not engaged on manual labour. And they have, of course, learnt to read—apparently for the sole purpose of perusing a dozen newspapers a day, since they never read anything else. Yet it was one of these fellows who told me, with a patronising smirk, not to judge the island by the villagers:

"They're a backward lot, you know. Why, they still kill each other on the slightest provocation!"

I could not resist pointing out that the two major crimes of that winter had both been committed by members of the Canea middle-class. The young man who had entered a school and, in front of a whole class of children, had fired three shots into a schoolmaster's stomach was that schoolmaster's own nephew. And it was a retired army officer who, when attacked by a political rival in the middle of the market-place, had defended himself with a hand-grenade (which he carried as a matter of course in his pocket), killing himself, his assailant and half a dozen others, including a nine-year-old girl who was enjoying a glass of beer in a café a few feet away.

It was a wonder that more people were not killed in the market that morning, for the place is crowded at almost every hour of the day. The large cruciform building, with each arm about as wide and as long as a station platform, resembles a busy terminus in other ways as well. Whenever I entered it I felt more like a passenger about to take a train than a householder doing his morning's shopping. The grocers' shops lining the main thoroughfare are each equipped with a bar, marble-topped tables and chairs, so that there seem to be more cafés than market-stalls; and the butchers here in their scarlet check aprons look as incongruous as a fancy-dress party on a boulevard.

My only objection to drinking in this unconsciously surrealist atmosphere was the noise; not the comforting noise of humanity herded together, but the incessant clamour of the ubiquitous loud-speaker. I feel that a law should be passed in Greece against the misuse of radio. In Canea the screech of atmospherics woke me up every day as punctually as an alarm-clock, and the din never sub-sided until after dark. It pursued me whenever I went out into the street, chasing me from one blaring building to another. Each time that I turned a corner I thought that I had eluded it; each time it would catch up with me from another direction. Every shop in the centre of the town seemed to have a wireless-set which was always on at full blast; every office, every tavern, every restaurant. Even the row of shoe-blacks at the entrance to the market had a large, loud set of their own.

After running this gauntlet it was always a relief to get back to the harbour. Here I could also avoid another of the town's nuisances— the beggars and hawkers. They never came near this poorer quarter. Elsewhere I was always scared of meeting the ghastly barefoot boy with half a face; I sometimes used to feel my sleeve being plucked from behind, would turn round and be confronted by this bandaged wretch whose left eye, and the cheek below it, were liquefied into an open, incurable sore. Then there were the peanut-sellers, two importunate little girls, as nasty as the almond-sellers—boys—were nice; and the palateless, hair-lipped half-wit with the shaven pate and the three-quarter length trousers, which seem to be the standard dress of the mentally deficient in every part of Greece.

The freaks in the harbour area were at least less repulsive in appearance. There was a pleasant piratical quality about the old fisherman without any hands, whose two arms ended not in conventional hooks but, respectively, in a large iron fork and spoon. And the giant black stevedore, Sali, the only negro in Crete, was a splendid, unique relic of a vanished Arab community which had settled in Crete when Canea became the capital. Even the crippled little dwarf Vittoria, who worked as a chamber-maid in the brothel round the corner—"a perfect job for me," she used to say, "I could use a French letter as an overcoat"—even she tried to make the best of her deformity by wearing a fresh ribbon in her hair every day.

———

But life in Canea was not all "cream-cheese and honey."[5] Overnight I found myself involved in a parochial political feud, unimportant in itself but symptomatic of the diseased condition of Greek bureaucracy.

The whole thing had started in 1945. At the end of the war all the nationalist partisan groups and guerilla bands which had operated during the occupation were officially recognised by the Greek Gov-

5. The local equivalent of "beer and skittles."

ABOVE: *Sphakia beach, scene of the British evacuation of 1941*

LEFT: *Father Nicholas of Anopolis*

Andreas Athitakis, the only fisherman in Loutro

ernment—except, for some reason, those belonging to the resistance organisation of Canea. The veterans of this prefecture were naturally shocked by the omission and, now that I had returned to Crete, asked me, as their war-time liaison officer, to see what could be done to rectify it. I explained that I no longer had any official position—a fact which they either chose to overlook or openly disbelieved—but agreed to send a letter to the local newspaper, expressing my amazement at the Government's failure to recognise the splendid resistance in Canea and citing, as examples of this resistance, a number of local leaders such as Vasilis Paterakis and Petros Petrakas.

I thought that this letter could do no harm and might possibly even do good. I was wrong. As somebody said to me later: "Good intentions don't work. Just look at the result of yours. You tried to make the Sign of the Cross and all you've done is poke your own eyes out."

It was not quite as bad as all that, however. If I was maimed at all, it was only metaphorically—by the mild abuse of a few minor leaders whose names I had failed to mention in my letter to the press. The more virulent abuse they reserved for those whom I had mentioned. For weeks afterwards the correspondence column was filled with claims, counter-claims, accusations and complaints from self-appointed leaders anxious to prove the superiority of their own war record over that of their rivals.

I began to understand why resistance in Canea had not been recognised. There was no head to the organisation—or rather there were too many heads, all at loggerheads, and none willing to allow another to be officially elected. And without an official election, no official recognition. Well, that was their business. I had done my best. In any case the matter was of no importance, merely a question of petty jealousies and petty pride; it could have no far-reaching consequences.

Or so I thought; and once again I was wrong. To the pensioner, I discovered, this selfish squabble was a matter of life or death. So many false claims for pensions had been submitted, and accepted, at the end of the war that the Greek Government decided a few years later to cease further payment, *even to the claimants who were known to be genuine*, until their claim was proved valid. But in Canea there was no way of obtaining such proof. Elsewhere it could be furnished by the recognised head of the resistance organization; a statement endorsing a claim and signed by him would be sufficient to ensure immediate payment. In Canea there was no one to sign such a statement.

So, as a last resort, the claimants now began to approach me. "Surely the authorities will listen to you," they said, "after all you were with us at the time; you knew who was killed or wounded and who wasn't. You can tell them if our claims are valid or not."

That was true; I did know these people. But I felt sure that no official in Athens would attach the slightest importance to my opinion of them. I told them so, and again explained that I could only endorse their claims in an entirely unofficial capacity; that therefore, as far as the Greek Government was concerned, my signature would be completely valueless.

"But our lawyers have advised us to come to you," they persisted, "and they know what they're doing, don't they? Anyway a statement from you can do no harm."

They were right; it did no harm. Neither did it do any good. Of the many hundred statements that I signed during the winter, not one had produced the slightest result by the time I left Crete six months later—apart from lining the pockets of the lawyers, who presumably charged a fee for forwarding each useless document to the authorities.

Perhaps I had laid too much emphasis on my unofficial position. Though the Cretans may never have heard of the adage "*Qui s'excuse, s'accuse*," though not one of them ever said of me "he doth protest too much," they are all past-masters at reading between the lines, even the lines of a blank sheet of paper. And so my insistence on my present inability to help them struck them, no doubt, as suspicious; they would not believe that the purpose of my visit (which they invariably referred to as "my mission") was to write a book, and apparently preferred to imagine me engaged on some high-level clandestine activity. Possibly they thought that I was even in touch with that God-like figure whom they call "Tsortsill"; but of this I am not really sure. All I do know is that as soon as I had endorsed a few pensioners' claims, I was immediately pestered with countless other requests.

Most of these were in connection with the free issue of clothing, a recent gift from the Government of New Zealand to Cretan families which had helped Allied stragglers and escaped prisoners-of-war. Of course, I had nothing to do with the distribution of these goods;

this was the responsibility of a specially formed committee. Nevertheless, I was continually being buttonholed by people asking me to see that they got their fair share. The most brazen request came from Nikos, the waiter at "The Seal."

"Of course, I'm not entitled to a thing. I wasn't even here during the occupation, I never saw an Allied soldier. But I could do with some new clothes. A shirt or two, perhaps—you'll help me over this, won't you?"

The most violent pleas, however, came from those who had already received the free issue. They complained that it was inadequate. These people, it seemed, not only looked a gift-horse in the mouth but even examined its teeth in the hope of extracting a few gold fillings. They now claimed that the young New Zealander, who had come to Crete two years earlier in order to launch this scheme, must have been a Communist agent—a sequence of thought which I did not attempt to follow. They also accused the distribution committee of misappropriation, conversion and general malpractice. On this point, at least, I could set their minds at ease; I pointed out that the committee included the British Consul. This information did not impress them at all favourably—some of them had seen that gentleman—but I think I succeeded in assuring them that he really was quite honest, in spite of his appearance.

Schemes of this sort are rarely appreciated in Crete. Those well-intentioned New Zealanders would have put the money which they contributed to better purpose if they had provided the island with a hospital or an orphanage, some sort of communal establishment which could not have been partitioned among the individual citizens. As it was, their gift caused nothing but disorder and discontent.

Further discontent was caused a little later by the free issue of American wireless-sets to the more remote villages. There were not enough sets to go round; the communities which had been left out of the deal at once approached me in order to lodge their complaint. I explained yet again that I had nothing to do with this distribution either; and again was met with disbelief:

"But America and England are allies, aren't they? Couldn't you write to Truman and tell him what's going on over here?"

Their faith in my purely imaginary powers may have been flattering: it was also extremely embarrassing. I was used to the locally recognised system of *rousphetia*, the request for personal favours; but the people who now approached me refused to accept the fact that I was in no position to meet their demands. And since they would not believe in my inability to help them, they concluded that I was denying them assistance simply out of laziness or malice.

9

Nippos

S<small>TILL</small>, <small>THERE WAS</small> someone in Canea who realised the true purpose of my visit—Yiannis Vandoulas, a young civil servant, who had been one of my couriers during the war. When I told him I was collecting material for a book, he at once offered his services in any capacity and, as a start, invited me to come to his village and have a look through some old documents which a relative had left him in his will. He asked his office to extend his Christmas holidays for a few days, and early in the New Year we set off for his home.

In the main-line bus on the Herakleion road I tried to identify the "pleasant plaine" which Lithgow called the "Valley of Suda"; but the only district recognisable from his description was the plain of Apokoronas, several miles east of Souda, which still contains the trees and crops that he noticed over three centuries ago:

The Olives, Pomgranets, Dates, Figges, Orenges, Lemmons, and Pomi del Adamo growing all through other: And at the rootes of which trees grew Wheate, Malvasie, Muscadine, Leaticke Wines, Grenadiers, Carnobiers, Mellones, and all sorts of fruites and hearbes, the earth can yeeld to man . . .

The Villages [he continues] for losse of ground are all built on the skirts of Rockes, upon the South side of the Valley; yea, and so difficile to climbe them, and so dangerous to dwell in them, that we thought their lives were in like perill, as he who was adjoyned to sit under the poynt of a two handed sword, and it hanging by the haire of a horse tayle.

One of these was Nippos, Yiannis's village. It stands on a cypress-crowned natural acropolis, which has been made more easily accessible since Lithgow's day; in fact, a motor road of sorts winds up right into the village square. The Vandoulas family lived lower down, in a small dip which divides the village into two separate communities.

Yiannis had once had three brothers, but the youngest—one of the strongest men I have ever known; it was he who used to carry our wireless batteries—had been killed in a German ambush towards the end of the occupation. The two survivors had recently married; their houses, which they had built with their own hands, were both brand new. The elder asked me to stay with him; Yiannis had a room in his father's house next door; but for meals we all met in the other brother's house, where the food and wine were said to be better.

That first evening in Nippos was unlike any other that I spent in Crete. After an excellent dinner of egg-lemon soup and chicken I glanced through Yiannis's books; then, with the three brothers, sat up until midnight quietly sipping wine and talking; and for once the conversation was not confined to fighting the war all over again or rectifying the mistakes of politicians. Instead, Yiannis steered it onto subjects which he knew I would find more interesting, such as the history of the district and local customs and superstitions.

He was, of course, far too young to have taken part himself in the insurrections against the Turks—he was born, in fact, a few years after Crete was finally annexed to Greece—but he remembered how they had been described to him by the old men in the village. What he now told me confirmed what I had heard from Uncle Theodore in Azoyires.

Every one of those uprisings in the last half of the nineteenth century had been prompted by unjust taxation. The *karatch*, or *impot de capitation*, levied on the head of every Christian male over thirteen years of age, had been abolished at the same time as slavery, in 1856. But this did not prevent the local pasha from acting independently of the Sublime Porte and imposing an additional tax in the area under his own personal command. No doubt he would have suffered had this unauthorised action come to the ears of his superiors for, like the Japanese in the last War, the Turks could be almost as brutal in punishing their own offenders as in dealing with rebellious Christians. Up to the end of the eighteenth century, for instance, a Turkish subject sentenced to death would be put to the extreme indignity of being executed—the recognised method was strangulation—either by two Greeks or two Jews; but occasionally he managed to avoid this ignominy by persuading a couple of Moslem friends to kill him instead, before the date of the execution.

The large Vandoulas family—there were two or three other branches in the neighbouring villages—had for years been the leaders of those local rebellions; the present generation, every member of which had distinguished himself against the Germans, must have inherited their war-like qualities from them. But none of them was belligerent in appearance. The heavy-boned, fleshy faces of the elder brothers would have looked coarse but for their gentle expression; Yiannis's features differed from theirs only in size and weight—a pocket edition, as it were, of the twin original.

The essential difference between them lay in their respective manner of speaking and tone of voice; the slow, almost struggling speech of the two older men was in direct contrast to Yiannis's effortless machine-gun delivery. The former were obvious peasants; the latter, a product of the town. Intellectually, Yiannis lived in a world which his brothers could only dimly imagine; he had been the only one in the family to complete his education.

Next morning I was woken by an invasion of winter sunshine. When I opened my eyes I was dazzled for a moment by the reflection from the bare whitewashed walls. In this new house everything was spotless, and the scarcity of furniture gave it an almost clinical atmosphere; there was nothing to absorb the light streaming in, not even the usual thin coating of dirt and dust.

I had just finished breakfast (two lightly-boiled eggs) and was licking the yolk off my fingers (there had been no egg-cup), when Yiannis called to show me round the village. Framed in the doorway, he looked like the conventional conception of an ancient Greek, incongruous in modern dress against the classical background of artichoke bushes lining the courtyard, each plant as stylized as the acanthus on an Ionic column.

Outside, I saw that almost every house was decorated with a wild squill nailed to the lintel over the front door—the relic of a New Year ritual. This bulb, with its broad strap-shaped leaves, is a symbol of eternity: it looks like an enlarged onion and, according to a Cretan tradition connected with Alexander the Great, an onion can never dry up and shrivel since Alexander's sister once sprinkled a bed of onions with the water of life. For this reason an *askillitoura*, as it is locally called, is fastened on to the house at the beginning of every year to ensure long life to the household.

Yiannis told me that it had other magical properties as well: when gently applied to the male sexual organ, it produces an immediate swelling. "It's absolutely true," he assured me, "I once tried it myself at school." Of course it is true; an erection is surely the natural result of such manipulation, whether a wild squill is used or not.

Outside some of the houses, I noticed piles of broken crockery, more than the normal amount of litter found in a village street. "The New Year again," Yiannis explained. "At midnight you toss an old plate or dish out of the window; when it breaks, that means your bad luck is broken for the year. For good luck you bring in a heavy stone, the heaviest you can carry—then the same weight of gold will come rolling in during the next twelve months."

Below the terraced fields, which were now being sown, we came to the vineyards, scarcely recognizable as such at this season. It was hard to imagine that these bare knotted roots, these wizened and deformed fists of wood, would ever be clothed in soft green, half-stained with the blue-green of copper-sulphate, and patterned with the arabesques of yellow-green grape-tendril. The earth here was waterlogged but not, so Yiannis told me, with rain; these pools welled up of their own accord from deep underground and sometimes yielded a miraculous draught of eels.

These could only come from Lake Kournas, ten miles away. It is incredible that Crete should ever suffer from a shortage of water; the whole island seems to be riddled with a vast network of subterranean aqueducts. But they are left untapped, unexploited; most of the villages rely throughout the year on a single, often insufficient, spring.

The one at Nippos is unusually splendid. Its water gushes in a controlled jet out of an edifice of Cyclopean marble blocks set deep into a fern-fringed bank of earth; the overflow from the broad troughs below it drains away over horizontal slabs of stone, worn smooth and neatly hedged with oleander. For shade there is a giant walnut tree, its trunk deeply gashed to allow for still more growth, the scars in its bark showing proudly, like tribal markings on the cheeks of a bushman. This setting is clearly the work of a naturally-gifted landscape gardener; and the people of Nippos do indeed claim that their spring was designed by an artist—none other than Raphael! Yiannis even showed me where the painter is supposed to have been buried; in a derelict Venetian chapel a little further up the hill. It seemed a far cry from the Pantheon in Rome.

After a midday meal of pork chops cooked in wine (the quality of the food in Nippos made me note with appreciation almost everything that I ate while I was there), we climbed up to the coffee-shop in the centre of the village. This establishment was larger, but in no other way different from those in the remotest highland hamlets. Yet one glance inside was sufficient to show that here the capital was far closer—all the customers looked like townsmen.

Young men in pin-striped trousers and pointed shoes sat crouched over card-tables, intent on the gambling which in a few days' time would once again be declared illegal; playing for money is allowed only during the fortnight after Christmas. Even the older men, who would have looked more at home in breeches or traditional Cretan "crap-catchers," were dressed in what they imagined to be the latest businessmen's fashion—*le dernier cri de La Canée!*—and had consciously assumed an urban, metropolitan air as they sat there reading their newspapers.

It was their reading that gave them away. Each one of them, as he scanned the headlines, was moving his mouth and emitting a vague, bumbling noise. Like most villagers, he was unable to take in what he saw before him in print without first tasting the sound of it on his lips. This bumbling habit has been shared by early Christian Fathers, such as St. Chrysostom, and even by modern statesmen like Lord Curzon, whose lips, when he read, have been described by Harold Nicolson as "moving rapidly in a faint, but not unpleasant, whisper . . ." So the Cretan peasant is in good company and need feel no shame. It is a wonder that he can read at all, living, as he does, in a world without books, in which the only library is the lips of the people round him and where, apart from newspapers, the only word is the spoken one.

———

Yiannis had only one more day's leave; we decided to spend it in Vaphes, the larger village just above us, where two of his uncles lived and which had been a home-from-home for me during the war.

It was an easy climb through the deserted olive-groves. The trees were still in fruit but there was no one collecting it; the harvest seemed to be at a standstill. No doubt the women who should have been engaged on it could not be spared from the sowing. But we did run into someone: a small boy who, as soon as he saw us, tried to hide what he held in his hands.

It was a rusty rifle-barrel, which he was re-converting into a weapon of sorts. The butt he had fashioned already, from a small tree-trunk; he was now working on the bolt and trigger-action—a primitive contraption of wooden cylinders and elastic bands with a fine-pointed nail for the firing-pin. This was no mere toy; it was just conceivable that the finished article would be able to fire a round; and I had no doubt that the child had plenty of those up his sleeve. I could not help admiring this example of typically Cretan ingenuity.

Vaphes is the highest village on this northern section of the range, but, since the ground here slopes evenly and gently to the plain, it is easily accessible by road and has its own bus-line to the capital. In feeling, however, it is still very much a mountain village, although not tucked away in a fold of the hills like Koustoyerako or Asi Gonia. The view is blocked only from one direction, from the south, where the range rises to its greatest height, not in a series of gorges and minor peaks, as in Selino or Sphakia, but in a single concave sweep. Its position gives Vaphes an air of grandeur and expanse.

We walked along the main street, past almond-trees already in blossom, as far as the coffee-shop where the bus stops. We were hoping to find one of the two uncles there, but both were out at work in the fields. So, to pass the time until they returned Yiannis suggested a visit to a cave nearby, the scene of a famous Turkish massacre. He bought a couple of candles from the shop and led me to the top part of the village, from which a miniature canyon cuts into the mountainside for a distance of about a hundred yards. We climbed up the left side of this until we reached a small ledge with an inscribed plaque let into the rock above it:

HERE IN THIS COLD-WATER CAVE
ON THE NINTH OF AUGUST 1821
THE PASHAS RESIT AND OSMAN
PUT TO DEATH BY SUFFOCATION
130 MEN WOMEN AND CHILDREN OF VAPHES

CHRISTIANS FLEEING FROM A TURKISH ONSLAUGHT
AFTER THREE DAYS OF VALIANT RESISTANCE.

Almost every Cretan cave has its history; this was the only one that I had seen with a permanent plaque to commemorate it. Yiannis described what he knew of the incident, which must have been quite commonplace during the early years of the War of Independence.

There are, I know, several pseudo-psychological theories about caves, one of which claims that people who use them are simply satisfying some atavistic urge of mankind to take refuge in the womb of Mother Earth. Another interprets this urge as a death-wish, a longing to be underground, to be in a tomb, buried. I prefer the less pretentious theory offered by the wording of the plaque. Those citizens of Vaphes who took refuge in this cave were certainly prompted by an atavistic urge: the urge to save their own skin. I very much doubt if any other subconscious process was at work within them at the time.

And they nearly did save it. The cave was unknown to the Turks; its small entrance, well off the beaten track and camouflaged by bushes, was invisible only a few yards away. It was a child that betrayed the company in hiding there; just as the raiding forces were entering the village, it began to cry. The story goes that the advance guard of the column took pity on the unseen but only too audible fugitives and went straight past them after shouting a word of warning:

"Silence that child, mother! Those behind us won't spare you, if they hear!"

But the child continued to cry, and attracted the attention of the main body of troops that followed. The hide-out was discovered and the Turks adopted their usual time-saving method of dealing with the people inside; they set fire to the bushes at the entrance to the cave and asphyxiated their victims with the smoke.

I wanted to see for myself how those people must have felt; Yiannis and I decided to go in and have a look. The entrance was wide enough but so low that, although neither of us could ever be described as fat, we could barely wriggle through. With the rock above us scraping our backs, we thrust forward horizontally, in a swimming motion, while our chests were scraped by the rock below.

The tunnel in which we were lying was about ten yards long and lined with a sort of shiny moss as cold and clammy as the deepest

oceanic clay, over which we found we could slide forward fairly easily in spite of the effort required to keep our candle alight; but I soon
discovered why this cave had been named the "Cold-water." Icy drips
from the tunnel's roof punctuated our progress; I could feel them tap-
ping along my backbone as regularly as a Chinese torturer's hammer.

Presently there was nothing in front of us but a six-foot drop.
Over this we slipped head-first, since there was no room to turn
round and negotiate it otherwise, and found ourselves in a roughly
globe-shaped chamber—a damp little air-bubble in the earth's
bloodstream. No light penetrated here; the only sounds were a drip
when the water hit hard stone, and a splash when it landed in one of
the many pools which it had formed already. The air, with only two
of us breathing it, felt heavy; I could well imagine how it must have
felt to 130 people.

Most of their remains had long since been recovered; but a few
skulls and twig-like bones, which glowed dull orange in the candle-
light, were piled up in one corner as though for immediate disposal
or salvage. Yiannis and I disregarded them and struggled back into
the sun.

The little canyon, though only a few minutes' walk from the village, still looked as gaunt and isolated as it must have been when the
Christian craze for eremitic life was at its height. Suitably, the chapel built into a cavern in the opposite cliff was dedicated to St. John
the Hermit. We climbed up there and left our candles burning in
his honour.

Back in the village, Uncle Antonis was waiting for us. I remembered him during the war as a fierce little white-haired gnome with
a white beard and tobacco-stained moustache always quivering with
hopeless rage. His leanings had been fanatically, impatiently pro-
British; every Allied reverse had sent him storming up to the vineyard above his house, which I was then using as a hide-out. There
he would remonstrate and call for vengeance, as though I had been
personally to blame for the catastrophe; the fall of Tobruk in 1942
almost caused a permanent breach between us. I had always been a
little bewildered by Uncle Antonis.

His moustache was now more tobacco-stained, his beard still
quivered—but with mirth instead of wrath. "Welcome back to the
British Consulate," he chuckled as he led us past his own house and
into the house next door, which belonged to his brother Nicholas.

Uncle Nicholas fully deserved his unofficial consular rank. At the beginning of the occupation his home had become a regular transit-camp for our stragglers and escaped prisoners; later it had been one of our most frequently-used secret meeting-places and an almost permanent personal base for me—too permanent for the liking of some people in the village, who were scared of the reprisals which the Germans would have taken had my presence there been discovered. Uncle Nicholas had simply ignored their threats to denounce him; his stubborn attitude had shamed them into silence.

He, too, had always been deeply affected whenever the Allies were forced to withdraw on any front. But, unlike his brother, he would give way to despair instead of anger. My main recollection of Uncle Nicholas was of a man broken by bad news, his whole body heaving with sighs of philosophic resignation.

This natural pessimism had not deserted him. He now looked far older than Antonis, who was his senior by several years, principally because his moustache, identical in size, drooped down instead of curling upwards. He still sighed and, as though leaving everything in the lap of the God in whom he fervently believed, finished every sentence with his favourite aposiopesis: "Well, when all's said and done . . ."

There was nothing remarkable about the rest of that day which I spent with those two old men. I was happy simply to be with them again and asked for nothing more—except, perhaps, for the presence of the third brother, George, Yiannis's father. If only we had brought him with us. Since he was absent, the best we could do was to talk about him. This discussion served to illustrate the essential mental difference between Antonis and Nicholas.

Yiannis knew better than anyone else the reputation which his father had for letting his imagination run riot. Old George was a sort of local Baron von Munchausen; every day he invented a new fantastic story about himself. He could hardly read or write, but the latest rumour in Nippos, spread of course by himself, claimed that years ago he had once been a schoolmaster. Yiannis now asked his uncles for their comments. Before Uncle Nicholas could say what he thought, Antonis—who had never been outside Crete in his life— gave Yiannis his considered opinion:

"Of course, your father was once a schoolmaster. It was when I was working in New York."

Yiannis wanted to take this good news back to his village at once, so we prepared to leave. As we made our way downhill I had a feeling that something had been wanting in the ceremony of our departure. I was haunted by the memory of a certain night during the war when I had been woken up in the vineyard by the sound of shooting a few yards away; next morning Uncle Antonis had come to me and announced: "Did you hear that rifle? That was me!" For some reason, I had been tremendously impressed by this completely pointless *feu-de-joie*; I wanted something of the same sort to happen now.

Uncle Antonis must have been a mind-reader. We had left the village far behind us by the time that I had begun to analyse these irrelevant thoughts of mine. Suddenly the silence of the evening was shattered by a burst of rifle-fire: six rounds in rapid succession. Then, winging over the olive-trees, came the sound of an old man's voice, shrill with the effort of shouting. I could distinguish only the two words: "Bravo! Eengleesh!"

10

ZOURVA

THE ORANGE SEASON was now at its height. Lorries unloaded the fruit into the market at almost every hour of the day; passengers on every bus from the plantation villages brought more of it in as personal luggage. People selling it sold for next to nothing, and those who gave it away gave a hundredweight at a time. For weeks the orange flow into the capital continued; the groves at its source seemed inexhaustible.

My landlord was the owner of one of these groves, in the foothill village of Meskla. He invited me to drive out there for the day and to eat as much as I could. Even my gluttonous passion for oranges had been amply satisfied lately, but I agreed to accompany him; Meskla would make a good starting-point for the visit that I had planned to Zourva, an isolated hamlet just below the snow-line.

Along their western arc the White Mountains dip down to the Canea hinterland, not in a single sweep as on to the Apokoronas plain but in a series of tentative radial thrusts. The rocky fist of the range is here, as it were, unclenched; and between its out-stretched fingers lie the foothill villages, invisible from the coast. The fringe of the orange-groves is roughly in line with these widespread finger-tips; their area corresponds to the wedge-shaped expanses of flat land between them. Meskla lies at the base of the first of these successive broad re-entrants.

The bus took under an hour to drive up the valley, but in that short time we were plunged into a world quite divorced from the rest of Crete, a green-and-gold landscape in which visibility in any direction was restricted to a matter of yards. It was impossible to tell what lay behind the encircling curtain of dark leaf and flashing fruit until the road began to run along the left bank of a stream, which was so obviously a mountain stream that we divined what we could not yet see: the slopes of the valley closing in on either side. Where the two sides came together, leaving only a narrow passage for the water, the road came to an abrupt end; this *cul-de-sac* was the main street of Meskla.

In the coffee-shop, which served also as a bus-stop, I was surprised to see most of the people whom I had expected to find further inland. There were the two Tsirantonis brothers, Yiorgos and Yiannis, with whom I had hoped to stay when I got to Zourva. "You can stay with us here instead," they said, "we've left Zourva for good. The old man still lives up there, of course; you can go and see him tomorrow if you like, but stay here with us tonight."

Since the end of the war, most of the young men of Zourva had left their homes and come to settle in Meskla where, as Yiorgos put it, there were "more opportunities. Down here, you see, there's the main road. It's easier to get supplies from Canea, Yiannis and I have now got a small shop; we don't do so badly. But up there in the hills there's nothing but the sheep, and when you've got no sheep left there's nothing at all."

I could see his point. The inhabitants of these highland villages had, for generations, been shepherds; sheep were their most secure, indeed their only, means of livelihood; and none of them had dreamt of living otherwise. But entire flocks had disappeared during the occupation—either stolen by thieves when their owners were away at the war, or confiscated and commandeered by the Germans; or, like that of the Tsirantonis family, sacrificed to the Allied cause and slaughtered to provide food for Allied missions such as mine. When the war was over, some of the shepherds had not a single sheep left. Rather than start again from scratch, many of them decided to abandon their previous profession and seek their fortune elsewhere, in the capital or one of the larger villages in the plains.

Yiorgos and Yiannis certainly seemed to have prospered through their shop. Their new house was a solid building of three separate rooms, with proper glass window-panes instead of wooden shutters. Yiorgos was married, but his wife could not receive us; she was still in bed after giving birth to a boy two days previously. So our dinner of jugged hare and cheese-cakes was served by the elder sister, Maria, who had been living in her brother's house ever since her husband, a former mayor of Meskla, had been murdered by a Communist band which had occupied the village during the post-war civil disturbances.

The black kerchief which Maria wore in mourning enhanced her good looks. She was not a beautiful girl—her over-wide mouth drew attention to the incipient moustache above it—but sorrow, which seems to disfigure most Cretan women, gave Maria's face an attractive expression of poignancy which it otherwise might not have had. Her voice was in keeping with her appearance; when she spoke of her husband it was in a tone of quiet resignation, without a trace of that hysterical whine—herald of an emotional outburst—which most peasant women affect when they discuss their dead relations.

Soft-spokenness was characteristic of the whole Tsirantonis family; the brothers' voices were never raised above conversation pitch, which they managed to maintain quite effortlessly and not, like so many others, as though they were simply repressing a shout.

Such modesty is unusual in Crete. Since my return I had heard so many "patriots" boasting about their war-time exploits—like the man in Canea who had recently stopped to talk to me in the street. I had never seen him before in my life, but he had taken pains to remind me how, at great personal risk to himself, he had hidden me from the Germans during a raid. Or like the one whom I had met in a bar on the day of my arrival—taking me for a tourist, and anxious to impress even a complete stranger, he had spent some time telling me how he had served as right-hand man to "the English spy, Alekos." I had not bothered to unmask him, but had enjoyed his embarrassment when, a few minutes later, I was introduced to him as "Alekos," the *nom-de-guerre* which I and no one else used in Crete.

The Tsirantonis brothers really had been right-hand men, but their reticence almost made me forget this. Yiorgos was a survivor from the ambush in which Yiannis Vandoulas's brother had been killed. I had not seen him since that day, when he had been wounded; and he would not have mentioned it now had I not asked him to tell me about it. He described it in detail and added:

"I knew something bad was going to happen as soon as I woke up that morning. I'd had a dream and it was a bad dream—I dreamt that a lot of people were eating figs and I was the only one who wasn't given any. That was a bad sign."

In spite of his worldly appearance Yiorgos was a peasant at heart still affected by peasant superstition. He firmly believed in *lavoma*, the power of the evil eye, not as practised by malefactors but, on the contrary, as a natural attribute of certain well-wishers. "It's not that they want to do harm," he explained, "they just can't help themselves. And it's when they're at their nicest that they do their worst. Take my father-in-law, for example. Last year he congratulated the neighbours on the state of their vineyard; and it certainly looked like a bumper crop. Well, two days later, for no reason at all, all the vines were shrivelled. It was father-in-law's admiration that had done it."

There was also a woman in the village who had the same unwelcome power; in praising the beauty of her newly-born grandchild she must have all-unknowingly cast a spell over it, for the baby had immediately fallen ill, and would almost certainly have died if the grandmother had not had the presence of mind to spit on it—spittle from the owner of the evil eye being the only known cure against the accidental curse of *lavoma*.

I was secretly pleased, then, that Yiorgos's baby was not yet on view. I never feel really at home in a nursery; its gurgling inmates fill me with embarrassment; I can only pretend to admire them. And now that I had been told that admiration could be dangerous, even admiration as feigned as mine, I felt that pretence would have been even more of an ordeal than it usually is. But I need not have worried—only blue eyes, Yiorgos assured me, have the power of evil.

I would have climbed up to Zourva first thing in the morning had I not been disturbed by an early visit from two old peasants in tears. This lugubrious couple had called to ask me for my assistance in releasing their son from prison. At first I thought that their approach was yet another example of the pointless *rousphetia* which had occupied so much of my time in Canea, but after listening to what they had to say I realised that here at last was an occasion on which I could, for once, be of service.

Two years before, their son Panayiotis had been arrested during the civil disturbances and subsequently condemned to death. His crime: anti-nationalist activity and membership of the proscribed Communist-controlled guerilla organisation. He had appealed against the death-sentence, which had later been reduced to one of life imprisonment; a second appeal was now being prepared, in the hope of securing his final release. His parents wanted me to attend the hearing and give evidence in his favour.

I was quite prepared to do so—Panayiotis had worked for me during the war. He, too, had been in that ambush with Yiorgos, and had shown equally exemplary conduct. I knew him only as a gallant, if slightly simple youth, who would have found any form of political theory as complicated as the theory of relativity. It was sheer folly, then, to suspect him of Communist sympathies—and perhaps not only folly but also wickedness; for why had Panayiotis and a thousand others like him been condemned to death, while a certain Cretan general who, more than any outside influence, had been responsible for the so-called Communist movement in the island, was not only living in freedom but was still indulging, unmolested, in subversive politics?

I arranged to see Panayiotis's lawyer as soon as I returned to Canea, and promised his parents that I would do my best as a witness at the impending court of appeal. Then, at last, I set off for Zourva.

Considering that the path here zigzags straight up the base of a mountainous *cul-de-sac*, I found the going surprisingly easy; in fact, from where I stopped for a moment to glance back at Meskla, the two side paths out of the valley, which lead respectively to Therisso and Lakkoi, seemed far steeper than the one that I had to take, although the slopes up which they climb are not so high.

From above, Meskla looks like a shanty town in stone: jerry-built and half-built houses dotting the groves, every one of them apparently of recent construction and constituting, it seems, not so much a permanent village as a provisional settlement hastily put up to last no longer than a single orange-season. Not a building of any age in the place. So there may be some truth in the local myth (though there is no historical evidence to support it) that the fine old town which once used to stand on the banks of this fruit-fostering river disappeared without a trace after the Kandanoleon catastrophe, when the whole population was massacred with the exception of one man, who eventually returned alone to rebuild the village and to found a new dynasty of villagers. There is no record, of course, of how he accomplished this feat which, without the assistance of a woman, must have been even more difficult than parthenogenesis.

Compared to the lower village, Zourva is a compact fortress bearing traces of the Middle Ages, its buttressed front soaring upwards and backwards like the inclined walls of the Potala at Lhasa. For want of space on this rocky slope, the houses here are crowded together side by side and one on top of the other, so that the agglomeration is more like a single solid block than a collection of individual buildings; as I entered it I felt I should have been crossing over a drawbridge.

The front door of the Tsirantonis' house opened on to a courtyard formed by the roofs of the houses below. To reach it, I had to negotiate a series of haphazard obstacles: pyramids of small tiles, broken baskets lined with baked clay, broken wine-jars and hollowed-out tree-trunks. Smoke issuing from one of them was the only immediate indication that these oddly-assorted objects served as chimney-pots.

As I stood there surrounded by these ingenious devices, I must have looked like the only human figure in a Dali landscape. An additional touch of surrealism was provided by the presence of other incongruous contraptions made of wood and metal: the pipes and cauldron of a dismantled still, the bits and pieces of an abandoned plough which seemed, in their present state, to belong to a mediaeval siege-engine rather than a modern agricultural implement. And, to crown it all, I found myself confronted with the upper half of a gigantic olive-tree, each branch of which appeared to taper off into a living female head, like the mythical *wikwak* of Persian legend—the oracular tree which spoke with human voices. This olive-tree spoke to me now with the voice of the youngest Tsirantonis sister:

"Just let me finish gathering; I'll be down in a moment."[1]

She and the other girls with her were the only people that I had so far seen in the village, which at this season was almost deserted; those that had not emigrated down the valley to Meskla were absent in winter pastures nearer the coastline. But presently I was joined on the terrace by her father and her husband, two men diametrically opposed both in character and appearance.

Old Yiannis Tsirantonis would have looked his best in traditional Cretan costume, but even in these remote villages that dress is rap-

---

1. In Zourva the women climb the trees to beat the olives down with bamboo poles; in most other villages they wait for the fruit to fall and then simply pick it off the ground. The difference in the two methods is not, I believe, due to the qualities of the respective harvesters; it is dictated by the properties of the respective types of olive being harvested.

idly losing its popularity; when the few members of the generation which still wear it die, the fashion will die with them—and perhaps even sooner, for in the whole of Canea there is only one man left who can make these clothes: Balladinos, the last *terzis*, or "Turkish tailor" (as opposed to the *frangoraphtis*, or tailor of European-style suits). Nowadays, alas, the cost of full Cretan costume is beyond the means of all but the richest; old Tsirantonis wore ugly wide-flapped breeches of hairy black wool and, on his head, a plain black *sariki*, unfringed and "sensibly" tied in distinction to the negligent manner of the Sphakians whom he appeared not to admire as much as I did. But he spoke about them in a peaceful, detached sort of way, as though they were a barely-remembered blight of the past.

His son-in-law, however, was anything but peaceful. This bullet-headed fellow with the permanent frown had retired quite recently from the gendarmerie and seemed incapable of dealing with his empty hours of unaccustomed leisure. In this half-deserted village there was no communal life in which he could take part, no civic activity in which to dissipate his energies. So he had turned into a frustrated handyman; while we sat and talked he kept fidgeting with bits of wood, knives and chisels, interrupting this haphazard carpentry only to air a banal opinion on whatever subject we happened to discuss.

Like everyone else in this area, he took a poor view of the Sphakians, who had come to be regarded as a menace even greater than the Turks. Zourva, being the nearest village to the Sphakian border, had for centuries been the main target for Sphakian sheep-thieves, so that little love was lost between the shepherds on these northern slopes and the raiders who descended on them from the frontier-ridge a few hundred yards behind. These raids were the chief cause of the present inter-provincial strife; and although that cause no longer exists, the strife continues—fostered solely by memory and tradition.

The people of Zourva still recall how the Sphakians behaved during the great revolution of 1866, when Meskla and Lakkoi were the main centres of resistance. The Turks in the plains below might have been routed if the revolutionary forces had not been compelled to defend their rear against treacherous attacks from the highlands, attacks which were launched not for political reasons nor for material gain, but simply out of spite, out of resentment against anyone else assuming revolutionary leadership, a privilege which the Sphakians chose to consider exclusively their own. It seems incredible now that such pettiness could ever have existed, yet in the history of Crete it crops up time and again; the inevitable Ephialtes of each heroic period was moved not necessarily by cowardice nor yet by cupidity, but by envy—like the Sphakian chieftain Roussos who, in a fit of jealousy, murdered a rival leader, Antonios Melidones, who had come to Crete from Asia Minor to support the 1822 revolt.

This discussion seemed to enrage the bullet-headed amateur carpenter. The scraping and slashing of his wretched bits of wood grew progressively more violent as we talked. Fortunately for his fingers, in constant danger of accidental amputation, we were interrupted by the arrival of a pair of visitors. The younger of the two was a schoolboy recovering from jaundice. Bullet-head at once ordered him to open his mouth and show me the tendon inside his upper lip. This, I noticed, had recently been severed.

"The only possible cure," said Bullet-head dogmatically. "Cut that tendon and your jaundice disappears overnight. Of course, I know that there are more scientific methods," he hastily added, as though fearful of appearing ignorant of the latest medical developments, "but give me the practical cure every time."

He then enlarged on the respective virtues of the "practical" and "scientific." Although clearly inclined by nature in favour of minor operations on the lip, he was prepared to admit the possibility of less drastic ways of dealing with disease. As far as medicine was concerned, he kept what he pleased to call an open mind. But when it came to religion he made no concessions, and forthwith showed his intransigence in this respect by starting an argument with the second visitor. For this man, it appeared, had the effrontery to call himself a Christian, although he belonged to no established religion.

I regarded the man now with renewed interest; he was the only Cretan that I had ever met who did not belong to the Orthodox Church. I wondered what such an eccentric could be doing in this out-of-the-way village where his unorthodox views would naturally be considered suspect, if not heretical. His appearance, too, was against him. The flabby face, the flashy suit, the reserved manner hinting at urban sophistication—none of these was calculated to earn him affection or respect in Zourva. Yet he was no stranger to the place, in fact he had been born here; but he had left as a child and been brought up in Athens, where the doctors had recently given him only a few more years to live. So he had come home to die.

But so long as he held his present views he was not going to be allowed to die in peace. He belonged, he told me, to an international sect, whose members hold no allegiance to any particular church, but believe in Christ and try to live in strict accordance with His doctrine. The sect had been declared illegal in Greece, and many of its members arrested and imprisoned on a vague charge of "proselytising." But I was not so interested in the official action that had been taken against the "Christians." More significant was the attitude towards them of private citizens, such as Bullet-head. If the personal views which he aired were any guide to public opinion, no wonder the authorities had felt compelled to legislate against the religious rebels.

The objection to them, however, seemed to be not so much on religious as on political grounds; their alleged heresy was construed as lack of patriotism. Since they could not be charged with jeopardising Christ, they were accused of endangering the State. The case against them was summed up in Bullet-head's unreasonable taunts:

"How can you be a Christian when you don't even go to church? How can you be religious when you don't even have a religion? Why, even Turks have a religion, the religion of their own country; if they hadn't they'd be traitors. Here in Greece it's the Orthodox Church; you're a Greek so you ought to belong to it—if you don't, you're undermining the country. And what about the priests, eh? What would happen to them if people like you had their way? What would they do for a living?"

Bullet-head's stream of nonsense, poured forth in a stern, "no-nonsense" manner, flowed on long after the "Christian" had left, and went on flowing for several hours, all through dinner, and later still.

"That cuckold!" he objected. "He never even went into mourning after his wife died; said there was no need since he knew she went to Paradise at once. Just like that, in a flash! As if he knew how long it takes! Even the priests aren't sure, but they say it's forty days at least! What do you think?"

The question was put to us in deadly earnest, which made our replies more ribald than they need have been. What surprised me most was the broad-minded, almost blasphemous attitude of old Tsirantonis, an essentially religious man but mercifully unbigoted. With elaborate wit he worked out an imaginary itinerary for a hypothetical soul, based, so he claimed, on the time he had himself taken to get to Paradise (which happened to be the name of the highest cliff above the village)—a unique contribution to the eschatological discussion, which we kept up in this vein until bed-time.

———

I woke up earlier than usual next morning, a premonition of spring acting as an alarm-clock. From the roof-tops I could see, as though through a telescope, the shimmering coastline; and beyond it the island of St. Theodore ablaze in the water. As I watched, the sun swept over the Alikianou plain and into the funnel of the valley below, which slowly filled with daylight, then suddenly overflowed; in a flash the curtain of darkness round me was drawn back, and the horse-shoe ridge of mountain where I stood was revealed like the view from a vast bay-window.

The bright blue dome of a church and a few white walls scattered along the western spur were all that could be seen of Lakkoi, the village directly above Meskla. Eastwards, the ridge formed an even, shallow saddle, which I planned to cross later that day in order to reach the village of Therisso and from there make my way back to Canea down the gorge on the other side.

But no one would go to Therisso with me; and old Tsirantonis would not hear of my going down the gorge alone. "There are bad men there just now," he said, "those bandits are still at large. They've been driven off the highest slopes by the snow; the gorge is their next best hide-out. We can't let you take the risk . . ."

I was sure that the outlaws had disbanded long ago; if they were not already safely behind the Iron Curtain, they were probably lying up in the Peiraeus or in Athens, or even in Canea, where they could live more easily unnoticed than in an isolated cave in the open. In any case, I felt that they had been mentioned simply as an excuse; the real reason for this attempt to dissuade me from entering the gorge was based on nothing more than the deep-rooted native objection to any foreigner travelling in these mountains by himself. It was almost as if the inhabitants wanted to romanticize their district by peopling it with imaginary villains for whom the solitary unprotected stranger would be easy meat. Pashley and Sieber were both advised against travelling alone; so was Sir John Myres—and that was during the nineteenth century, long before the Communist menace had been imagined. I regarded the present threat, therefore, as traditional rather than actual.

But old Tsirantonis was adamant: "Even if you get to Therisso, who will you stay with? We've got no friends there; the village is full of Reds. And there's another danger: supposing you lose your way? It might be days before you get back to Canea. You've got to get back pretty soon, remember, to give evidence in that case."

This was a more cunning argument! It was unlikely that I should lose my way, since Therisso lay only a few miles beyond the saddle, which was in sight; and from there I simply had to follow the one path leading to the coastal plain. But it was, I suppose, just possible that I should be delayed in the village itself—possible, though unlikely. But the barest possibility of delay implied an equally slight risk of my reaching Canea too late to attend the Court. Had I taken that risk, I should have proved myself willing to jeopardise Panayiotis's chances of freedom. Old Tsirantonis had framed his argument as a subtle appeal to my *philotimo*; naturally it was successful.

I took the next bus back from Meskla, smugly priding myself on my sense of duty, and telling myself, though without much conviction, that the argument to which I had succumbed was morally valid besides being personally cogent. At heart I realised I had simply been worsted; and to make up for this defeat I vowed that I would walk up that gorge as soon as Panayiotis's case was over.

It was over more quickly than I could possibly have imagined. I was asked to present myself at the Court at nine o'clock in the morning. When I arrived I was ushered into the waiting-room, a small walled-in balcony, where for the next three hours I shared the icy draughts with a dozen other shivering witnesses, all from Meskla. We whiled away the time discussing perjury, a subject which, naturally enough, lay temporarily uppermost in our minds.

"There'll be no need to lie in this case, however," said the village priest, "the whole thing's cut and dried. Panayiotis has made a declaration, renouncing his political views. He'll be let off, it's all settled."

"Then what are we doing here?" I asked.

"Just a formality."

Fortunately the formality, once it started, did not last long. One by one, we entered the Court and gave our evidence. I was delighted to see that each witness in turn spoke up for the accused although several of them had suffered at the hands of the band to which he had once belonged—yet another example of Cretan charity. Even if Panayiotis had not been a fellow-villager he would have had their support, simply because he was a man in trouble and in need of their help. Once a criminal is caught, he ceases to be an enemy.

My own cross-examination lasted less than five minutes. There was no witness-box; after swearing on a heavily ornate Bible laid open in a glass case, I gave my evidence standing in front of a bench of five judges, the normal complement for a Court of Appeal. Panayiotis sat behind me, in a dock railed off by ornamental wrought ironwork: he looked more like a holiday-maker taking the air in a park than a prisoner on trial in a courtroom. Grinning happily at the prospect of certain freedom, he was the only person present who appeared to be enjoying the meaningless ritual.

My evidence was in every way superfluous. But I had been asked to give it and I had given it. Now for that visit to Therisso!

PART THREE

Winter–Spring

Les montagnes ont été, dans tous les temps et chez tous les peuples, le dernier asyle de la liberté, comme elles ont toujours été l'apanage de la force et de la santé. Un sol scabreux, pénible, qui offre peu de subsistence, qui oblige l'homme à un travail long et opiniâtre, qui le soumet à la sobriété et le condamne à toutes sortes de privations, ne tente guère les peuples conquérants, lorsque chaque rocher d'ailleurs est transformé en forteresse, lorsqu'il faut combattre à chaque pas des hommes vigoureux, énergiques, qui defendent avec opiniâtreté le terrain qui les a vu naître et l'independance qu'il leur procure.

Olivier

11

Therisso

Defiance was not my only motive. I had no intention of going to Therisso to beard the so-called Communists in their den; I wanted to see the village because of its association with Venizelos. Besides, it would be pleasant to walk up the gorge, which was reputed to be as magnificent as that of Samaria, though on a far smaller scale.

I was lucky to find a companion who was prepared to face the hypothetical bandit menace with me: an Englishman, Anthony Baynes, the only other Englishman in Crete—unless, of course, one counted the British Consul, a Levantine who said he came from Somerset. Anthony was then in charge of the English School in Canea and could not spare the time for a long jaunt through the mountains; we had to plan a rigid itinerary. It seemed pointless to go up the gorge and then come back to Canea by the same route, so we proposed to strike eastwards from Therisso, across the never-never land behind Malaxa Ridge, which we would pierce again through its only other opening on the further side, and so re-emerge on to the coastal plain twenty miles away.

We took the morning bus to Perivolia, a village just behind Canea, from where the entrance to the gorge showed clearly in the sun, the shadow of the rift so black against the surrounding grey that it looked like a vertical stripe painted on to the rocky wall. The Perivolia plain was the best-irrigated area that I had so far seen in Crete. Water flowed everywhere, past us and round us, rippling in the river-bed, gliding over mud channels, gurgling along metal pipes and at one point, through a break in the pipe-line, gushing into the air in an extravagant fleur-de-lis fountain.

We followed the path by the side of the stream, past two ruined churches, orange-gold outside and dust-black within (a colour scheme peculiar to every ruin in these regions), past walnut-trees and boulders and bushes of oleander, until we came to a spot where the water abruptly ceased to flow above the ground. This was not the source of the river but only a haphazard subterranean exit: a large pool fed by smaller whirlpools welling up from beneath the surface.

We sat down at its edge to eat the food which we had brought with us. It was so warm out in the open that we took our coats off with our packs; a single yellow butterfly, seen for a second against the green of oleander leaf and the pink of almond-blossom, seemed to confirm that spring was here. But looking backwards into the mouth of the gorge, we were reminded that the month was still February; the sunless grey walls were roofed in by a glazed-glass dome of not-so-distant snow. A turn of the head was all that was needed to switch from one season to another. We retreated, as it were, into winter as soon as we entered these walls, and the cold continued until we reached the village several hours later.

I found the gorge indescribable, simply because it resembled any other: the same awe-inspiring landscape of contorted rock overhead, levelled rock underfoot, pitted rock on either side, and wood weathered to the semblance of rock wherever any tree was visible: and not a soul did we meet in the whole length of that winding crack in the mountains, except one old woman, whose sudden appearance in this confined wilderness was as startling as the apparition of a phantom.

She, too, was surprised to run into us there, and more surprised still when we told her that we were English; so surprised, in fact, that she refused to believe us. To her, of course, it seemed highly improbable that two foreigners should be wandering about this remote part of the countryside; therefore—I could almost hear her thoughts working along these lines—it was highly improbable that we really were foreigners. Now, improbability is only one step short of impossibility; it was as good as impossible, therefore, that we should be foreigners. But we had told her that we were—all the more reason, then, not to believe us!

I had come across this method of reasoning so many times before. Because I speak Greek without a strong foreign accent, because I am

A visiting caique in the normally deserted bay of Loutro

The "stink-lily" or dragon arum (dracunculus vulgaris)

The Church of St. Nicholas at the entrace to Kyriakosellia

less than six feet tall, because I have brown eyes and what was once brown hair, because my skin is tanned by the sun—for all these reasons I had often been disbelieved after saying that I was English. Because, of course, as any fool in Crete will—and invariably does—tell you, every Englishman is six-foot six, his eyes are blue, his hair is fair, his skin when sunburnt is painfully pink, and he speaks Greek like—well, like an Englishman.

It was not the rudeness implicit in this disbelief that annoyed me, nor the slyness and suspicion underlying the curt retort: "No, you're not!" What I resented most was being taken for someone posing as an Englishman—a pose which I have always looked upon as an exclusively Levantine prerogative. So I was delighted when the old woman suddenly modified her views. "Well, *you* may be English," she said, turning to me, "but your friend certainly isn't!"

Strange that she should have picked on Anthony who, if his knowledge of Greek can be discounted, is blessed with almost all the features essential to the Cretan conception of "English." Or had his nose not peeled enough in the sun? Anyway, I enjoyed seeing someone else, for once, taking the medicine that was usually doled out to me.

The river re-emerged on the surface just before we sighted a grove of cultivated olive-trees, sure sign of a village in the vicinity; the walls of the gorge slowly opened as though to make room for these plantations, and presently the outlying houses appeared. Since we knew no one here we made for the coffee-shop, indistinguishable from the rest of the damp stone buildings but for some tables and chairs on a level patch of ground outside, where half a dozen men sat watching our approach with open curiosity.

It is always a slight ordeal to enter a strange Cretan village unaccompanied by a local guide. After the gauntlet of brazen stares has been run, and the conventional words of greeting exchanged, an uneasy silence falls. Then, suddenly, out of the blue, the leading question: "What are you doing here?" Although I was prepared for it each time, each time it startled me as much as the Customs' official's: "Anything to declare?"—a demand which always makes me feel, and look, more guilty the more certain I am of my innocence.

For what is the correct answer? And what is the best manner to adopt to allay such deep-seated distrust? Pashley once tried the jocular, without much success. "One of the women," he writes, "asked me, What our business was, and why we had come there. I replied, laughing, 'to see you to be sure.' But her fears were too serious to be trifled with, and I could not at all quiet the suspicion with which she regarded us."

But the serious approach invites a similar reaction, even in official members of the community. During his search for antiquities Pashley tackled the Albanian commandant of a large village, who, at once on his guard, "wondered what could be my object in asking questions about the country." A subsequent appeal to the village priest merely led to further misunderstanding; for he, "supposing like most of his fellow-countrymen, that my journey could have solely a political object, addressed me very warmly on behalf of his fellow Cretans of the Christian faith, expatiating on the injustice they had suffered, at the hands of the Allied Powers, by being transferred to the dominion of Mohammed Ali."[1]

So in Therisso, with its reputation for hostility towards strangers, I was prepared for the worst. I need not have been; our arrival there was taken for granted. There was plenty of curiosity, admittedly, but no trace of suspicion in the way that we were welcomed at the coffee-shop, not even when I began asking questions about Venizelos's activity here during the 1905 rebellion.

The historical background I already knew. The turn of the century was a period in which Great Britain was linked for the first time with the internal administration of Crete. As long ago as 1878 a major revolt had been averted by British intervention, when a pact was drawn up between the Turks and the Cretan chieftains under the auspices of the British Consul. During each of the three rebellions that followed within a space of twenty years, the British again intervened, inducing the Turks to introduce milder methods of government. And when, in 1897, a Greek expeditionary force under

---

1. It is unfortunate, though typical, that this grievance should have been aired to a travelling scholar who, naturally, could do nothing about it; for the complaint of "injustice" was not unreasonable. The independence of Greece, to which Crete had made a generous contribution, was declared in 1830; but the Cretans' heartfelt wish to share that independence, by being united to the mother country, was opposed by the Allied Powers who, since they recognised that some action had to be taken to curb Turkish misrule, adopted the unhappy compromise of transferring the island to Egypt, and then only for a period of eight years. Its reversion to the Sublime Porte in 1840 led directly to the disastrous insurrection of 1866.

Colonel Vassos landed on the island and proclaimed the occupation of Crete in the name of King George of the Hellenes, British
troops were among the Allied forces which occupied the principal
towns to restore law and order. In 1898 Prince George of Greece was
appointed High Commissioner in Crete under the auspices of the
Allied Powers, but still no step was taken towards achieving union
with the mother country. In 1901, therefore, Venizelos formed an
opposition party pledged to secure that union, by force of arms if
necessary; and four years later he resorted to arms by convening the
Revolutionary Assembly at Therisso.

Venizelos was, of course, declared an outlaw by the authorities,
including the British, but I like to think that, in spite of this, we
held him unofficially in high regard. Certainly our Consul in Canea
did; while the rebellion was still at its height he managed, by devi-
ous methods, to supply the leader in his hide-out with delicacies and
copies of *The Times*. Years later Venizelos declared that those newspapers had taught him to read English, and he always dated from
our Consul's indiscreet attention his affection for the British race.[2]

I wanted to find out more of these personal details from the villagers who were with him at the time. Very few of them were still
alive, of course, but two old men who were sitting with us said that
they remembered him well, and even before the rebellion. Although
Venizelos was not born in Therisso, it was his mother's home; so he
had many friends and relations here. His popularity in the neighbourhood was an additional reason, then, for establishing his revolutionary headquarters in this village, the closest one to the capital
with natural defences.

He had come here three years running, before the rebellion, and
spent all summer studying and reading, in an isolated hut above
the village on the track leading to Meskla. This hut, alas, no longer
exists. I should love to have seen the place where, in self-imposed confinement, the simple provincial lawyer had worked out his schemes
for the Greater Greece which he was later destined to govern.

At the peak of his career, when he had proved himself to be one
of the greatest statesmen of this century, Venizelos used to wear a
distinctive headgear similar to that worn today by Pandit Nehru,
but black instead of white. I wondered when he had first taken to

2. For the information contained in this paragraph I am indebted to Sir Harold
Nicolson, to whom Venizelos himself related the event I have described.

this fashion, and asked what sort of hat he had worn fifty years ago in Therisso. Neither of the two old men could remember, but one of them produced a photograph of a contemporary group which included Venizelos. In this he appeared to be wearing not even a Cretan *sariki* but, disappointingly, a European cloth cap.

The 1905 rebellion must have been a more highly-organized affair than the previous uprisings in the mountains. Neither of my informants made a single reference to any fighting, which is generally a survivor's main recollection; what had impressed them most was the vast camp, "a second Canea," into which their village was transformed. The problems of administration must have been immense, but food had not run short and the men had even received regular pay.

"Where did the money come from?" I asked.

"We printed our own."

A "patriotic loan" of 100,000 gold drachmae had apparently been raised, and, on an old hand-press, twenty thousand five-drachma notes had been run off to serve as immediate cash. On each note it was stated that the loan was to be repaid, at an interest of six per-cent, "six months after the settlement of Cretan question." I was not told what happened to this money. The notes, I imagine, were practically valueless. For the rebellion was suppressed in a few months; it was not until 1912 that the Cretan question was settled, when the island was officially annexed by Greece.

I had been too engrossed in the talk to notice the early sunset, until the cold drove us inside long before it was dark. I had wanted to see something of the village, but was told that it was not worth the visit. At this season most of the houses were abandoned, like those in Zourva; their owners absent with the flocks in the plains. So not more than a dozen people gathered round us in the coffee-shop, while we warmed ourselves with the *tsikoudia* which they offered, and waited for the meal which the shopkeeper had kindly promised us. We spent the rest of the evening happily drinking.

With most of the inhabitants away, and almost every house locked up, there was not a spare bed available; sleeping accommodation for us presented a problem. This was solved by the gendarmerie, who commandeered some blankets and invited us to doss down on the floor of the police station, a damp draughty building on the other side of the river, which we crossed by one of the many slippery planks laid along the bank to serve as bridges. But the blankets were warm and we were both tired. We went to sleep soon enough, lulled by soft dance-music from the station's wireless-set—an incongruous sound which, coupled with the sight of the bamboo supports in the unfinished roof overhead, transformed the place for me, in my last moment of consciousness, into an artificially-primitive sophisticated night-club.

I woke with a shiver to the reality of morning. The sun was not yet high enough to penetrate the gorge, but it was too cold to lie there and wait until it did; we decided to set off at once. After a double *tsikoudia*, to restore our circulation, we started the long ascent up the eastern slope.

Once over the ridge, we were moving in another climate. Not yet hot enough for us to feel it, the sunshine created at least an illusion of warmth as it sparkled on the snow just above us and coloured the countryside just below. We were again on the borderline between two seasons, where a single glance embraced both spring and winter separated only by an elevation of a few hundred feet. But our view was continually restricted by a succession of deep folds in the ground, which we took all morning to cross, folds intersected by a whirl of transverse valleys further down the slope, which gave the whole district an air of untidy, haphazard planning. An aerial photograph of these gigantic convolutions would probably resemble a close-up of a peeled and flattened walnut, or of an exposed human brain.

It was not until midday that we came across signs of human habitation and saw our first human being since the dawn: a young shepherd protected by a savage dog, which kept me at such a distance that I had to shout to find out where we were.

"Drakona," came the reply.

We descended another valley and climbed another hill surmounted by a group of houses, at which I again made enquiries.

"This is Drakona," I was told.

We walked on, or rather up and down, for about another hour, past solitary houses and through isolated olive-groves, in one of which was an olive-press operated by a couple of gleaming, glorious red-faced drunks, who insisted on our sharing their wine.

I was not surprised to hear that we were still in Drakona. From here the houses which we had passed over an hour ago were within hailing distance; a bridge across the intervening space would have made them accessible in a few minutes. The village is certainly dispersed, but not to the extent that one would imagine; on a map it would appear perhaps less than a mile wide. But on foot, I felt it was more like ten; I was grateful for this excuse to stop and rest.

It was cool and dark inside, and noiseless save for the occasional movement of a mule, blindfolded and harnessed to the press, and the answering squeak from the cogs of the mechanism. The glasses which we were given were slippery in our hands, for our hosts were covered in oil from head to foot. I could not tell, nor did I care, whether this was due to drunken messiness or was the inevitable result of their work; the wine tasted delicious.

These chance encounters on the road are one of the joys of Crete. They never last long enough to allow the friendly curiosity of the people to become irksome; at the first sign of boredom there is always the excuse of having to continue the journey. In the olive-press Anthony and I felt no urge to move on; the wine added zest to the conversation. The owners, in their fuddled state, seemed to take our presence here for granted; their only surprise was that we should have arrived on foot.

"But where are your horses?" they kept repeating. "Where are your . . . here, have another glass, but do please tell us, where are your horses?"

They refused to believe that anyone could walk for pleasure. Understandably enough: I would not have believed it myself, if I had had to live in Drakona. And then, in Crete, no one ever walks, even in the plains, unless he is compelled to by poverty; riding or driving is as much a social distinction as the wearing of a gabardine raincoat instead of a shepherd's cloak, or a *republika*[3] instead of a *sariki*. And here were Anthony and I, calling ourselves English, hatless and travelling on foot—naturally, it was hard to understand.

For, in Crete, every Englishman is still taken for a millionaire; when he travels, then, he must travel in state. Up to the end of the last century, I suppose, most Englishmen did so travel. Professor Raulin was accompanied by pack-animals and guides during his tour of the island—equipment which today would be considered quite a luxury—yet he prided himself on "*mes goûts simples et mon*

---

3. The name given to that ludicrous bit of felt, which in England, I believe, is called a "trilby."

habitude, extrèmement peu anglaise, de préférer à tout autre chose en
voyage l'imprévu de la fortune de pot." And even at the beginning of
this century Englishmen, when they wandered in the more remote
parts of the Mediterranean, wandered in reasonable comfort. Norman Douglas may have set the fashion for rough Calabrian travel;
he was still the English *milord* who dispensed advice, cigars and
soldi to a native peasantry.

———

Beyond Drakona we entered a country with a more reasonable natural pattern, where each view was a landscape and not just a section of
strangely shaped earth. The horizons here were less hampering than
the succession of blind ridges behind us; and soon there appeared a
permanent feature, distant but never out of sight: the cloud-ringed,
snow-capped cone of Mount Ida. But, as before, there was little sign
of human habitation; the nearest village might have been a hundred
miles away. Our encounter with the American, then, was all the
more unexpected.

We found him sitting by the side of the path, near a derelict
church which looked as if it had been left there by mistake. He
must have heard us talking as we approached, for he greeted us with
the words:

"You American boys?"[4]

"No, English."

"Same thing," he cheerfully replied, though his face betrayed his
disappointment. He motioned us to sit down beside him, shook our
hands and thumped his chest with a proud, superior gesture.

"Me American!" he declared.

I had met this sort of bore before—the boastful, loud-mouthed,
ubiquitous and unavoidable Greco-Brooklyn boy, the fellow who
emigrates as a young peasant to one of the industrial centres of
America, lines his pockets there through a decade or so of gruelling labour and no less gruelling economy, and then returns home, a
musical comedy version of a small-town Yankee commuter, to enjoy
a life of ostentatious leisure and to plague, with the few words of

4. The fact that he spoke first also showed he knew that we were foreigners. Had
he taken us for locals he would have expected us to address him instead; for in
Crete the conversation is opened by the person walking past, *never* by the one sitting down. This is an invariable rule.

English that he manages to remember, any English-speaking foreigner whom he happens to meet. His sort is to be found in the most
unlikely places; in the big towns, of course, but also in the smallest villages, and, as I now realised, even in an empty wilderness of
untilled earth and stone.

These fake Americans usually appear so scornful of what, on
their return, they call "the home-town" that one wonders why they
ever come back, or why, once they are back, they do not immediately leave again. But they do come back, and for good; this hom-
ing instinct of theirs is universal. The attraction does not lie in the
idea of home as we know it; not in the sentimental dream of a cheerful fire, muffins for tea and a faithful spaniel on the hearth-rug. The
Greek peasant home provides none of these emotional and creature
comforts, it is merely a place in which to sleep and shelter. What
drags the Brooklyn boy back to Greece is the thought of the village
square, the coffee-shop, the vineyard; proximity to the earth and
mankind; talking and gambling and drinking in the sun; in short,
the easy uncomplicated life of the *agora*—and a very pleasant life it
is too. Most of them, I am sure, find it so, even those who appear to
despise it most.

From his clothes I could tell that this one had been back in Crete
for many, many years. If he had ever owned a brown Homburg, a
gold tie-pin or a pair of brown-and-white shoes—which are normally essential items in a Brooklyn boy's wardrobe—he must have
long since worn them out or lost them; he now dressed, and looked,
like a shepherd. This pastoral appearance made his harsh Bowery
accent sound all the more incongruous: it was only lack of practice,
I suppose, that made it unintelligible as well. After listening for several minutes to what I took to be whole sentences, in which I could
distinguish no more than an occasional "sonofabitch" and "goddam," I suggested that we might come to understand one another if
we continued the conversation in Greek. He was amazed:

"Wha! You know Greek? Wha! Goddam hard! Greek goddam
harder than any sonofabitch! Wha!"

Quite a common opinion, this; though usually voiced in milder
terms. The richness of the Greek language has gone to many a good
Greek's head and filled it with a number of extravagant ideas, one of
which is that Greek is a difficult language to learn since it has several words to describe a single object. When I point out that this
phenomenon exists also in other languages I am immediately shown

the second great difficulty, namely that in Greek there are no less than six ways of writing the sound "ē." My only retort to this is that in English there are no less than five ways of pronouncing the syllable "ough." And so it goes on, an unrewarding argument at the best of times, and certainly not one that I wished to pursue with a mouthing character in the middle of a Cretan field. I got up and prepared to leave.

"Wha! So soon!" he exploded. "Sonofabitch soon! No talk? Wha! American talk, eh? Fine, goddam fine! Pittsburgh! Detroit! Chicago! Wha!"

"Some other time," I said; and moved off.

We were now on the last lap of our journey, walking mainly down-hill, approaching the large village of Kampoi. On the lower slopes the olive-groves grew increasingly abundant; but I could never have enough of them. Of all trees the olive is the most individual. However large the grove, each separate dust-grey growth maintains a character of its own; just as every Greek man or woman, in however large a crowd, remains a distinct personality. Looking at these trees, I found my thoughts revolving round the possibility of a direct link between national character and national landscape. A far-fetched conceit, perhaps; but another instance at once sprang to mind—Christmas-trees, the epitome in arboreal form of the Southern German mentality. I had always found the fairy-tale atmosphere of the Black Forest perfectly in keeping with the sentimental heartiness of its people; each Christmas-tree had appeared to have about as much individuality as a tin soldier; walking through a whole forest of these silly toys had been like living on a nursery diet. But here, amongst the olives, my visual palate was happily free from the taste of rice-pudding.

We reached the outskirts of Kampoi in the late afternoon. It was still warm enough to have our drinks served outside the coffee-shop, where the first person I met was the very man that I was looking for: Costis Athousakis. It would have been hard not to recognize him, even if he had abandoned the full Cretan costume which he had insisted on wearing, as a sort of gesture of defiance, throughout the occupation; no one else that I knew in this area had red hair, a grey beard, a scarlet face and a nose squashed so flat that the forehead was joined by a concave slope to the flaming upper lip.

His obviously picturesque appearance had appealed to every amateur photographer in the *Wehrmacht* stationed in Canea. The sentries on the road blocks into the town had always welcomed the sight of this rollicking little gnome who passed them regularly once a week on his way to market. They had stopped him every time, of course, on the pretext of examining his identity card, but in reality to take another snapshot of him perched on top of his heavily-laden mule. He had always obliged them by posing for as long as they liked, with an expression on his face that was luckily far more innocent than the contents of his saddlebags. Costis had been one of my most successful couriers.

He had also been one of my most entertaining drinking-companions; the flush on his cheeks was not due entirely to a healthy life in the open. It was now, alas, too late in the day to renew that companionship. In formal, declamatory tones—for he was proud of his prophet's voice—he asked us to stay and drink with him there all night; but we had already decided to go on to Kyriakosellia, a hamlet at the base of the outlet to the plains, so as to be nearer the main road for the early morning bus back to Canea.

It was pitch dark by the time we reached the little group of houses, and only just light when we left it on the following day. So I did not see much of Kyriakosellia during that visit; certainly not enough for me to do justice to it here.

But I have tried to make up for this in a subsequent chapter.

12

SPHAKIA

SOMETHING WENT WRONG with the weather that year. A fortnight detached itself from the middle of summer, and intervened
between winter and spring. Local geniuses attributed this climatic
phenomenon to a recent atom-bomb test in Nevada; in Crete it was
then the fashion to blame nuclear fission for even the smallest cos-
mic irregularity.[1] Whatever the reason, the whole island, which
had just been subjected to an exceptionally late and enduring cold
spell, suddenly became the target for a scorching gale which, for two
weeks on end, blew straight across from Africa.

In that short time the whole mountain range was stripped of its
winter coat: from my room in Canea I could see the contours of
the highest peaks changing their shape from day to day as the snow
which had camouflaged them melted and subsided, like huge *bombe
glacée* at the mercy of a blow-lamp. Within a few days everything
was warm to the touch, warped and desiccated. Flat surfaces, which
had lately been smooth and damp, felt like sand-paper. I used to
be woken up by the loosened plaster cascading into powder down
the walls; when I put on my shoes in the morning, I would find the
leather of the inside soles curled and crinkled.

---

1. Another example: the latest consignment of D.D.T. had proved less effective
than usual. Immediately Canea was swept by the rumour that the component
materials essential to that insecticide had been kept back for the manufacture of
a new atomic pile!

This visitation of the *lyvas*, or Lybian wind, was the earliest and longest within living memory. Winter pastures dried up overnight; the shepherds' return to the highlands was advanced by several weeks; and the tracks and roads over the topmost passes were uncovered, drained and scoured all at once. Here was my chance to get to Sphakia at least a month earlier than I had hoped. Daphne was due back from England; we set off together a few days after her arrival.

As the crow flies, Sphakia village is only twenty-five miles from Canea—a little more perhaps, for even a crow would have to describe a high arc over the mountains to get there. By road, the journey takes a whole day; Cretan buses are not designed for speed—just as well; for on the Sphakia route, at least, one of the passengers usually has to get out and run in front of the vehicle in order to shift the larger boulders out of its path. Besides, there are the frequent stops to allow the poor old seething engine to cool.

There are certain fixed rules which seem to apply to every bus journey in Crete. To begin with, no bus ever starts less than twenty minutes late; yet there is always one person who arrives even a few seconds later, and the departure is further postponed for the inevitable argument that follows between him and the driver and any of the other passengers who cares to participate. In consequence, the driver invariably starts off in a blazing temper, which he vents on the gear-box and steering-wheel. The complement of every bus includes at least one small child, who at some stage of the journey is sick all over the floor; and one hysterical adult, who throughout the journey shrieks advice to the driver and warnings to his fellow-passengers.

The bus that took Daphne and me to Sphakia contained an additional source of noisy disturbance: a young mother with a babe in arms which was apparently about to die—that, at least, was what she told us as she sat there suckling it and sobbing. Her announcement provoked a chorus of condolences and admonitions. "It is God's will," said one; said another: "Don't take on so, you'll only poison your milk." But she would not be comforted. Though she was quiet enough on the move, at each stopping-place she gave vent to a fresh outburst of myrologies, as though she considered the child she held already dead and buried.

These conventional lamentations are the most hideous sounds of which the human voice is capable. The grief which provokes them is genuine, no doubt, but the stylized doggerel in which they are composed, and the ham-actor's manner in which they are delivered, arouse in me, I regret to say, scorn rather than sympathy. The suffering of this young mother was pathetic so long as it was silent; her face had an appealing loveliness while the tears coursed down it noiselessly, the great blue eyes blinded by the horrors of the thoughts behind them. But the loveliness was there only when she was not attracting attention to herself; it vanished as soon as she opened her mouth to scream out her misery—and this she did in every village at which we halted on the way, her cries being echoed by those of half a dozen captive goats bleating in a misery of their own from their prison on the roof of the bus.

It was an unpleasant journey; we found we could endure it only by what Daphne called "going Yogi," by deliberately "rising above" the crowded confusion of our immediate surroundings in the hope of achieving a trance-like state in which every sensibility is dulled. And here the motion of the bus was helpful; the gentle lurching lulled us both into a comatose condition which rendered us more or less oblivious of the din and discomfort, but oblivious also of the places which we passed on the way.

I had intended to note every detail of this road, in order to form some idea of the impression that it must have made in 1941 on the defeated British troops who withdrew along it to reach the evacuation beach on the south coast. The only note I made, however— and this one merely mentally—was of the great plain of Askyphou at the head of the main pass over the mountains: a miniature Omalo, the highest elevation in Crete at which the vine is cultivated. From here a second, deeper pass leads southwards to the sea; but it has ceased to be a main thoroughfare now that the motor road constructed along the edge of the ravine follows a more direct line to the coast.

This road had not yet been completed as far as Sphakia, but there were signs that it soon would be. From where the bus stopped— about a couple of miles short of the village—we could see where the rocky slope had been excavated and prepared: a red ribbon of freshly turned soil curved and zigzagged down to the last small saddle, over which it disappeared out of sight. A single church and a small group of houses straddled the sky-line there, as though to signpost the harbour which, invisible from this height, occupied the cove below.

The province of Sphakia has not always been the size that it is now. In statistical records as recent as those of 1890 it is referred to, not as a province at all, but as a prefecture, with boundaries extending from Koustoyerako to Asi Gonia and embracing the present province of Apokoronas. Sieber mentions it as being divided, for administration purposes, into twelve *kapetanata*, or headmanships—no doubt the last remaining trace of the mediaeval method of local government and land-division.

When the Venetians occupied Crete in 1204, the island was arbitrarily partitioned into 234 *cavallierie*, or baronies, each the personal responsibility of a Venetian noble; further subdivisions occurred in the course of the subsequent century, so that in 1367 the administrative areas had been increased to the number of 394. Three of these, the baronies of Sphakia, Ayios Niketas and Anopolis, then covered an area equivalent to the whole modern province. The foreign rulers soon found this method of governmental decentralisation ineffective in dealing with the rebellions organised by such large clans as the Skordylis family, whose sphere of influence far exceeded the parochial boundaries of any individual Venetian; the three baronies were therefore united so as to come more directly under the jurisdiction of the *Rector*, or Governor of Canea; and Sphakia was made the capital.

Why this should have been considered a cause for rejoicing, I cannot tell. The fact remains that the union was celebrated in the new capital by a spate of ecclesiastical building, each of the forty-five outlying villages being asked to contribute a church at its own expense. Clearly the scheme was not universally popular; for a long time the village of Patsianos refused to subscribe to it. But the whole weight of public opinion was brought to bear on the reluctant inhabitants, who were subsequently compelled to provide a church dedicated to the Holy Apostles, and to build it with mortar in which wine instead of water was mixed with the lime and sand.

Over a hundred churches were eventually erected among the houses in the cove and above the little harbour, so that every three days or so the people of the capital had a pretext for feasting in honour of a saint; by the beginning of the seventeenth century the Sphakians had won an enviable reputation for idle merrymaking. "But now they delight in ease, in shades," observed the pious Sandys, "in dancing and drinking; and no further for the most part endeavour their profit, that their bellies compel them."

But most of these buildings are now in ruins. Acres of rubble and a single street are all that remains of what was once the largest town on the south coast. Large numbers of its original population of 3,000 fled from Crete to Melos to avoid the Turkish reprisals that followed the 1866 rebellion; their abandoned homes either collapsed or were pillaged by the villagers who remained. By the beginning of this century Sphakia was reduced to a mixed community of 500 fishermen and shepherds; and these numbers were further depleted, and further material damage done, by the German air raids of June 1941, when for almost a week the whole of the British force which had withdrawn from Canea was concentrated on this narrow strip of beach to await evacuation.

In spite of its derelict appearance, Sphakia still retained an urban atmosphere foreign to any of the other villages I had so far visited. There was clearly some semblance of a plan in the lay-out of the buildings, in which natural hazards such as outcrops of rock and inland caves had been catered for and incorporated; the double row of houses at the water's edge was separated by a properly paved path which could almost be termed a street, in which there was something unique in a village of this size—a tavern.

It had recently been opened by an old friend of mine, Nikos Douroundous, who had realised the possibility of making a quick profit by catering for the hundreds of labourers imported from elsewhere in the district to work on the road. They were still at work outside when Daphne and I arrived; the little room overlooking the sea was empty; but Nikos, when he came round from behind the bar to greet us, seemed at once to fill it all by himself.

At the best of times—or rather at the worst, for it was during the occupation that I mean—he had never been particularly small; he was now outrageously, indecently large. In Crete, more than anywhere else, a man's affluence can be judged by his weight and shape; Nikos must have prospered since the war. I found myself wondering how many bank-notes had gone into the making of all that blubber, which heaved and quivered in the constriction of a six-foot leather belt with an outsize buckle. This brand-new belly was a really outstanding acquisition; to go with it Nikos had also developed a rich, juicy voice. But his mournful, black-shadowed eyes and his sickle-shaped moustache—which had once made him look like any French character-actor and now made him look like the one and only Raimu—these at least had not altered.

We did not have Nikos to ourselves for long. The labourers on the road knocked off at sunset; soon all the tables and the chairs and the standing-room round the bar were occupied by a crowd of gobbling, gabbling, wine-swilling, loud-laughing navvies, white from the dust they had raised with their picks since morning. Nikos attended personally to the lot of them, in a manner that was more dictatorial than servile. He was the only person in the room without a perpetual smile on his face; the rest behaved as though they had just struck oil or found a gold mine. Perhaps it was pay-day. Whatever the reason, there was an exhilarating "gold-rush" atmosphere in the air, which I found a refreshing change from the gloom and boredom of the usual village coffee-shop.

But there was one man there who did not appear to regard himself as a successful pioneer. He must have been working on the road for he was as dusty as the others; he was also far more ragged. Barefoot, in three-quarter-length trousers, he shuffled up to us and gurgled over the food, pointing at a piece of bread and then at his own mouth in a gesture of desperate hunger. I assumed that he was the local village idiot, although his head was not shaved in the customary mentally-deficient's style; in fact his locks were so long and unruly that they were tucked into a woman's hair-net. I gave him the bread and he scuttled off with a smile to try his luck at the other tables, where he received a few crusts and also a few insults. "Cuckold of a deaf-mute!" was the cry that followed him as he made his rounds of the room.

At first I thought that this attitude was simply a manifestation of peasant cruelty; such treatment was generally reserved for dogs. It was just as well that the poor fellow could not hear what was said to him, though he could understand the looks of hostility he received; I pitied him for not being able at least to answer back. But my pity, I soon learned, was misplaced.

"We've known this cuckold for years," a friendly labourer explained. "He's the biggest sponger in the district, turns up at any celebration—uninvited, of course. He'll hear of a wedding or baptism even before it's planned, no matter how far away it is; when it does come off, there he'll be—begging as usual. And there's nothing wrong with him at all, except that he can't hear or talk. He can do a job of work when he wants to; he's working with us now on the road. And the pay isn't bad at all."

"But if he's paid," I asked, "why does he have to beg?"

"Force of habit, I suppose. He's done it all his life."

This combination of gate-crashing and mendicancy was an unusual form of enterprise, and apparently a highly successful one. From force of habit the deaf-mute begged although he had no need; from force of habit, and equally needlessly, his fellow-workers gave him part of their food. In his own way the man was a pioneer, after all.

It was nearly eleven o'clock by the time Nikos locked up for the night, having first tucked a loaded revolver into his shirt-front. "I've got lots of personal enemies," he explained. This might have been an act designed to impress us, but I did not think so at the time. It seemed quite likely, indeed more than probable, that Nikos should have enemies; there were people who might resent his massive arrogance and importance. And on the long climb in the moonlight to his home in the upper town he would have made a sitting target; he panted and stumbled even more than we did as he led us slowly and deliberately up the hill.

Nikos's wife, Anna, was a suitable match for him. To begin with, she was almost as large, and just as handsome. More important, she had a voice to rival his. His simple request for coffee, delivered in ringing, cavernous tones which made it sound like a threat, was answered by an echoing blast which was her way of indicating assent; their conversation continued like an antiphony of thunder and wind until the appearance of the coffee caused a lull in the verbal storm.

By peasant standards, Nikos's house was almost luxurious. It was well-kept too; even the floor was freshly whitewashed. On the walls hung the inevitable family photographs, one of a young dandy with a tame ibex at his feet. It was the ibex that gave me a clue to his identity—that and the unmistakable Viglis features, which not even the straw boater and ludicrous townee suit could disguise.

"Yes," said Anna in confirmation, "that's Theodore all right. He was my brother."

I should have realised the relationship in the first place; she was a typical Viglis herself. She showed no sign of sorrow over her brother's death, which she discussed quite dispassionately, as though murder and violence were the two human factors which everyone took for granted. Her attitude was in the true tradition of Sphakian lawlessness; I admired her for it. In other districts people had talked about their crimes either boastfully or with sham regret; some even tried to put forward excuses for them. But here breaking the law was taken as a matter of course.

Nikos also maintained this tradition, both in his activities and in the way he described them. Piracy was once the main occupation of the sea-going members of the Sphakian community; it has now been superseded by smuggling. Cigarette-papers are worth a small fortune in Crete where, despite a Government monopoly, excellent tobacco is illegally grown by almost every male of smoking age; and the Coast of North Africa, where these papers can be picked up dirt cheap, is within range of the smallest caique. Nikos had recently financed an expedition to Sollum, but on the return journey the vessel which he had chartered was intercepted by a police launch; the cargo had to be jettisoned; and contraband worth many times more than the seventy-five million drachmae[2] which Nikos had invested went straight to the bottom of the sea.

Still, he had obviously not done so badly for himself. There on the table, respectfully covered with a cloth as though it was a sacred tabernacle, was an unmistakable sign of prosperity: a brand-new wireless set. For Nikos, alas, it was not the simple decoration that it is in most peasant homes; under the table were two batteries to which it could be, indeed was, connected. As soon as we finished our coffee he switched the thing on and started fiddling with its many knobs. For several minutes the room seemed to be filled with packs of wolves, Chinese fire-crackers and the massed bands of a hundred lunatic asylums. Rather regretfully, I thought, he let these noises recede into the background and tuned in, more or less, to a programme of gramophone records; Sophia Vembo's throbbing voice could just be heard above a crackling accompaniment of static.

"Oh, what a whore of a singer!" he sighed in admiration.

At last the programme came to an end. Nikos turned to us and asked if we were sleepy. We said we were. He nodded sympathetically and started twiddling the knobs again. He continued to twiddle for at least half an hour. Finally even he had had enough noise for one day; he got up and prepared for bed.

Sheets and blankets had been made up for Daphne and me on the polythrone, a vast piece of furniture without which no well-to-do

2. This sounds a formidable sum, but at the time of this smuggling operation the rate of exchange was about 40,000 drachmae to the £.

Cretan house is complete. It can best be described as a cross between a sofa and a bed, though it fails to serve the function of either; it is too upright for one's back, too narrow for one's seat. Lie in it or sit in it, either way it is an instrument of torture. This one was about five yards long and two planks—I could feel them both—wide. Daphne and I lay there, end to end, and rigid for fear of falling off, like a couple of entranced fakirs stretched out on a church-pew.

Sleep would not have come easily in any circumstances; it hardly came at all, thanks to the noise of our heavy-weight hosts in the loft above us. The boards groaned as they turned and twisted in what sounded like a struggle to the death. Anxiously I awaited its outcome, which I imagined would be announced by the collapse of the roof. But the tussle overhead seemed to be lasting as long as the courtship of a pair of hippopotami; I could feel no change in the regular rhythm of those embarrassing Leviathan movements, which slowly rocked me out of my wide-awake, eavesdropping tension into a state of sporadic unconsciousness.

———

Nikos left the house at first light; I heard the stairs creak as he came down, then the door slam behind him. But it was not his departure that woke me up; at least an hour earlier I had been disturbed by noisier movements from above. Only half-awake, I was under the impression that the gigantic copulation of the night before was still in progress, an impression which seemed to be confirmed by Nikos's thundering demands:

"Give us a kiss now! Why won't you give us a kiss? Oh please, please give us a kiss!"

Then his tone had suddenly changed; the thunder grew even louder; the storm was directly overhead;

"Come here at once, you little cuckold, and give your father a kiss!"

If his son had been asleep until then, he could not have slept any longer; no one could. Anna was certainly awake, and proved it blowing a gale of abuse; this noise frightened one child, who immediately burst into tears; and I fancied I could hear through the din the vague protestations of another. Having thoroughly roused the household, Nikos had got up and left. But a three-voice chorus of complaint continued long after his departure. Further sleep was out of the question; Daphne and I decided to get up as well.

Presently the cause of all the trouble came downstairs—the small boy who had refused to kiss his father. He showed that he was still in a bad mood by kicking Daphne hard on the shins. But his sister, a few years older, was embarrassingly affectionate; she would not leave Daphne alone for a second, and clung to her side even in the outdoor lavatory where there was scarcely room for one person at a time. When we went down to the beach she followed us.

The strip of shingle from which our army had left Crete in 1941 was still littered with rusty steel helmets, rotting respirator-tubes, old boots and empty bully-beef tins: in over ten years no attempt had been made to clear up this depressing mess. It was a hateful place in which to stay for long, so we climbed up to the only attractive spot in sight: a pine-grove overlooking the harbour. Having visited the remains of an old fort there, we seemed to have exhausted all the sight-seeing possibilities of Sphakia; we climbed down again and spent the rest of the day in the tavern. Nikos's daughter, of course, was still with us.

Daphne had noticed that the little girl was wearing bracelets of red and white string round her wrists, and a necklace of the same material. I asked what these were for. "To protect me from the March sun," was the reply; "if I wear them until Easter, I shan't get sun-burnt. But I take them off then and burn them in the oven when we bake the Easter bread."

I was grateful to Daphne for calling my attention to these amulets, which I should never have noticed myself; for I was beginning to take everything for granted in Crete, even many of the strange customs. Familiarity does not necessarily breed contempt, but it certainly dulls perception. Now that I had been reminded of one superstition, I decided to make a note of some of the others, while I still remembered them.

Almost every household activity in these villages is bounded by some sort of custom. During bread-making, for instance, the dough and the flour-sieve must be protected from starlight, and before the bread is put into the oven, salt is strewn over the fire as a protection against malignant powers which might cause the baking to fail. The water with which the women wash out the baking trough is at once used to wash their own faces; for this is considered an aid to beauty.

The simple act of washing also has a particular ritual of its own. Soap is never handed directly by one person to another for fear of its washing away friendship between them. Wherever we stayed the soap was always placed on a window-sill beside the front door, although our hosts themselves usually poured the water over our hands while we washed.

Many of the customs are simply a question of peasant etiquette. Bread is always laid on the table with the top crust facing the guest, who would know that he was unwanted if the bread were placed before him upside-down. But then he could easily retaliate, by folding his napkin neatly on leaving the table; a neatly folded napkin is considered an insult to the host. Even the table cloth is never folded after a meal; the housewife simply gathers it up at the corners, so that the crumbs do not spill.

Some superstitions are exploited as a good excuse for not working: a woman will refuse to sweep the floor on a feast-day, not on religious grounds, but because she would thereby fill the house with malignant spirits. Similarly, a man who forgets an essential tool of his trade when he goes out to work will not return to fetch it—that would bring bad luck. And unlike the notoriously forgetful plumbers in England, he will not send his mate back to fetch it either.

There are other superstitious beliefs in Crete that are reminiscent of our own: broken mirrors for bad luck, for instance. Putting on a piece of clothing inside out also has a special significance in both countries; but whereas people in England consider this a good omen, in Crete it is construed as evil. Again, Cretans, like us, regard Friday as an unlucky day, but to them Tuesday is equally unlucky; moreover, on Wednesday no baking should be done, nor should vegetables such as beans be sown, for these would then never soften in cooking. On any of these days a man who wants to get on in life should avoid cutting his finger-nails; and if he has been a good man during his lifetime he can prove it on his death, by dying on a Saturday or Sunday, the two most propitious days of all.

Birth and death naturally provide numerous examples of peasant superstitions, some of which are often disguised in the form of religious ceremonial; the sacred period of forty days is always in evidence. During the forty days preceding Easter the Gates of Paradise remain open; that is the best time to enter them. During the forty days that follow the birth of a child, its mother should not visit her neighbours; if she does, her recent pregnancy will turn their wine into vinegar or cause some equally bleak catastrophe. For forty days after a man's death, his spirit still visits his old haunts on earth; he is still half-attached to his corporeal part and so, while his body is laid out for burial, a wax cross is put inside the mouth to prevent the Devil from entering it and turning the dead man into a vampire.

Most of these customs, of course, are not universally preserved; nor does everyone subscribe to the beliefs. Yet I found that, among the older generation at least, disbelief in the existence, say, of vampires seemed to be based not so much on a certain knowledge that such creatures have never existed as on the assumption that they have become extinct through the greater efficacy of modern exorcism.

The Cretan vampire, the *katakhanas*, was endowed by popular superstition with the ability to visit a wife in her husband's absence, and to enjoy with her what was normally the husband's privilege. It is said that a virgin once attributed to such a visit her otherwise inexplicable pregnancy; and her parents believed her. But I doubt if any Cretan would nowadays be taken in by that sort of easy explanation.

Of all the theories propounded concerning the origin of the Sphakians, the one that I like best is the improbable shot-in-the-dark of Hakkim Ismail Pasha. This gentleman, who rose to be Governor of Crete in 1861, was a Greek by birth. Captured at the age of twelve on the island of Chios, he became a Turkish subject and subsequently the favourite of the Sultan, who sent him to be educated in Europe at the expense of the Sublime Porte. The extent of his ethnological studies may be judged from a pronouncement which he made in all seriousness. The Sphakians, he declared, were descended from those Saracens who had invaded Crete in the ninth century; proof of this was the derivation of their name—from Sfax, in the town of Tunisia.

Nonsense, of course.[3] But at least obvious nonsense, and more entertaining than many a contribution from more learned sources. The list of alleged Sphakian connections reads like an incantation: Eteocretans, Kydonians, Kouretes, Corybantians, Pelasgians, Achaeans—not to mention our old friend, the Dorians. But who, when it comes down to brass tacks, are all these people? "Lost" tribes, every one of them, but with names which provide convenient tags for the theorist with a card-index mind. This sort of classifica-

3. Nevertheless the nonsense was believed so implicitly that Hakkim's successor, Reouph, took action on it; in 1870 he imported 300 toughs from Benghazi to form a human stud farm in the hope of creating a new race to rival the Sphakians!

tion looks neat enough on paper; to a layman like myself it is valueless. Until I can identify the dead man behind whose mask the living Sphakian lies concealed, I shall still be unable to trace what relationship there is between the two.

Not that I find this inability a burden; I am quite content simply to be aware of the basic difference that clearly exists between the inhabitants of Sphakia and those of the other Cretan provinces.

Their wild independence has been noted by every foreign traveller who has come into contact with them. On Venetian maps their province is marked "*Sfachiotti popoli bellicosi*"; and their reputation was such that in 1575 Foscarini, the General Proveditor, granted them a general amnesty in order to keep on good terms. For some time Sphakia became the most peaceful region in the island; Foscarini tried to exploit his success with these "warlike people" by sending Venetian instructors to train them in the use of the harquebus, but the Sphakians preferred to rely, as they had always done, on bows and arrows.

At the beginning of the Turkish occupation the Vizier followed the Venetian example and adopted a policy of appeasement; by granting the Sphakians special privileges, he hoped to prevent them forming an alliance with the *khainides* who were still under Venetian protection. This policy was successful until the fall of Grabousa and Souda, when the nucleus of the resistance movement was automatically transferred from those two coastal fortresses to the mountains. It was not until 1769 that the Sphakians once more emerged, after almost two centuries of comparative peace, as leaders of revolution. They have maintained that reputation ever since.

Their distinctive appearance, too, has provoked a comment from almost every foreign observer. "They are of great stature" wrote Buondelmonte in his description of the fifteenth-century shepherds, "incredibly active in their mountains, and bold in war. They attain the age of a hundred without any infirmities; instead of wine they drink almost always milk."

Foscarini also praised "their purity, bravery and beauty." Captain Spratt went even further and claimed that "the blood of the Sphakians is undoubtedly the purest of all the Cretan race, its purity having been preserved by their mountain location and jealous clanship, that has maintained amongst them exclusive habits and manners and a dialect, some of the peculiarities of which may have descended from the days of Minos." Even Sieber, who was apparently not easy to please, grudgingly admitted that "one cannot help admiring them in spite of their rough ways." His scientific eye also noted the absence of disease among them: "no leprosy, but only people disabled in local feuds."

All these remarks, of course, applied in particular to the Sphakians of the mountain villages. While we remained on the coast, Daphne and I had no chance of confirming them by personal observation for, apart from the labourers on the road, there was scarcely anyone living in the village of Sphakia itself. Even the fishermen seemed to have deserted these shores; during our stay there we saw no more than one at work—an elderly one-armed buccaneer in a wide straw hat—and his only catch in three days was a solitary gigantic lobster. As for the shepherds, they had vanished altogether, driven by that scorching wind to seek their summer pastures several weeks in advance.

Daphne and I decided to follow their example.

13

ANOPOLIS

THE CLIFF PATH which we took, westwards from Sphakia, winds inland after a few hundred yards so as to circumvent the first of the many gorges which furrow the coastal plateau as far as Souyia. Soon the sea dropped out of sight, its proximity still proclaimed by the abundance of wild thyme, a plant which is supposed to flourish only in maritime regions.

The stony dreariness of the ravine was relieved by other plants which lined our path: camomile which, could the rocks here have been lawns, would have looked like daisies; white anemonies, too, already past their prime, and sage-grey *phaskomilia* heavy with crisp green galls, which left an acid tang of pear-drops on our tongues as we munched them to extract their juice. Cistus, like the device on a flowery coat-of-arms, canopied the slope with a repeated heraldic design—merely a decorative shrub these days, although once of commercial value: its aromatic gum used to be highly prized by the Arabs as an ingredient in the manufacture of incense. According to Herodotus, this product was collected by combing the beards of the billy-goats which browsed on the plant. There were no goats to be seen here now.

No humans either: nothing but *maquis* and rock for mile after mile of this twisted, steep, narrow cleft aptly named the Dizzy Gorge. It was a revelation to emerge at its furthest end, in a sudden blaze of noon, on to the fertile upland plain of Anopolis.

The plateau of Askyphou might have been equally impressive before the motor-road through it was built; for it is just as large and mountain-locked as this. But its approach by bus eliminated any element of surprise which I might otherwise have felt at the sight of it. Anopolis, which can only be reached after a stiff climb on foot, was consequently far more rewarding; more rewarding even than the Omalo, which affords little comfort apart from a flat surface on which to rest a pair of tired feet.

Anopolis provided something on which to feast the eyes as well: an oasis balanced aloft in a bone-coloured desert of limestone; green acres of wheat well advanced and almost waist-high; vineyards and wells; fruit trees—mulberry, pear and apricot—and, among the first group of houses we saw, a blue and white coffee-shop with chairs and tables outside it beneath an awning of vine-covered trellis. Mercifully this was not a mirage.

Surprise then followed surprise. In the first place, our arrival caused not the slightest disturbance among the group of bearded giants sitting there in black shirts, black boots and black breeches; after a friendly nod and a word of greeting they went on with their conversation without another glance in our direction; and the owner who brought us our *tsikoudia* seemed to take us completely for granted. Then the sergeant strolled over from the police-station next door; I thought he was going to ask us to show him our papers— quite a normal demand to make of a stranger—instead, he asked us to have something to eat. A table was laid outside in the sun and presently food was produced: a bowl of fried eggs, a dozen at least, and a platter of fried potatoes.

The explanation did not come until after the meal, when the sergeant admitted that he had known me before, in Selino, during the occupation; he was from one of the villages near Koustoyerako and had been a member of the Paterakis gang. But this explained only his own hospitable behaviour, not the surprisingly worldly attitude of the others. I asked him how he accounted for that.

"You know what the Sphakians are like," he replied. "Of course they're surprised to see two strangers turning up off the beaten track like this—who isn't? Especially when one of them's a woman. They've probably never seen a foreign woman before in their lives, but they're too proud to admit it! You say you're writing a book— they may believe you, they may not. You may be fooling them, you see; and they'd rather die than be made to look foolish. So they don't commit themselves either way!"

There was something in what he said. Proud the Sphakians certainly are, but I was glad their pride took this particular form; an attitude of indifference, however simulated, was preferable to the open disbelief which I had sometimes encountered. Here, in a village which I had never before visited, my presence seemed to cause less distrust than in some of my old haunts where the people, who had remembered me as an officer with apparently unlimited funds, now saw me return as a civilian whose purse was quite clearly restricted—a highly suspicious transformation! But in Anopolis, where I was known only by hearsay, I was taken at my present face value, ostensibly anyway. And whether my reasons for coming here were believed or not, Daphne and I were at once invited to have a look round the village.

The mayor, a young man wearing sandals and a cavalry moustache, volunteered to be our guide. He was at once joined by the two schoolmasters—village intellectuals, plainly, for both were clean-shaven. At the last moment, the youngest of the three priests, in pale grey robes instead of black, announced that he, too, would accompany us. With this escort, singularly un-Sphakian in appearance, we set off on our conducted tour.

"Where to first?" I was asked.

There was no doubt in my mind: I answered without hesitation: "To the house of Daskaloyiannis."

The first and greatest hero of Turkish-occupied Crete would have remained unknown forever but for the ballad which celebrates his martyrdom. *The Song of Daskaloyiannis* was written sixteen years after his death, in 1786. It is not a great work; in fact there is so little literary merit in the whole of its thousand-odd lines that it was overlooked even by such enthusiastically philhellene scholars as Passow and Fauriel, who introduced the klephtic compositions of the mainland to the Western public during the first half of the nineteenth century, at the time of the Greek National Revival. *The Song of Daskaloyiannis* was not published until 1880. But it is in the true tradition of Greek folk-poetry; the epilogue states how it came to be written.

An illiterate Sphakian cheese-maker, "Uncle Pantzelio," was the author. He must have known Daskaloyiannis personally; and the verses which he made up to while away the long hours in his remote hut in the mountains were without doubt based on the true facts as he remembered them. He could not record them himself, however, since he did not know how to write, so day by day he dictated them as they came into his head to a scribe, whose identity is disclosed at the end of the narrative: "Anagnostes, the son of the priest Siphis Skordylis."

Uncle Pantzelio was a typical *rhimadoros*, one of those uneducated natural rhymsters which the provinces of Greece seem capable of producing in thousands. Anagnostes, sitting under a pine tree with a pen in his hand, describes how the old man's eyes streamed with tears as he dictated the verses; how his speech failed him at times and how he fell into a bleak reverie at the recollection of his hero's fate. But he had what his scribe refers to as "the greatest of God's gifts," a faultless memory. In his own language, then, the language of the illiterate shepherd, old Pantzelio's verses were preserved and handed down, unedited, to posterity. So if the meter is sometimes shaky, if the verses fall flat, the reader is asked to remember that it was an old cheese-maker who composed them. "They were not," his scribe hastens to add—with rather undue emphasis, I feel—"they were certainly not composed by me." But he need not have been so ashamed of them; old Pantzelio's doggerel is of paramount importance, if not as verse, then at least as a unique slice of history.

By the middle of the eighteenth century the hero of *The Song*, a native of Anopolis, had come to be acknowledged as the leading citizen of the whole of Sphakia province. He was rich and respected, the owner of a prosperous fleet of trading schooners; he had the distinction of being the only man in Crete who wore European clothes; he spoke four foreign languages and was considered so learned that he earned the name of Daskaloyiannis, which can be literally translated "John the Teacher."[1]

1. This name does not, of course, imply that its owner was a schoolmaster; it is simply a title of respect, for which I find it difficult to find an English equivalent. "Master John" is one suggestion. Professor Dawkins has furnished another: "John the Clerk." I shall simply avoid the issue by keeping to the Greek. Daskaloyiannis, as I shall call him, then, had yet another *paratzougli*, or nickname: that of "Tselepes"—but rather than add to the confusion, let us consider him as having dropped it quite early in life.

His real name was Yiannis Vlachos. A patient genealogist would probably be able to trace his relationship to at least half a dozen of the most famous families in Sphakia; for his own family, following the recognised Cretan practice, had changed their identity several times through the centuries. In Venetian times, for instance, they had been known as Papadopoulos, which was a branch of the Kallergis family and also of the Kandanoleon; under the Turks they were called Manousellis; which, for all we know they may well have adopted after relinquishing Mousouros, the name that disappears so mysteriously early from every official document. Daskaloyiannis, then, was a Sphakian aristocrat as well as being an influential businessman; by birth and upbringing he was well equipped to deal with men of importance on equal terms.

It was on one of his regular professional visits to the Black Sea that he first came into contact with Orloff, emissary of the Russian Empress Catherine the Great. The meeting took place in Odessa, just after Russia's declaration of war on Turkey. Orloff's mission was twofold: to incite the nations under Turkish rule to rise in arms against the Sublime Porte; and to support the consequent rebellion from the sea. In Daskaloyiannis he found an enthusiastic collaborator.

Units of the Russian fleet were transferred to Trieste, where a second meeting took place between Orloff and his new Cretan ally; detailed plans for the operation were discussed, and a final agreement reached. Daskaloyiannis was to organise a Cretan uprising to synchronise with the proposed rebellion in the Peloponnese; at the same time Orloff would sail with his navy into Greek waters.

Daskaloyiannis at once sent a cargo of arms at his own expense to Crete, went himself to confer with the local leaders in the Peloponnese, then sailed home with the tidings of impending liberation. His plans were not universally welcomed in Anopolis; his own cousin, the village priest, was fearful of the consequences of probable failure. But Daskaloyiannis persisted, confident in Orloff's promises; he calmed every fear, according to Pantzelio's *Song*, with the words "I'm bringing Moscow here." At a general meeting held in Sphakia he was unanimously elected to lead the revolt; arms were distributed, and a special raiding force formed—the famous "Night Fighters," who were later to be christened by the Turks "*Saitan Takimi,*" in English "Sons of the Devil."

In the early spring of 1770 a report was received from the mainland: the Russian fleet was off the coast of the Peloponnese, the re-

bellion was about to be launched. On the 25th of March,[2] the day
on which the Feast of the Annunciation is celebrated, the standard
of revolt was raised in Crete. A few days later, on Easter Sunday,
Daskaloyiannis concentrated his troops in Krapi, the little plain
north of Askyphou just off the modern main road; then moved
them down to a temporary camp on Malaxa Ridge. By this ma-
neuver he hoped to contain the Turkish forces which had taken
refuge within the walls of Canea—an easy target for any Russian warship.

But no warship appeared; Daskaloyiannis was compelled to withdraw back to Krapi, there to await the inevitable Turkish counter-
attack. A few days later the Moslem troops broke out, advancing
behind a screen of 4,000 Christian hostages. With his small force of
800 irregulars Daskaloyiannis succeeded for two days in withstand-
ing the onslaught of the organised Turkish army 25,000 strong; then
withdrew once more to prepared positions in the Askyphou pass.

Every dreary detail of the ensuing campaign is related in Pantzelio's verses: the arrival of the Turkish forces from Rethymnon, the
heroic resistance of the rebels, the fall of Kallikrati on the 26th of
April, and the subsequent fall of every other village on the route
to the Sphakian coast. Defeated by the Turkish pincer movement,
Daskaloyiannis gave orders for all women and children to be evacuated from Loutro, the small port below Anopolis. But the Turkish
advance was unexpectedly rapid; and the helpless non-combatants
were surprised during the steep descent by a Moslem fighting patrol.
The massacre that then took place on the cliff path was the turning-
point of the whole rebellion.

Most of the women and children who were not slaughtered were
taken prisoner. Daskaloyiannis's personal losses in this action were
particularly heavy: his wife was wounded, his two eldest daughters
were captured, and so was his brother Nicholas. It was at this psychological moment that the Turks called on him by name to surrender. He refused. And the rout continued.

The whole of Sphakia was now in Turkish hands as far as the Aradaina Gorge, the rebels' last line of defence. The gorge might have
been held indefinitely since the only path across it was a closely-

---

2. A favourite date for rebellion, it seems. It was on the same day, 51 years later,
that the War of Independence was declared in the Peloponnesian village of Ka-
lavryta.

Goats waiting to be milked in a mountain pen

ABOVE: *The last of the goats in the pen, still waiting*
BELOW: *The author with police-escort on the Omalo*

guarded Sphakian secret, guarded now as well by Sphakian troops;
yet somehow the Turks discovered it—the inevitable Ephialtes was
at work again—and at once forced their way across.

A second Turkish demand for Daskaloyiannis to surrender was
accompanied by a letter from his captive brother Nicholas, who
urged him in the strongest possible terms to give himself up and
thereby save the lives of the many hostages. This letter, however,
was signed with three capital M's: a private code indicating that
the Pasha's promises were false and that therefore no action should
be taken. But Daskaloyiannis's position was already hopeless. He
now had nothing to lose but his own life; by sacrificing it, he might
still be able—despite his brother's warning—to save the lives of his
friends and relations. To the amazement of the Turks, he walked
into their camp and announced:

"I surrender myself to the Vizier."

At first he was treated as an honoured prisoner and cross-ques-
tioned about his relations with the Russians. He was then asked to
sign a truce, which the Turks had drawn up on the following terms:[3]

1. A capital tax to be levied on the insurgents.
2. All rebel arms to be surrendered forthwith.
3. Any individual found guilty of breaking the truce to be given
   up to the Turkish authorities.
4. All contact with foreign elements hostile to Turkey and Islam
   to be discontinued.
5. Any foreign agent discovered on Cretan soil to be handed
   over to the authorities in Herakleion.
6. Any such agent avoiding arrest to be excluded at least from
   Sphakian territory.
7. Supplies of food and water to pirate ships to be discontinued.
8. All Sphakians to be tried henceforth in accordance with
   Turkish law.
9. Rebuilding of damaged churches to be forbidden.
10. Building of new churches to be forbidden.
11. A tithe of all Sphakian crops and other agricultural produce
    to be paid to the Turkish authorities.

3. These are not mentioned in *The Song*, but appear in a recently discovered Turkish archive, which is, as far as I know, the only historical document in existence
relating to the Daskaloyiannis Rebellion.

12. All Sphakians to wear normal *rayah*[4] clothing.
13. No houses of more than one storey to be built.
14. No church bell to be rung.
15. All Turkish prisoners to be set free at once.

Had he agreed to these terms, Daskaloyiannis might have managed at least to postpone his own execution, but he was too proud to consent to such unconditional surrender—why, it is hard to tell; the surrender, after all, was already an accomplished fact. Anyway, he refused to sign the document—and thereby signed his death warrant instead. A few days later he was led in chains to the main square in Herakleion, tied to a four-post scaffolding which had been erected under a plane-tree, and there flayed alive.

It was a noble death; and pointless. His quixotic gesture in giving himself up in fact was defeated by his stubborn refusal to surrender in theory. By sacrificing his own life, he saved the life of no one else and secured the release of not a single prisoner; of the 82 rebels captured by the Turks, most were to die miserably in their dungeons within the next three years.

But his two daughters, at least, were spared. For many years after their father's death their fate remained unknown and became, in the absence of all historical record, largely a matter of individual conjecture. Changebug, for instance, had a theory that they both escaped and took refuge in Asi Gonia with a man called Markos, who subsequently married one of them and assumed the name of Daskalomarkos, a name which exists in the village to this day. More reliable authorities claim that one of the girls, Maria, was given in marriage to a Turkish bey, by whom she was well treated. She was not even forced to change her religion and, after her husband's death, became a nun on the island of Tenos.

What became of her sister, Anthousa, remained a mystery right up to the present century; established historians, like Papadopetrakis and Psilakis, have had to admit their inability to trace her or any of her children (she is believed to have been married at the time of her capture). It was not until the end of 1939 that a certain Mr. Zondianos of Herakleion came forward with the claim that he was

---

4. The ordinary everyday clothes of the Christian Cretan. This particular clause was presumably inserted for personal reasons to put an end to Daskaloyiannis's practice of wearing a European suit.

one of Anthousa's descendants; according to him, she was married to a cobbler by the name of Pakhynakis and was safely returned to her husband on condition that she stayed in Herakleion and never again set foot in the province of Sphakia.

This information is not of vital interest, I admit, but it does serve to show how many gaps there are in Cretan history which still remain to be filled. Little, for instance, is known about the conditions in Sphakia immediately after the suppression of the Daskaloyiannis rebellion. Many of the inhabitants must have fled from the province, since the population of Anopolis and that of Sphakia village were both reduced to a fraction of their previous total; it is almost certain that a large proportion of them found refuge among friends in Odessa. It was in that town, years later, that the secret patriotic organization known as "The Society of Friends" set up its headquarters to prepare, in the safety of neutral territory, for the Greek general insurrection of 1821. Among the most influential of the Society's members were some of the refugees of the Daskaloyiannis *débâcle*, men who had since enriched themselves on commerce, whose wealth, then, was due indirectly to the outcome of a rebellion that had failed. It was only poetic justice that they should now contribute that money to a rebellion which was destined to succeed.

The remains of the Daskaloyiannis house were unimpressive. Of the original building, only the back wall was still standing; the rest had been reconstructed in 1926. Its present occupants invited us inside and showed us with pride the upstairs room, the largest that I had seen in any Cretan village. But this unusual space had not been exploited; the place looked as bare as an empty barn. I was disappointed. I had expected something more than this; though exactly what, I could not specify.

My spirits lifted once more as we climbed to the top of the hill which separates Anopolis from the coast. The steep slope is chequered with the relics of an ancient town; the foundations of what must once have been the vaulted homes of a thriving community serve now only as obstacles across the path we took. The elements in Crete reduce an abandoned building to ruin within a few years but, having reduced it, preserve it in that state for centuries; it is difficult to distinguish here between a genuine antiquity and the rubble of a much later date. So now I was unable to tell whether the stones belonged to a pre-Christian settlement or to the Anopolis which was destroyed during the Kallergis rebellion of 1365. It was at times like this that I most regretted the abysmal gap in my knowledge of archaeology.

On the summit of the natural acropolis we came to an isolated chapel separated only by a few yards from the shell of a small fort, part of the long line of coastal defences erected by the Turks after the 1866 insurrection. Catherine, the saint to which this little church is dedicated, is credited with more than the recognized quota of supernatural power; if it had not been for her, the chapel would have been disfigured or engulfed. For the Turks had planned to build their fort right on top of it; but each time that they tried to put a stone in place, the saint at once dislodged it. In revenge, one of the builders decided to defile this Christian shrine in the approved Moslem manner. He succeeded, but only up to a certain point, and at the cost of his own life: it was his entrails that fell out on to the floor, not his excreta.

From this vantage point the whole plain was visible, cupped in the curling palm of the foothills, with the white shoulders of Mount Theodore hunched above it over six thousand feet further up. In the afternoon light the bright green of field, the dark red of earth, the blue of painted woodwork were colours that seemed to have occurred almost inadvertently: accidental dots and patches in a monochromatic landscape. But a backward glance substituted for this sunny pastoral scene a dizzy view of sea and cliff.

Loutro lay so much further below us, so unexpectedly further than Anopolis, that at first sight the line of houses curving round the bay appeared to be constructed on a different scale, diminished several degrees beyond the usual effect of distance. It seemed impossible that the little promontory directly at our feet should be in fact so far away: no visual measuring-rod normally in use on the flat can be adapted to deal with such a vast vertical gap.

I was at once enchanted by Loutro, and not only because of its Lilliputian appearance. From where we stood it looked like a model fishing-village—model in both senses of the word: a miniature reproduction and a perfect design. Had I been able to alter its shape or plan—and from here I felt that I had only had to bend down a little for those toy buildings to fall within my grasp—I would not have shifted a single feature. A Turkish fort on the headland stood sentinel over the bays on either side, in the nearest of which the

port lay otherwise unprotected, with the houses prodigally dispersed
along the beach instead of being concentrated into an undignified
commercial block, as at Palaeochora, or huddled together as though
for mutual defence against an imminent attack from the sea. The
sense of danger implicit in the lay-out and architecture of most Cretan villages was absent in Loutro; even the solitary palm-tree there
conveyed an impression of security and peace.

By comparison, Anopolis appeared almost forbidding as we descended again into the inland bowl. Our rucksack had been left in
the coffee-shop, so we returned there to collect it and to spend the
remaining hour of daylight drinking with the shepherds who had
come in from the pasture-land nearby. Once more I was amazed by
our reception. I had expected these bearded giants to be bores, with
conversation limited to conventional subjects such as the respective
merits of different makes of fire-arms, the state of the crops, the
conditions of the flocks and, inevitably, their own individual prow-
ess during the war. This part of Sphakia, fortunately, had been relatively unaffected by the occupation; during the whole evening the
Germans were not mentioned once.

Darkness fell, but Daphne and I still did not know where we
were to spend the night; and as uninvited strangers to the village,
we could not very well ask. Sleeping arrangements in Crete, where a
traveller normally has no luggage, are left to the last moment; there
is no business of unpacking or being shown to the guest-room; food
is considered a more important factor than a bed. It was the mayor
who finally invited us to dinner and hinted, by taking our rucksack
with him, that we should also be staying in his house.

So far we had seen no sign of the lawlessness with which the
Sphakians are romantically credited; their reputation for wildness
seemed to be based on their appearance alone. Those that we had
met behaved far less riotously than, say, the people of Selino; their
conversation was more civilised than the banal chatter of Canea
society; their living conditions were much less primitive than those
to be found in many of the main-road villages. The mayor, I admit,
might not have been truly representative of his mountain community, and it was from his household that I drew my conclusions; but
even after making the necessary allowances for any superiority that
there might be in his personal manner of life and thought, I could
still find no cause for regarding the Sphakians in general as more
backward than the rest of their compatriots.

Dinner was prepared for us in a room unwittingly converted into a bower by a ceiling of mulberry leaves. These were slung on planks from the roof, to house and feed a colony of silkworms; cocoons, distaffs and an enormous wooden loom were further evidence of the household industry. A pleasant susurration accompanied the meal, which was served by the mayor's sister, a pretty young widow. In spite of her brother's apparently advanced ideas, she was not allowed to sit down with us. With her face half-concealed by a black kerchief, she hovered in the background attending to our needs; when our glasses were empty it was she who refilled them on her brother's orders, although the wine-jar stood within easy reach at his elbow. His peremptory commands were the only indication that he still recognized the peasant custom of exercising masculine authority in the house.

Normally these social duties would have been undertaken by his father, as senior member of the family; but the old gentleman asked us to excuse him. He could not eat with us, he explained, since this was the period of the Lenten fast; and as a priest, he added with a roguish grin, he at least had to set a good example. So while we ate, he talked.

Father Nicholas was an entertaining talker and, like every other priest in Crete, untainted by sanctimoniousness. On entering the house he had discarded his *rasso*, to reveal the homely black sweater and Turkish trousers which he was wearing underneath; since he also affected a rakish velvet fez in preference to the normal ecclesiastical headgear, he now looked more like a pagan prophet as he sat there envying our food and drink. With his bright pink face and snowy beard, he reminded me of the late Bernard Shaw; but Father Nicholas was no vegetarian.

"Come, now, you wouldn't want me to starve, would you?" he replied, when I asked him if he had ever eaten stolen meat.

My question was not altogether impertinent; we had just been discussing sheep-thieving, the present attempts to prevent it and the measures taken against it in the past. Suspect thieves in this district, I had been told, always confessed their crime when confronted with the icon of the Archangel Michael in the Byzantine church of Aradaina. I was anxious to see this church which, besides its thaumaturgic property, was of architectural interest as well. "Wonderful wall-paintings there," the mayor assured us. Aradaina was only a few miles away: Daphne and I decided to walk over there in the morning, visit the church and the famous gorge beneath it and then, perhaps, move on to Ayios Ioannis, the most remote village in Crete. With our host's assistance we began to map out an itinerary for the next three days.

We might have kept to it if the mayor had not casually mentioned another church, that of Saint Paul, on the beach between Loutro and Ayia Roumeli. "A lonely chapel half-buried in the sand" was how he described it; and he made it sound so pathetic and precious, so helpless against its gradual interment—for the sand, it appeared was encroaching daily—that it was almost with a feeling of desperate urgency that we immediately altered our route. The Archangel Michael could wait; we would have to hurry if we wanted to see Saint Paul.

There was, I admit, a subsidiary motive behind our apparently hasty change of plan; the chapel in itself was not the only attraction. The mayor had told us that the best way to reach it would be to go through Loutro; and Loutro had been haunting my imagination ever since I had first caught sight of it. That little port had appealed to me so strongly that I envisaged it, however unreasonably, as a haven of exceptional significance: a sort of maritime Shangri-la. Here was an immediate chance to test the accuracy of my conception.

I was slightly put out to hear that there was a telephone line to it—that prosaic instrument did not fit into the picture—but I managed to stifle my romantic disappointment. The mayor rang up and arranged for a fisherman there to put his motor-boat at our disposal for a day, to enable us to reach Saint Paul's in comfort by sea and so avoid the precipitous coastal path.

This last attention was typical of our host's worldly thoughtfulness—an additional crowning gesture of hospitality. When I thanked him for it when we said good-bye in the morning, he replied:

"Words are superfluous; the only way you can thank us is by coming to stay with us again."

14

LOUTRO

I MAY AS WELL say at once the Loutro was all that I had hoped and expected. The promise which it held began to be fulfilled even before we reached it. At each bend of the path on our two-thousand-foot descent, a new feature, hitherto blurred by distance, was brought into proper focus—an arch over a front door, the reflection of a rowing-boat in deep water, the pattern of nets on white rock, black rock imbedded in earth the colour of paprika—these and a dozen other visual delights were gradually welded into position, fixed as component parts of the general view, from which, as the distance between us decreased, they melted again one after another, to reappear finally, when we were down on the shore, as a succession of individual close-ups.

The mayor of Anopolis had told us to ask for Andreas Athitakis. We found his house, which was also the village coffee-shop, halfway along the arc of the bay. Our arrival had been notified, and our approach observed: a glass of *tsikoudia* was thrust into our hands as soon as we entered, and we drank to the chorus "It is well you have come."

Most of the villagers seemed to have taken refuge here from the midday sun. The beach had been deserted; in this cool, vaulted room every chair and bench was packed. One of the drinkers was a young man whom we already knew. George, the Sphakia postman, easily distinguished in the crowd of trouser-wearing beach-dwellers by his breeches and mountaineer's boots. His weekly round of the neighbouring villages was calculated to last three days. He always managed to get through it in two; the spare day, and the living allowance for it, would be spent in Andreas's coffee-shop. He had been here since six o'clock in the morning; his blue eyes were already happily glazed; he made an exaggerated ceremony of introducing us to our host.

Andreas would have looked like a buccaneer if it had not been for his eccentric headgear; instead of the usual black *sariki*, he wore a carefully tied pink dishcloth—a sort of piccaninny bonnet, in effect, and more in keeping with a printed cotton smock than with the grey fisherman's jersey which covered his barrel-shaped chest. It gave his weather-tanned face an infantile expression, which made wrinkles and moustache scarcely noticeable; the gruffness of his voice, too, was mitigated by his childishly shy manner of speech.

"No boat, I'm afraid," he told us. "Engine's broken. But there's no hurry, is there? Stay as long as you like. Here, I'll get you something to eat."

He returned a little later with plates of fried eggs, some fish and two glasses of wine—but not the small thimbles that are normally used for a quick succession of short drinks; these were *coupas*, the traditional Sphakian measure, each of over half a pint. Daphne and I started to sip, but the postman shouted:

"None of that! Bottoms up! You've got to have a round with me!"

We had that round, then several more. The visit to the church in the sands began to appear less urgent. "You can go there tomorrow," the postman assured us, "I'll come with you. Andreas's engine won't be ready for days; it's got to be repaired in Palaeochora. But there's a caique here that'll take you, just in from Sphakia. I'll have a word with the skipper."

He went out to make the arrangements. A quarter of an hour later he was back. "All fixed," he cheerfully announced, "we start off at six in the morning. Now let's have another drink; then I'll show you the sights of Loutro."

There is not much to see on the little peninsula apart from the ruins of Phoenice, "which is an haven of Crete, and lieth towards the south-west and north-west"; it was here that Saint Paul landed after barely escaping shipwreck during one of his many propaganda tours. And when he did land he barely escaped with his life; for he was looked upon as a busy-body and promptly beaten up. That, at least, is what they say in Loutro today: and I can well believe it. The preaching of the apostle could certainly not have endeared him to such happy-go-lucky pagans.

We wandered listlessly over the ancient terraces, occasionally stubbing our toes on the remains of a Roman wall or early Christian tomb, unable to work up much enthusiasm over all these scattered stones. In the hot sun, our thirst for culture was very soon quenched, our physical thirst correspondingly quickened. After a superficial study of the Turkish fort—the same stones again, but on a vertical plane—we found ourselves retracing our steps.

Siesta-time. The coffee-shop was almost empty; Andreas was asleep upstairs; his wife was now in charge. Despoina Athitakis was obviously accustomed to such responsibility; her husband's fishing expeditions, and the odd hours which he was consequently forced to keep, had made her more independent than the average peasant housewife; she was an efficient partner rather than a connubial drudge. In fact, with her determined air and complete lack of shyness, she looked the more capable of the pair.

But she had once been completely under her husband's thumb, more so than most young women. When we came to know her better, she told us the story of her marriage. She had been a "stolen bride." She had known Andreas only by sight when he, quite literally, swept her off her feet. With a gang of his friends he had abducted her one day as she was coming down the path from Anopolis, and taken her off to a hide-out high up on the slopes of Mount Theodore. There she had remained for sixty-six days while her relations combed the countryside for her. One of the search-parties had once come within ear-shot of the cave in which she lay confined.

"Did you still want to escape?" I asked her.

"Of course, I was frightened."

"Then why didn't you shout?"

"You don't shout when you've got a pistol held to your breast!"

It was hard to imagine Andreas as a romantic desperado, or this shrewd middle-aged woman as a damsel in distress; even harder to envisage a successful outcome to such an adventure. Marriages by capture still occur occasionally in Crete, but they almost always end in disaster; either someone involved gets killed and the death culminates in a family-feud, or else the girl becomes forcibly reconciled to her fate—the discomfort of imprisonment in the mountains is calculated to break down anyone's resistance—and marries, of necessity, against her will. Even then her troubles are not over; she has

only avoided death at the hands of her abductor; there is still the risk
of her being killed by one of her male relations if her acceptance is
considered adulterous or harmful to family honour.

Despoina's relations, fortunately, had not resorted to such extreme
measures. They had simply disowned her; thereby showing a stubborn lack of foresight, for her marriage had proved a success. "But
even I never thought it would," she admitted, "so I don't altogether
blame them."

Later that afternoon Father Nicholas came down from Anopolis.
There was no resident priest in Loutro, so the village took advantage
of this visit; the whole population began to prepare for church—the
whole female population, that is. Daphne was dragged off to the service with the rest of the women; I joined the men in the house next
door, where a basket of sea-urchins had just been brought in to serve
as *mezes* for the evening *tsikoudia*.

Andreas, meanwhile, had rowed out again to lay down his nets for
the night. He seemed to be the only person here who did any work
at all. Apart from fishing, there was no industry in Loutro: nothing could grow from the rocky soil which, at this season, provided
not even enough scrub to feed a small flock of goats. The men who
were shepherds had left; those that remained, then, were presumably
fishermen. Yet none of them, except Andreas, ever put to sea. In
this respect they resembled the inhabitants of Souyia. But their leisure was very different from the neurotic indolence of those Selino
mountaineers who had migrated to the coast to wait for a main road
that never reached them. In Loutro no one expected a road; no one
wanted one. Perhaps the men here were lacking in ambition, idle and
effete; I found their company a refreshing change from the usual
Cretan atmosphere of swaggering virility.

A drink with them was not the exhausting challenge that it had
sometimes been elsewhere. There was no ceremonial about it, no
continuous clinking of glasses, no conventional toast; there was not
even any singing. My appreciation of the absence of such *panegyric*
trappings came as a slight shock to me; it made me realise that the
novelty of Crete was beginning to wear off. Perhaps I had been here
too long at one stretch. Whatever the reason, the fact remained: I
was enjoying Loutro simply because it was untypical, if not of the
whole of Crete, then certainly of the White Mountain district. This

was a sobering thought. I fought against it and, with the postman's help, defeated it. By dinner-time we were both splendidly drunk.

We reeled back to the coffee-shop, where Despoina and Daphne had been waiting for us for over an hour. The two Athitakis daughters were also there: Evangelia, a silent fair-haired girl of eighteen, and Ioanna, an ash-blonde imp of five. Seeing them, I realised how Despoina herself must have appeared when young. I imagined that at Evangelia's age she, too, had had that aloof, purposeful expression, the attractively sly half-smile that was now on her elder daughter's lips; and as a child she had probably behaved with the same intrepid lack of inhibition noticeable in little Ioanna. The contradictory features in her own character—the silent efficiency on the one hand, the brazen worldliness on the other—seemed to have been sorted out and re-grouped between the two daughters, in whom they reposed, as it were, properly filed and catalogued, each in its respective pigeon-hole.

While we ate and drank, Evangelia never said a word; Ioanna was not silent for a minute. She chatted away in an extraordinarily deep, manly voice, swore, giggled and swigged, addressing everyone with her favourite endearment: "My little red mullet." Finally, she burst into song:

You have broken my heart,
My little red mullet . . .

"I'm afraid she's been at the wine again," Despoina apologised. "She's always at it; helps herself from the barrel when no one's looking. And listen to her language; she's picked that up from the men. I can't do a thing with her; she's always fooling about with the men, tries to do what they do, always copying. Sometimes I think she's a little off her head. She's so wild. Do you think there's anything really wrong with her—that voice, I mean?"

Poor Despoina seemed genuinely worried. I assured her that she need have no anxiety: Ioanna, in spite of her voice, was perfectly normal—and perfectly delightful. Maybe she did drink a little too much, but then who was I to talk?

By midnight, when someone shouted through the door that Andreas had just landed with his catch, we had all of us drunk a little too much. Unanimously we decided to go out on to the beach and help with the nets. We were too late; they had already been hauled in by an excited group which, for some reason, had gath-

ered at the water's edge. Ioanna ran on ahead of us and presently we
heard her rapturous screams of obscenity mingling with the general
torrent of abuse.

Even in my tipsy condition I could sense the upsurge of bloodlust
emanating from those people; somewhere in their midst there was a
victim. We soon saw what it was: the fisherman's arch-enemy, a con-
ger. This one, luckily, had not damaged the nets. But it might have
done; and that possibility was sufficient reason for the present hatred
in the air. The crowd cursed and spat at it, kicked it and battered it
with rocks; but even when its head was smashed, the beast still scattered the pebbles round it with frantic sweeping movements of its
tail. I had never before seen anything struggle so desperately against
death. For Ioanna, the evening had been made.

Andreas joined us in a final drink to celebrate the miraculous
preservation of his nets, then we all went to bed. Daphne disappeared upstairs with the women; the postman and I dossed down
on a couple of benches. "We shan't have much sleep in any case," he
said, "we'll have to get up at five o'clock."

"Five o'clock," he repeated after what seemed like a few seconds.
"I'll just go and wake the skipper." As he opened the door I saw
that it was already daylight. I turned over and closed my eyes again;
we were bound to start several hours late. But presently I heard
the cough of a caique engine. I shouted upstairs for Daphne to get
dressed and roused myself into a sitting position. I was putting on
my shoes when the postman came back.

"Everything ready?" I asked.

"Everything; except that the skipper now says he's going to Sphakia. I think I'll go with him. Do you want to come as well?—no, I
thought not. Ah, well . . ."

He said good-bye and left.

I was still too fuddled to ask for an explanation. None had been
offered; presumably none was intended. Daphne came down in time
to see the caique chugging out to sea, in exactly the opposite direction to St. Paul's; our chance of visiting the church in the sands that
day disappeared into the horizontal glare of the sun.

By now the whole house was astir. Despoina appeared, holding
her head like a sick monkey, and produced a large bowl of yoghourt,
the perfect hangover breakfast. But Andreas did not need it; he
cheerfully took another glass of wine before settling down to the job
of sorting out last night's catch. His fish were scattered on sacking

all over the floor. He threaded them through their eyes into conve-
niently portable bundles, which he then hung up for sale; in a short
while the room was decorated, as though for Christmas, with loops
and coils and pendants of shimmering red and silver.

Loutro was a village of early risers. When Daphne and I went out
a little later, groups of people were already assembled round tables
in the sun—among them Father Nicholas, sitting over a coffee. He
greeted me with a wink: "I hear you knock it back a bit. Well, so
do I." In the morning light he looked as if he did: were those red-
rimmed, yellow-glazed eyes of his, I wondered, signs of an interrupted fast? We wandered on, aimlessly, with no fixed destination,
happy that there was no need to hurry. I began to understand, that
morning, the attraction of a beach-comber's life, the twin temp-
tations of sunshine and drink. I was filthy dirty, furry-tongued,
unshaven; yet I had no desire to wash, only an overwhelming urge to
go to sleep somewhere in the shade. While Daphne went on with her
walk, I settled down in some bushes at the foot of the Turkish fort.

But not to sleep. No one could have slept in the stanching miasma
that suddenly rose from the plants around me. For a nightmarish
second I imagined that I was lying on a corpse; the smell of carrion
was all-engulfing. In panic I jumped to my feet. From the patch of
green below me there protruded a skinny phallus, so dark green as
to be almost black. This shameless organ appeared to be sheathed
in rotting tiger-skin, a maculated green-and-black cylinder hemmed
with a fleshy purple ruff. It seemed impossible that such an animal
object could belong to the vegetable kingdom: yet it was, in its own
way, a beautiful flower, a real *fleur du mal*. Its decadent appearance
would have been delightful if only it had not smelt quite so awful.

The stink-lily, as I christened it—it was only later that I learnt its
real name: dragon arum (*dracunculus vulgaris*)—was one of the few
plants in Crete that excited my dormant, almost moribund, botani-
cal curiosity. A sad confession to make, I know, especially since the
island is considered to be a botanist's paradise, but my ignorance of
plants is such that their appeal lies only in whatever theatrical, musi-
cal-comedy quality they may have. I wish, for instance, that I had
seen the squirting cucumber which, when touched, is said to fire its
seed (accompanied, rather alarmingly, by a poisonous juice) more
than twenty-five feet into the air. Mandrake, too, I should like to
have gathered, if only to follow the instructions laid down by the
Father of Botany, Theophrastus.

"On cutting the root," he advises, "one should draw three circles round mandrake with a sword, and cut it with one's face towards the west; and at the cutting of the second piece one should dance round the plant and say as many things as possible about the mysteries of love."

If plant-collecting were always as gay as this, I should no doubt show more interest.

We could, of course, have gone to St. Paul's on foot; but I soon fell into the habit, exclusive to Loutro, of regarding the sea as the only highway. The coastal path did not provide a gentle walk along the shore; there were cliffs and chasms on the way, difficult to scale without a guide. And no guide could be found among the small population of charming idlers. I dare say the obstacles were not as formidable as they were made out to be; they were simply put forward as an excuse, which I was only too ready to take. Daphne and I decided to wait until Andreas's engine arrived.

Waiting here was no hardship. There was privacy as well as shelter in the Athitakis house, which consisted of several small rooms instead of the usual single barn full of visitors and noise. Andreas we scarcely saw, and Despoina was not an exacting hostess. Here at last was an opportunity to sit down and read or write in a silence broken only by the homely thud of Evangelia's loom and an occasional outburst of bad language from Ioanna. Since we were both treated as members of the family, no effort was made to entertain us. We therefore escaped the alternative afflictions which Cretan hospitality sometimes imposes: the boredom reminiscent of a genteel tea-party and the sort of heartiness generally associated with a rugger team on a Saturday night.

The rest of the village showed us the same considerate reserve, as though we were part of the population. There was no staring when we strolled along the beach. On one occasion only were we treated in any way differently from the other inhabitants: an old woman looked at us with pity as we passed her house. "Oh, you poor, poor people," she said; and forced us to accept a gift of half a dozen eggs. Otherwise we wandered about unmolested, taking photographs without the usual gang of would-be models dogging our footsteps.

Loutro is the same size as Souyia. Like Souyia, it lies at the water's edge. And there the similarity between the two ends. Both communities are equally isolated, but whereas the isolation of those make-shift warehouses littering the Selino beach is regarded as grounds for complaint, the seclusion of this pretty little Sphakian port is jealously and appreciatively guarded. The buildings here are established homes, lived-in, well-designed and properly maintained. Apart from a Venetian construction, a miniature of the Canea arsenal—a relic perhaps from the days when this little harbour was a flourishing centre of shipbuilding—there is nothing of outstanding architectural interest; there is also not a single eye-sore.

But it could not have been its architecture alone that first attracted me to Loutro; nor its position in relation to the sea and the adjacent coast-line. When I had gazed at it from the cliff above Anopolis, it had been too far away for me to form more than the vaguest idea of its physical attributes; yet even at that distance I had been conscious of a particular quality which I knew I would not find elsewhere. I had prepared myself for a revelation; and although even now I was unable to define it, I knew that I had experienced it.

Put in its simplest terms, that experience was the discovery of an attitude to life unique in Crete, an easy-going—degenerate, if you like—approach to things and people, but an essentially worldly one. I was disturbed to find that I much preferred it to the more primitive peasant outlook which I had hitherto romantically championed. I began to have doubts about the bliss of an Arcadia uncontaminated by the touch of civilization. In Loutro the lightest touch had been sufficient to endear the place to me.

There was no sign that Andreas's engine would ever arrive. We might have waited there indefinitely for it, if I had not been roused from my contented stupor by a recurrent twinge of conscience. I had promised to be in Kyriakosellia for Easter, and Easter was almost upon us. Our visit to the church in the sands therefore, would have to be postponed, and the return journey over the mountains undertaken instead.

Our first lap would be as far as Sphakia, almost a day's march by the overland route up to Anopolis and down the Dizzy Gorge. Andreas arranged for us to go by sea, only a three-mile voyage; we could accompany him when he dropped the nets, and be picked up half-way by George the postman in another boat.

We left in the late afternoon. Facing forwards and standing upright as he rowed, Andreas pushed the clumsy vessel along with short jabs of the oar—a deceptively easy movement. I realised what effort it required as soon as I took over to leave him free to throw out the nets. I only had to row, to his instructions, over a short zig-zag course, but the oars soon felt like tree-trunks in my hands, their full movement impeded by the rough thole-pins which served as rowlocks. I was grateful when George at last glided up to us out of the gathering darkness.

Half an hour later we were in Sphakia; and early next morning, after another seismic night in the Douroundous establishment, we took the bus back to Canea.

15

KYRIAKOSELLIA

On my previous visit to Kyriakosellia with Anthony Baynes, I had made up my mind to go back there for the whole of Holy Week. Loutro meanwhile had held us up; it was not until the eve of Good Friday that Daphne and I reached the little hamlet situated at the centre of a star-fish formation of minor valleys and indentations. We had climbed up the main gorge from the road for over an hour, penetrating so deep into the mountainside that at times we had the impression of travelling not up-hill but underground; in this quasi-subterranean passage it seemed unlikely that we should ever find habitation suitable for anyone but the most hardened spelaeologist.

At one point the path actually did plunge downwards, into a river-bed which would have been dry but for the overflow from a spring which inundated a small platform of level ground shaded by a giant plane-tree; it was this rude construction rather than the Byzantine church nearby that indicated our proximity to human dwelling. There was no other building visible, but a little further on, through the dense olive-groves, came the usual sounds of village activity: the bleating of sheep and the tinkle of their bells, a shepherd's cogent whistle and, nearer still, men's voices raised to the frantic pitch of normal Cretan conversation. We still could not see our destination which was less than a hundred yards away.

Though I had been through Kyriakosellia countless times during the occupation, I had scarcely ever seen it by daylight; certainly I had no recollection of the cultivated terraces, mere strips of wheat a few yards wide, nor of the orange trees bearing, at this season, fruit and blossom simultaneously. These I noticed now for the first time. I had forgotten, too, how the twenty-odd houses lay concealed both from the outside world and from one another, each in its own individual cranny. From the air, perhaps, they would have resembled separate bits of plaster inserted into the cracks of this mountain wall; on the ground it was impossible to tell their relative positions in the general design. Had I been asked to draw even the roughest plan of the village, I should have been unable to place the site of a single building, with the possible exception of the house of Levtheris Kourakis which had been my home during so many wartime nights.

Levtheris, alas, had died in our service just before the liberation; his widow, Kyria Phrosso, now lived in a new, half-finished house next door. When we arrived we found her looking even more ill and tired than usual; her face under the black kerchief was as smooth and yellow as a skull, her eyes sparkling feverishly in the depth of their sockets. She had been up for the last three nights, attending to a peritonitis case in the adjacent village of Ramni. Although suffering herself from stomach ulcers, she acted voluntarily as a nurse to everyone in the neighbourhood; she was the only person within miles who knew how to handle a hypodermic needle—a valuable qualification in this completely doctorless district.

When she was not engaged on these errands of mercy, she devoted herself to weaving. Her loom, indeed, was her only means of livelihood now that the Greek Government had withdrawn all pensions in the prefecture of Canea, including those due to clearly deserving cases. It was a mystery to me how she managed not only to keep alive herself but also to bring up two daughters. So often in Crete a household falls to pieces on the death of the male wage-earner; his widow, worn out by additional daily toil, soon turns into a bent old sluttish crone, her children go barefoot and in rags, the house itself becomes a slum.

Aided only by her elder daughter, Yiorgia—the younger girl, Costoula, was at school in Canea—Phrosso had contrived to maintain a standard of living far higher than that of her richer neighbours. Her two rooms were anything but luxurious; her kitchen, as in every other village house, was a roofless stone partition built against the courtyard outside, so that cooking in bad weather was always an ordeal;[1] but the food that she provided, even the simplest dish, was prepared and served with a rare and welcome attention to temperature and decorative detail. A minor manifestation of her epicurism was noticeable as soon as we entered the house: the Easter eggs on the table, besides being dyed the conventional purple and scarlet, were also patterned with an attractive floral design in white—an effect produced by applying a leaf or herb or flower to the outside of the shell before dipping it into the colouring agent. An elementary bit of panache, admittedly, but typical of the trouble that Phrosso took, in spite of her poverty, to give her home an atmosphere of comfortable ease in the absence of comfort itself.

The eggs, of course, were not for immediate consumption; these are forbidden during the forty days of Lenten abstinence, as well as all meat, milk, cheese, fish and oil. Fasting is universally practised in Crete, although no longer in strict accordance with the precepts of the Church. The forty days' abstention from meat, for instance, which once used to be observed by everyone in mourning, is now as unfashionable as the equally compulsory abstention from washing during the same period and for the same purpose. And few people nowadays are as punctilious as their parents were in their observance even of the main religious fasts, except perhaps on such risky occasions as the Feast of St. John the Baptist; on that day, August 29th, no one would dare to eat anything cooked in oil for fear of being seized by a sudden ague—such are the punitive powers of that particular saint, familiarly referred to in Crete as "Old Shiver-bones."

Though oil is forbidden during a fast, olives, strangely enough, are not; these, then, together with plain boiled vegetables, are the staple diet of strict observers during the forty days before Christmas, the fifteen days before the Assumption and the twelve days before the feast of SS. Peter and Paul, which constitute the principle "lean" periods of the year. There are, however, certain dispensations; for *bona fide* travellers, such as Daphne and myself, the rules may be re-

1. The alternative was to cook on the chimneyless indoor fire: an ordeal by smoke instead of by rain. All peasant houses in Crete seem purposely designed to impede rather than facilitate the housewife. The construction of a chimney would cost next to nothing; poverty, the usual excuse for discomfort, is not, therefore, entirely responsible for the peasant's lack of facilities. The real reason is the universal want of ingenuity in the domestic sphere, surprisingly uncharacteristic of the Greek who, in other respects, is a master of improvisation.

laxed. Phrosso offered to cook us a separate meal of chicken or rabbit: an unnecessary expense, not to mention the additional trouble entailed. We told her we would share whatever food she was preparing for herself and the rest of the household.

Our dinner, then, was exclusively vegetarian: broad beans, wild asparagus and edible blue flowers which I was unable to identify. We had been joined at table by Phrosso's sister-in-law, Sophia, a strong, dark, self-confident woman who reminded me of Katina Paxinou in the film of *For Whom the Bell Tolls*. (Hemingway's Pilar had always struck me as essentially Greek rather than Spanish; I was not surprised that a Greek actress should have been chosen to represent her on the screen.) Sophia was now a confirmed spinster—"why should I share my estate with a man?"—but men still figured apparently in her dreams. Her opening words to me were: "I knew I'd soon be seeing one of our old friends again. But I thought it would be Michalis,[2] not you; last night I dreamt he kissed me on the lips."

It was a novel experience in Crete to spend the whole of an evening in exclusively female company. It could have been unspeakably tedious; luckily none of the Kourakis women were representative of that vast black-hooded company of household drudges who, when they are not subjected into silence, raise their voices in a shrill, cicada-like clamour more objectionable even than the barking tones of their menfolk. Sophia spoke and behaved in a manner suited to her appearance; forcibly, humorously, but with an undertone of melancholy resignation. Yiorgia, whose mischievous little black eyes and two long plaits made her look younger than her eighteen years, had the quick untrained intelligence of a schoolgirl. Phrosso, in her conversation, showed a positively masculine gift for ratiocination and exposition; but then, compared to most peasant women in Crete, she was widely travelled and extremely well educated—it was to her, and not to any man, that the villagers came when they wanted a letter read or written.

She was the daughter of a well-to-do priest and, as a child, had accompanied her father on his journeys all over the mainland; at an early age, therefore, she had burst the narrow confines in which the female Cretan peasant remains, as a rule, imprisoned for life. The death of her father, the loss of the family fortune and her return to

2. Paddy Leigh Fermor's Cretan *nom-de-guerre*.

Crete occurred almost simultaneously. Then came her marriage to Levtheris, who was younger than she was, and poor: and she herself had little or no dowry—a combination of circumstances that earned her not the sympathy but the scorn of her fellow-villagers. "They used to throw their shoes at me," she said, "just to show how much they despised me."

Her description of their behaviour revealed an aspect of peasant mentality which I had never before imagined, and certainly never personally encountered—the reverse of the Cretan coin that I had known, whose obverse is Christian charity and more-than-Christian hospitality. I can only suppose that their attitude was prompted by fear, the primitive fear of poverty as personified in this new bride with an education but no dowry, whose action in marrying a poor man, and one younger than herself, must have seemed inexplicable to people who look upon marriage as a means of financial improvement.

By her utter saintliness Phrosso had eventually won them over; she was now, and with some justification, the most respected member of the community. So there was no need for condolences. In any case it had happened so long ago; it was no longer a subject for pity. But I still found it one of absorbing interest. For, unless Phrosso's experience had been an isolated exception, I saw that I would have to revise my judgment of Cretan character and examine still more closely its various qualities.

Charity, for instance, a quality which I had found in abundance all over the island—did it, I now asked myself, begin at home? After hearing Phrosso's tale I fancied not. Had she been a complete stranger wandering in distress through the village, she would have found immediate succour and support; as an ordinary resident with no apparent reason for her plight—for she was neither on the run nor in danger of her life, nor even at that time physically ill—she had found none. I began to realise that the Greek word for hospitality, *philoxenia*, should be interpreted quite literally: "love of strangers."

Clearly, then, I was still considered a stranger myself, for hospitality was lavished on me wherever I went. I had been priding myself on knowing Crete and the Cretans so well that I had long since come to be regarded as one of them; their persistently hospitable attitude towards me, and the discovery of my own incomplete knowledge of them, proved that pride to be premature.

A welcome drizzle was falling when we woke up next morning—
a favourable omen for Good Friday, especially after the weeks of
drought which had followed that scorching wind from Africa. This
change in the weather was the answer to the peasant's prayer:

> May Christmas time be bright and clear,
> Epiphany be white with snow;
> Fall, gentle rain, at Easter time
> To fill our larders here below.

For breakfast there was tea, then *tsikoudia* with quinces—an
essentially Cretan fruit and indigenous to this province of Kydonia, from which it derived its Greek name. Pliny refers to the quince
as "the apple of Crete," and so it is. But to the apple it stands in the
same relationship as the paw-paw to the melon; it is at once more
exotic and astringent—usually too astringent; the quinces of Kyriakosellia were the only ones I ever tasted which did not either shrivel
my tongue or buckle the roof of my mouth.

While Daphne and I sat over the bottle, Phrosso and Yiorgia
bustled about the room preparing the traditional Easter *koulouria*,
shortbread flavoured with sesame seeds and cinnamon. Through the
open door I could see a crowd of girls picking their way past the
damp undergrowth on the opposite slope. They descended in a long
line, one behind the other, like characters in a ritual procession. It
was as if a classical frieze had suddenly come to life—an impression
often created in Crete, where the narrow paths oblige any sizeable
group of people to move in single file. These girls came slowly down,
leaning even further backwards than the angle normally required to
compensate the forward drag of a steep descent. As they approached
I saw the reason for this exaggerated posture; they were all, apparently, enormously pregnant, overbalanced by the burden which they
carried tucked up in the folds of their skirts. This, however, proved
to be not the fruit of their womb but the fruit of their toil—a load of
edible snails, roused from lethargy by the unexpected shower.

All this activity round us prompted us to work as well. The relative solitude and quiet of Phrosso's house gave me a rare opportunity for attending to my notes, while Daphne was enabled to spend
the morning writing her monthly "Chatelaine" article for a London
magazine. Her contribution for that particular month was devoted
to the duties of a hostess in a large English country-house—a splen-

didly incongruous subject for someone who was then a guest in a small Cretan cottage. Her description of a weekend of luxury in Wiltshire sounded all the more nostalgic after the night which she herself had just spent in the primitive loft upstairs.

Half-way through the morning our work was interrupted by the sound of Easter carols. Two small boys were at the door, one of them carrying an icon of the Virgin wrapped in a clean white cloth and decorated with red carnations, the other with a dirty old can of oil in his hands. With solemn expressions and utterly toneless voices, they went through every verse of *The Sufferings of Christ* before collecting their dole of oil from Phrosso and moving on to the next house.

Their visit was a foretaste of the long paschal ceremony that was yet to come. I had warned Daphne to be prepared for hours on end in church; we were expected to attend the first of many services that evening. Luckily a break in the weather at lunchtime enabled us to spend the rest of the day out-of-doors; the terraced fields were steaming in the sun as we climbed them with Sophia and Yiorgia.

There was only one point from which the whole village was visible: a lofty acropolis crowned with the remains of yet another Venetian fortress. The houses below us looked as distant as a handful of pebbles thrown into an empty well—but a broad well, which the sun was able to penetrate right down to the vineyards and orchards lining the bottom and sides. The profusion of fruit-trees there was evident even at this distance: apricot and pear, and walnut of immense size and yield—the one in Phrosso's courtyard produced an average harvest of half a ton. Wild cherry and almond grew on the higher slopes. Though the fruit was still green, Sophia and Yiorgia both insisted on picking and eating as much of it as they could find: it was as bitter as quinine. I asked them why they did not wait until it ripened.

"By then everyone else will have picked it," they answered, "and besides, it's better in this state."

So that is how the taste of these villagers is developed! By beginning to prefer unripe fruit to no fruit at all, they end up by preferring it to fruit in condition.

This general view of Kyriakosellia was surprisingly pretty—a landscape in Crete is usually ruined if it includes any building—yet at the same time unsatisfactory. Apart from the obvious lack of design caused by its position, the village seemed incomplete, almost deformed; an essential part of it was missing. I felt disturbed by the sight, as though I was looking at a body without a head, until I realised the reason for this crippled appearance: the absence of a church. St. Nicholas's, the Byzantine chapel which we had passed on our way in, was a mile off at the bottom of the gorge; but a second church, that of St. Mamas, lay close at hand though likewise invisible. It had been built to commemorate the accidental discovery by a stray goat of a hitherto unknown water-hole in the face of the cliff below us.

Only a goat would have chosen such a spot. To approach it we had to lower ourselves over a precipice by clinging to the bushes on its side; fortunately these grew thick and firm. And when we reached it there was not much to see inside: a roughly walled-in cave containing a few dusty icons and a pair of unidentified skulls. But the view of the gorge alone was worth the journey. We hovered hundreds of feet above it, with no apparent means of access or support, as though we had got into this position by some miraculous feat of levitation.

The atmosphere of improbability was heightened by the sudden echo of a nightingale, so unexpected that it sounded almost discordant. In Crete nightingales seem to sing at all hours; and at all seasons, too, in defiance of the local adage that they fall silent from the moment the first vine-shoots appear until the time they finally stop growing: a period of annual mourning for these particular birds, ever since one of them ate a vine-tendril and choked to death.

As we descended into the river-bed, the frogs in the underground pools added their voices to the evening chorus. By the time we reached Phrosso's house, the dusk was noisy with a thousand croaks and trills.

There was only one priest for the three separate parishes in this area; for the midnight *Threnos*, or mourning service, we had to go to Ramni, a large village about a mile away on the saddle overlooking the plain of Apokoronas. We stumbled in the dark up the steep rough path, but when we reached the church we found that the priest had not yet come down from Kares, a remote community a couple of miles further up the mountain, where he had been conducting an evening service. These heavy threefold duties of his provided an excuse for unpunctuality which, for once, was perfectly valid; no one minded waiting.

An hour later he arrived and we filed into church, after buying a candle each at a sort of cashier's desk set up at the entrance. The whole congregation stood in a close-packed crowd round the central Easter symbol, the *epitaphion*, a miniature bier decorated with acacia, geraniums, stocks and roses, carnations and wild orchids. This floral edifice was surmounted by a single lily; its handles were bound with rosemary; the candles on it were the only ones in the church which still remained unlit.

The children swarmed delightedly round this beautiful new toy, stroking it and burying their faces in the petals; some of them, the smaller ones, even crawled under it, as though playing hide-and-seek. In this they were encouraged by their parents, who no doubt regarded it simply as a childish pastime without recognizing its true significance; for this apparently innocent game was an atavistic urge, and their encouragement of it was unconsciously prompted by the relics of a belief of which they were not even dimly aware, the belief that it is lucky to come between a dead body and the ground—the same belief which once induced superstitious people to stand beneath a victim of the gallows.

The service at last began. I was unable to follow every detail of the liturgy; the presence of the crowd and the deafening noise—both of chanting and incidental chatter—discouraged me from making the necessary effort. For about an hour the priest sweated over the threnody, supported by a trio of adult acolytes who stumbled and stopped and started up again, like schoolboys learning to read. Meanwhile the congregation, who understood not more than one word in ten, kept up a running conversation with each other, stopping from time to time to make the Sign of the Cross—an act of piety which, in this jostling throng, turned every candle into a potential incendiary weapon. It was not long before the smell of burning cloth mingled with that of the incense, whose perfumed smoke was noticeably thickened by a more acrid puff issuing, I observed with some surprise, from the top of Daphne's head. Her beret had been set on fire.

A few minutes later Daphne was again the centre of congregational interest. The priest's sprinkler, which serves, in the Orthodox Church, the same purpose as the Catholic *aspergillum*, was found to be blocked; he had swung it at us but nothing had come out. His acolytes at once seized it and tried to clear the obstruction by blowing down the nozzle and sticking matches into it, while the congregation encouraged them with contradictory advice. Their joint efforts were finally successful, the service was resumed. With a broad grin the priest once again raised the sprinkler, which at once proved to be in perfect working order: at the first swing it emitted a powerful jet of orange-scented holy water straight into Daphne's eye.

When the laughter had died down, the candles round the *epitaphion* were lit and the bier itself was carried out, followed by the whole congregation in symbolic funeral procession. Meanwhile the bell started tolling—a solemn noise which lasted at least ten minutes—while the priest stood at the entrance to the church receiving individual contributions of money for the prayers which he had undertaken to say for the dead. I took advantage of this interval to move to the edge of the crowd so as to light a surreptitious cigarette. I found that at least a dozen other men had had the same idea. At this sombre stage of the service, with the bell delivering its message of universal mourning through the dark Christian night, my urge to smoke had seemed almost blasphemous. My companions were evidently not disturbed by sentiments of this sort, which in me—I had to admit—were prompted more by the superficial trappings of mystery than by any inner sense of devotion. My feeling of guilt was at once dispelled by their gay refusal to be overawed.

This typically Greek attitude to religion—the outcome, I suppose, of a completely healthy spiritual state—was again in evidence as soon as we re-entered the church. All candles were now extinguished, save those round the bier; the absent body of Christ was lying in state before us. For the first time the congregation relapsed into complete silence. But the spell was not allowed to last for long; the silence was broken by a brief blessing from the priest, who then, almost jauntily, wished us all good-night.

This was the signal for an immediate outburst of communal horseplay; the end of the service developed into a sort of boisterous parlour game. The *epitaphion* was carried to the door of the church and held there at arm's length by two of the acolytes, so that the whole congregation had to pass underneath it on leaving—an adult version of the children's game that we had seen a few hours before, only more destructive; for everyone in turn made a jumping grab at the flowers (which are said to be an effective defence against the power of the evil eye), while the acolytes struggled to keep them out of reach of the laughing, leaping scrum. They were both tall men, but no match for Daphne either in height or determination; despite the special effort which they made when it came to her turn, she managed to get away with a handful of rosemary.

Twenty-four hours later we were back in church to attend the climax of Holy Week, the service of the Great Resurrection,[3] which proved to be a great disappointment. There was not a single bonfire or firework. Normally an effigy of Judas is ceremoniously burned in the churchyard at dawn, and the Resurrection is symbolized pyrotechnically; even during the occupation, when fireworks were unavailable, we used to make some show of celebration by firing our rifles and tommy-guns into the air. In Ramni there was not so much as a squib.

Nevertheless, as we emerged into the early morning light, we were conscious of an atmosphere of jubilant release; and when we heard the words "Christ is risen!" acclaimed on all sides, it was as if we ourselves had just risen from the dead. This greeting was repeated again and again as we made our way back to Kyriakosellia, and the joyful answer echoed round the surrounding hills: "Verily, He is risen!"

The meal that we had on our return was literally a break-fast: egg-lemon soup with rice, *kaltsounia*—mint-flavoured cream-cheese pasties, traditional Easter fare and exclusively Cretan—and, instead of the paschal lamb, a young kid stewed in wine. As soon as we had eaten we went to bed, for we had to be up again in a few hours. There was yet another service which we were expected to attend at two o'clock in the afternoon: this time, fortunately, not so far away—in the chapel at the bottom of the gorge.

At two o'clock the whole village had congregated in the little churchyard; the priest, of course, did not turn up till three. Not that that mattered: this period of waiting coincided with the one and only hour of the day that the sun's rays penetrate this part of the chasm, and it was delightful to sit there in the warmth.

Like most of the smaller Byzantine churches in Crete, St. Nicholas's had been disfigured by an excrescence built on to the west wall; but from certain angles this was invisible, and tile and stone appeared in original design with nothing to distract or offend. Every

---

3. The Small Resurrection had already taken place in the morning, while we were still asleep.

scar and sagging feature of this ancient edifice seemed humanized by the glare of the sun, the cracks in its lean walls showing like the furrows on an old man's cheeks, the tufts on its battered dome as sparse as the hair on a balding head; yet the only effect of this unkind light was to underline an expression of robust benevolence well suited to the vigorous peal of the bell which announced the priest's arrival.

The ceremony was mainly a family affair; almost every member of the congregation was interrelated. The liturgy was therefore even more haphazard and happy-go-lucky than it had been in the larger church at Ramni. No one objected to Daphne taking photographs throughout the service—in fact the priest interrupted it several times to pose in front of the camera—while the children were allowed to romp about as noisily as they liked. But there was one small boy who refused to play with them; he was too busy eating his honey-flavoured beeswax candle. Long before the service ended he had chewed it down to the wick.

Once again the most popular feature of the service was carnivalesque rather than religious. After dipping behind the iconostasis for a few seconds, the priest re-appeared like a conjuror, holding in his arms the remnants of the *epitaphion* flowers, which he then flung in handfuls to the delighted congregation, as though distributing largesse. When the pandemonium subsided, we all lit our candles and formed up for the final ceremonial procession outside.

Each tiny flame was anxiously guarded from the wind, for if it went out, we were told, its bearer was bound to die in the near future. Every one of us, then, who attended that service at St. Nicholas's must be doomed to an untimely end; for all our candles were simultaneously extinguished by a single sudden gust. But no one appeared worried by this fate in store; everyone was shaking hands and kissing each other in a general upsurge of joy, while the bell rang out its message of deliverance and hope, then abruptly fell silent—the children who had been pulling it had broken the rope.

The rest of the day was devoted to an orgy of hard-boiled eggs and *koulouria*, offered with *tsikoudia* in every house in the village which we visited in quick succession. There was to be singing and dancing all night: a lyre-player was expected from one of the neighbouring villages. But Daphne and I went to bed long before he arrived, for we were due to leave early in the morning. We had accepted an invitation from Changebug to a shepherds' feast on St. George's Day,

when all the flocks in the neighbourhood of Asi Gonia are concentrated at dawn in the village, to be blessed before being milked outside the church; we were expected there in two days' time.

————

Rather than walk down to the main road in the hope of catching a
bus—no one knew for sure if the buses would be running on Easter Monday—we planned to go straight across country through the
foothill villages overlooking the Apokoronas plain. If we started
early enough, I thought, we should have plenty of time. I was wrong.
I had not accounted for the heightened hospitality during this paschal season.

We set off from Kyriakosellia laden with Easter eggs and *koulouria*; and our load increased every time that we passed through a
village—each coffee-shop on the way was an obstacle, a trap, impossible to negotiate except at the expense of half an hour's delay
devoted to feasting and drinking and attempting to refuse still
more food thrust upon us or stuffed into our rucksack; for at least
a week afterwards I kept finding bits of egg-shell and crumbs in all
my pockets.

We had hoped to reach Asi Gonia on Tuesday night, the eve of
St. George's Day; it was nine o'clock in the morning of the day itself
when we at last tottered into the village. By then the flocks that we
had come to see being blessed and milked outside the church had
dispersed; but the service, which had started at dawn, was still in
progress. The villagers were all assembled in a nearby olive-grove,
for the church itself was not large enough to hold a tenth of the
present congregation; as we approached, an almost unrecognizable
dandy detached himself from the crowd and came forward to greet
us. It was Changebug, resplendent in a smart new suit worn in honour of the feast which was also his own name-day.

With him we joined one of the many groups standing and chatting in the sun. Vast copper cauldrons, into which the sheep had
recently been milked, lay drying all round us; loaves and cheeses
were piled like a buttress against the church wall. As I put my rucksack down beside them, I felt as though I had just arrived late for
a wonderfully organized picnic; I could not associate the pastoral
setting and the crowd's casual appearance with any form of ortho-

The path winding down into the Gorge of Samaria

The saddle at the head of the Gorge on the Sphakia-Selino border

dox religious activity. Nor apparently could anyone else: the priest's sermon, delivered from the garlanded church entrance, fell on deaf ears; the congregation was more interested in Daphne's camera.

The service came to an end with the distribution of the bread and cheese—a substitute donation from those shepherds whose flocks, in the highest and most distant pastures, were unable to descend to give their milk on the spot. Like everyone else, Daphne and I pocketed our share—it would be a change from the eggs and short-bread which had been our staple diet for the last two days—then followed George into his house, where still more food was waiting to be eaten. We spent all day eating it.

Non-stop assimilation of food and drink, which is almost the only recreation known in Crete, tends to make one holiday indistin-guishable from another. That afternoon of feasting in Asi Gonia was similar to countless other afternoons of feasting elsewhere, except for one memorable event: the unexpected arrival of a telegram. A small boy suddenly turned up and announced that I was wanted on the telephone; there was a message for me from Canea.

I was convinced at first that there must be some mistake or that this was one of Changebug's jokes, or that I was drunker than I thought. I did not know if Asi Gonia was even on the telephone, until Changebug took me to a house at the far end of the village and showed me where the instrument was. The receiver was off; I picked it up and was answered at once by someone in the Canea post-office. So it was not a hoax after all; there really was a tele-gram for me, addressed, I was told, to Asi Gonia from "somewhere in Europe."

As far as I knew, no one anywhere in Europe could have had the faintest idea that at this very moment I was to be found in this par-ticular village in the heart of the White Mountains. Then I suddenly remembered: a few days earlier Daphne had mentioned in a letter to Paddy Leigh Fermor that we were coming here on St. George's Day. Paddy was living in Normandy at the time; I wondered why he should now be wanting to get in touch with me so urgently. The telegram, alas, did not provide me with an answer. I hardly expected it to: a message despatched in English from a French post-office and relayed by a Cretan clerk ignorant of the Latin alphabet was bound to be difficult to decipher. I could make out no more than an odd word here and there "St. George . . . Crete . . . Daphne . . . English friends . . . David . . ." The mystery remained unsolved until several weeks later, Paddy wrote to me and asked:

> Did you get a telegram on St. George's Day at the Corner?[4] Daphne's letter had just arrived and I walked into Paçy with John Russell to have luncheon at the Étape with Duff and Diana,[5] David Herbert and Jaimie Caffrey. At the end of luncheon I read out D's letter and Duff said: "Tomorrow's St. George's Day, we must send them a telegram" and wrote out, almost without drawing breath, the following quatrain:
>
>> Long live St. George of England, Greece and Crete
>> And Xan and Daphne, sweetest of the sweet,
>> From English friends in France who sing Hosanna.
>> John, David, Jaimie, Paddy, Duff, Diana!
>
> which was despatched forthwith. Isn't that pretty?

———

The cult of St. George is more established in Asi Gonia than anywhere else in Crete. Most of the male population are named after the saint; two of the three churches in the village are dedicated to him; and apart from the flocks that are milked for his blessing on April the 23rd, others are sacrificed in his honour on November the 3rd. This annual slaughter takes place in the precincts of the second church of St. George, in a glade just outside the village, where the animals are killed, skinned and cooked during the service, and eaten on the spot immediately afterwards.

The victims are selected weeks in advance, the finest representative of each herd, and during that time they are said to develop an almost human understanding; each of them becomes aware of its impending fate and of the privilege implicit in laying down its life for the saint. Changebug cited a recent example of this heightened animal consciousness.

One of the shepherds in the village had earmarked the best of his rams for the sacrifice, but a few days before the ceremony he decided to substitute a less valuable animal—after all, there was no

4. Our war-time code name for Asi Gonia.
5. Lord and Lady Norwich.

one to know what his first selection had been; and the saint could not be expected to distinguish one potential victim from another. The argument, though immoral, proved valid. The lesser animal was duly slaughtered and no one was any the wiser. But the shepherd had reckoned without the old ram which he had thus deprived of an honourable end; that frustrated beast suddenly turned up in the middle of the service and, in a final gesture of denunciation and defiance, lay down at the church door and died.

Daphne and I visited the scene of this phenomenon on our way back to Canea next morning. In the enchanted glade of St. George it was difficult not to believe in the miraculous powers attributed to the saint. The huge ilex trees here are said to be under his direct protection and are consequently proof against the depredations both of man and goat. A villager once tried to cut one down with an ordinary axe; the tree, so Changebug told us, "just laughed at him." But when he fitted his axe-head with a shaft made of one of the tree's own branches, it succumbed to the first blow—a unique example of the effects of saintly power in human hands, and the only recorded instance of a saint's defeat at the hands of a man.

With goats, however, St. George has been invariably successful. Ilex trees elsewhere may be ravaged by these animals, those in the glade remain inviolate. A miracle? Possibly. Certainly none of the trees which we saw there bore the usual signs of goats' activity. But then neither did the ground underneath. As far as I could see no grazing animal had ever come near this glade—which accounted perhaps for the immaculate state of the wood. Not every miracle defies explanation.

Nevertheless St. George still rules supreme as a local thaumaturge. It was the vision of him standing guard at the entrance to the village that had frightened the Turks away each time that they had attempted to enter it; it was his unseen presence that had prevented the Germans, who later did enter it, from burning it down to the ground. And that was most certainly a miracle; for throughout the occupation Asi Gonia headed the German list of villages due for destruction in reprisal.

PART FOUR

Spring–Summer

These mountains of *Sfacia* are abounding in all things necef-
fary for life, and nothing can be more delightsom in the Summer time.

Randolph

16

THE OMALO

DAPHNE AND I were still feeling guilty about our failure to visit the church in the sands from Loutro. We now planned to reach it, as a subconscious penance perhaps, by a far more arduous route: straight over the mountains, through the Omalo and down to the west by the Gorge of Samaria. We had covered half this ground once before, in the autumn, but the plateau had then been almost deserted and the gorge shrouded in mist; it was worth repeating the journey in better weather. We chose, as our starting-point, the village of Lakkoi—the large collection of houses scattered over the ridge above Meskla—which we reached very late one afternoon; this was the highest point on the northern slope of the mountains to be served by a motor-road.

I had passed through Lakkoi several times during the occupation, but had never spent a night in the village—Zourva, next door, had always been a more suitable base—so I hardly expected to meet any old friends there; besides, Lakkoi had always impressed me—without reason, I admit—as an unfriendly sort of place. In spite of the pretty surroundings of hillside transformed into a giant staircase by countless fertile terraces—or perhaps even because of these—the houses here look as obscure and forbidding as an old hag in a girl's summer frock. Other travellers before me have noticed their exceptionally grim appearance; Spratt refers to them as "mean, comfortless hovels, sombre and dark as the slaty rock they are built of, without a patch of whitewash on any of their exteriors or interiors to denote within the appearance, the reality, or even the idea of cleanliness and comfort."

Things have improved since then, of course; whitewash has been applied—but not in sufficient quantities to create more than the barest illusion of cheerfulness or ease. As we sat in the coffee-shop at the bus-stop, Daphne and I both found ourselves shivering; the atmosphere was chilly, metaphorically as well as in fact. The usual gaping crowd at once gathered round us—the people of Lakkoi, unlike the Sphakians, are not too proud to stare—but was soon dispersed by the local police-sergeant, whom I happened, luckily, to have met once before. The presence of even a chance acquaintance in this antipathetic spot was as welcome as a sudden rise in temperature. The sergeant sat down with us and presently, when we were joined by the priest and the two local schoolmasters, all of them equally friendly, I began to feel that I had misjudged this village. Such abrupt transitions from one mood to another have affected me more often in Crete than anywhere else in the world.

Even the dullness of the conversation now seemed less discouraging. After the inevitable exchange of polite platitudes and war-time reminiscences, the police-sergeant proceeded to enlarge on the bandit menace and warned us, as so many others had done, of the terrible dangers which we would be courting by walking through the mountains unaccompanied. But his voice, I noticed, was tinged with envy; he was a true mountaineer and hated the confines of his office in the police-station. But, for Crete, it was an exceptionally comfortable room; there was no need for the apologies he made when he offered to let us stay there for the night.

It was strange that in such a large village—the population of Lakkoi is over nine hundred—no alternative accommodation was suggested. Perhaps no other building was considered suitable. When Spratt came here he was forced to camp out by the church, for "in so large and well-reputed a village we expected naturally to see at least one or two neat-looking houses, if not very large ones; but, as in many other villages, we looked in vain." The shortage of neat-looking houses was still apparent, but I felt that the lukewarm hospitality of Lakkoi—unique in Crete—was due not so much to the lack of accommodation as to the peculiar mentality of the villagers.

The inhabitants here are still over-conscious of the role their forefathers played in the various insurrections against the Turks; Lakkoi has probably produced more captains[1] than any other village in Crete, and the number of these self-styled local leaders is a standing joke to this day. When anti-Turkish activity was the only criterion of a man's value or virtue, it was naturally everyone's ambition to be recognized as a leading guerilla; nothing more than this recognition was required to invest him with a coveted "captaincy." Many of these "captains" fully deserved the respect which they eventually won; but there were large numbers who, if the phrase had been known in those days, would have been termed "plain bull-shitters"—men elected not on personal merit but on the unofficial votes of friends and relations.

I have often wondered how, in the absence of any government authority, these appointments first came to be recognized. What administrative machinery was set in motion to secure the necessary nominations? The system which I had seen in practice since my return to Crete affords a possible clue. I have described in a previous chapter how the resistance movement in the prefecture of Canea was not officially recognized after the war, mainly because none of the four or five candidates for leadership would stand down in favour of another. This did not prevent one of them, however, from setting up an office for his own "National Resistance Organization," from which he issued to each of his supporters a captaincy "certificate" bearing his signature. Unofficial and worthless scraps of paper, of course; each of the Paterakis brothers had received one and treated it with the contempt that it deserved. But many of the other recipients were delighted with the title conferred on them and exploited it for all it was worth; a new generation of "captains" was thus brought into being.

Whether a similar system was used during the Turkish occupation, it is difficult now to tell; hero-worship is incompatible with historical research. The descendants of such famous "captains" as Mandakas, Skoulas and Nikoloudes have no need to investigate their ancestors' claims to recognition, for their deeds have been recorded and substantially confirmed. There are others, however, whose right to the title is more open to question. But the awe in

---

1. This is not a military rank; the Greek for captain is *lokhagos*. *Kapetanios*, the word used to denote a local leader, is clearly borrowed, but I have here retained its English equivalent, since it is still universally used in this context. A more accurate translation, however, would be "chieftain."

which these men are held, whether justified or not, is of less interest than the effect of their reputation on the present-day inhabitants of Lakkoi. The parochial pride of captaincy may be a pathetic quality; it is still a sufficiently strong one to make this particular community deeply self-conscious and on the defensive. And this self-conscious-ness may possibly account for the local stand-offish manner essen-tially alien to the rest of Crete.

———

The police-sergeant was not a native of the village; nor were his men. From their meagre rations they produced food for us—six fried eggs each and a couple of bottles of wine—and two of them slept on the floor so that Daphne and I could use their beds. In the morning the sergeant insisted on our having coffee with him before leaving.

It was not yet six o'clock but the coffee-shop was already open; we sat outside on the terrace in the sun. "A perfect day for walk-ing through the mountains," said the sergeant, "but I feel quite guilty letting you go on your own." He repeated his warning of the previous evening; and again there was a note of envy in his voice. "My dog's a wonderful hunter," he added. This remark would have sounded irrelevant had I not divined his train of thought.

"Partridges?" I asked.

"Partridges, yes. Hares as well. He'll sniff them all out."

He gave the dog an affectionate pat on the nose. It was a nice dog, well-cared for and confident, utterly unlike most Cretan dogs, which are turned into snarling, cringing curs by the clouts and kicks which they receive if they wander into human range. This one, instead of flinching when we got up to go, wagged its tail in happy anticipation; and hopefully followed us for several hundred yards after we had left.

The craze for road-building which has swept through Crete since the end of the war must have reached its height in Lakkoi. The vil-lage was already connected by main road to Canea, but this solitary line of communication was no longer considered sufficient; no post-war "captain" was going to be satisfied until the road was prolonged right up to the Omalo—that would show those cuckolds on the Selino Ring what the citizens of Lakkoi were worth! Work on this ambitious scheme had actually begun and, like many other Cretan schemes, been abandoned—provisionally at any rate; there was not a sign of activity anywhere on the five-mile length of prepared ground when Daphne and I walked over it that morning.

It was easy to see why the work had stopped at the end of five miles. Up to this point it had been an easy walk round the head of the valley which separates the Lakkoi ridge from the main Omalo range; the real climb was yet to come. As we zigzagged up the first steep slope in front of us, my sympathies were all with those optimistic workmen: how could they ever convert this narrow rocky path into the main road of their dreams?

Even on foot it was difficult to follow the rough goat-track as it wound upwards through a mass of narrow defiles and enclosed valleys bristling with hawthorn, cistus and rock-rose. The compact stratified limestone of the smooth higher level was covered in these prickly plants, as though to make up for the absence of the shales and schistose rocks which we had left behind us on the lower ridges. But here and there the landscape relented and offered, by way of compensation for its stubborn spikiness, an occasional meadow luminous with asphodel.

We sat down to rest on the edge of one of these flat bits of ground hedged in on all sides by scrub and by a gorse-like plant which in the Western Mediterranean, I believe, is known as *tuechèvres*—so thick and impenetrable that even a goat will not approach it. But the ingenious peasants in Crete have found a use for it: stuffed into the neck of a water-jar, it acts as a cork and filter at once.

The thought of water reminded us of our thirst. Luckily we had brought some lemons to suck; we had seen not a single spring or well on the way. The lack of water on these slopes no doubt accounted for the complete absence of any herd or human being. We had been walking for four hours through an apparently deserted country, without sight or sound of the shepherds that I had expected to come across in these summer pastures; the flocks must have already assembled in the upland basins, where the melting snows could be trapped instead of draining away, as here, underground. Meanwhile the only living thing that I could see, apart from ourselves, was a solitary industrious dung-beetle.

This insect's behaviour was as comic as the antics of a circus-clown; it seemed deliberately to be making heavy weather over its apparently pointless task. The load it was pushing, larger than a golf-ball, obstructed its view; so it would have been unable to see where it was going even if it had been walking forwards in the normal way. But to make the job still more difficult, it insisted on walk-ing backwards, balancing on its front legs and trundling its burden along with its hind feet. Each time that it hit an obstacle in its path, the crash turned it head over heels. Undaunted, it would then pick itself up and go round to the other side of its burden, as though to push it forwards in the opposite direction. But instead of pushing, it clambered over it and fell once more into its original undignified position, its hind legs in the air. And the whole silly business would be resumed, until the next obstacle was encountered and it landed yet again upside down in the dust.

Until then all I knew of this insect's habits had been based on a single performance of Karel Capek's *Insect Play*, which I had seen years ago in London. I realised now how slack that production must have been: the actor playing the part of the dung-beetle had never once walked on his hands.

As Daphne and I were watching this miniature display of acrobat-ics, with our noses almost glued to the ground, a third nose silently intervened: the damp black nose of a dog. Even without looking up I recognized the police-sergeant's pet; no other animal here would have approached us with such natural confidence. It must have tracked us, then, all the way from Lakkoi—or so I thought until I heard the sound of footsteps, followed a few minutes later by the appearance of the sergeant himself accompanied by three of his men.

"We've been ordered to escort you," he announced with a happy grin, "the chief in Canea insists."

So he had wangled his trip to the mountains after all! It had been quite simple. All he had had to do was to ring up headquarters as soon as we had left and stress the danger of allowing two foreigners to wander about in Sphakia on their own; Canea had at once given the only order possible.

"It was my conscience," he explained, "I had to ring up. Those bandits you know. If anything had happened to you . . ."

But I noticed that he had armed himself for our protection not with a service-rifle but a shotgun.

Daphne and I would have preferred ambling along at our own pace, unaccompanied. We were also rather anxious about how we would now be received in the more lawless areas such as Samaria; there was no love lost between the Viglis clan and the police force. It was with mixed feelings, then, that we thanked the sergeant for all the trouble that he had taken on our account. But I was grateful to him for his knowledge of the country. He loved these mountains for their own sake and for the sport that they provided. Unlike the shepherds, who regard them with blind eyes simply as a means of livelihood, he appreciated their beauty and had taken the trouble to know something of their history. It was he who told me the use of the small forts perched at regular intervals of a mile or more on the highest crags overlooking the path.

"Signalling towers," he explained, "the Turks put them up after the '66 rebellion. They were manned by trumpeters. Orders blown on one instrument would be picked up and relayed by the next one, and so on right down the line. Like drums in the jungle. Primitive, yes. But the messages used to get through more quickly than ours now do by telephone; Canea could contact even Ayia Roumeli in a matter of minutes."

We came across the first occupied cheese-hut as soon as we reached the flatter ground leading into the Omalo. It was milking-time. In a circular pen built, like the shack beside it, of several thicknesses of stone without mortar, about a hundred goats were assembled waiting their turn to pass through the narrow gap in the wall and then through the narrower gap of the milkman's legs, which straddled each animal as it came along and held it in position over the pail. The pen was tightly packed: a ruffled pool of horns and beards and amber-coloured eyes, an ocean of goat, in which no one goat could be distinguished from another. It was only when each emerged from between the milkman's legs that its entity was abruptly established.

Like clients leaving a public-house at closing-time, they rejoined their kids outside, each resuming at once the individual character and distinctive features which it had temporarily cast off in the crowd. The first lurched away with a drunken seaman's gait; the second trotted off as though on tartish high heels; the third moved forward with the creaking dignity of an elder statesman. The fourth and the fifth and the sixth followed in rapid succession; for each of them a suitable human counterpart automatically suggested itself. With sheep, it would have been impossible to play this imaginative game. A sheep is a sheep and, apart from that statement, there is little else to be said for it. A boring beast deserves a boring background. Sheep, I feel, should be confined to a perpetual Christmas-tree climate; and the olive-tree landscape, the landscape of character, be reserved for the animals worthy of it, the goats.

The approach to the Omalo from Lakkoi filled me with less surprise or delight than I had felt last autumn when entering over the
Selino Pass. There was nothing abrupt about this second encounter
with the plain, whose presence was betrayed, as it were, in advance
by the length of the obvious entrance to it. An open slope, gilded
and burnished with flowering ilex and yellow broom, gently depos-
ited us on the very edge of the plateau, a few yards away from the
Katavothron; we were in the neck of the funnel through which the
plain is drained.

Only a few weeks before, the ground underneath us must have
been awash with melted snow irresistibly drawn, as though by a vac-
uum, into the gaping mouth of this thirsty cavern. Through its open
gullet we could see the descent of the water-course, a perpendicular
spiral, like the staircase of a mediaeval tower—tempting territory for
any spelaeologist, and virgin too. For no one, I believe, has ever tried
to discover what lies at the bottom; the ghost which is said to haunt
the place discourages such attempts.

The only building which distinguishes the Lakkoi Ring from the
arc of stone shacks on the Selino circumference is the house of Hadjimichalis Yiannaris, the Lakkoi chieftain who launched the rebellion of 1866. Hadjimichalis[2] must have been an exception to the
pallikari-class of that period; he created as much as he destroyed.
Apart from erecting the chapel of St. Panteleimon and the house
next door that still bears his name, he was the first Cretan leader
with a sufficient sense of history to record his activities in a volume
of memoirs. Unfortunately his book has been out of print for years,
and his home is now in ruins. Like every other national monument
on the island, it has been pulled apart so as to furnish building or
repair material for the present generation—a system of cannibaliza-
tion so prevalent in Crete that it will in time defeat its own ends:
when all the old houses have been sacrificed, new victims will have
to be found for this wholesale vandalism.

Most of the shepherds' huts were still unoccupied: it was too early
in the year for a general assembly of the flocks. But a few cultivators

2. The Cretan practice of referring to historical figures by their Christian names
alone is common but confusing, especially when two well-known namesakes are
near contemporaries. In a later chapter I refer to another leader called Hadjimichalis, who was killed by the Turks in 1823; he was not in any way related to the
Lakkoi chieftain, as his name might reasonably lead one to suppose.

were already at work in preparation for the potato crop. The ground at this season is normally in a perfect state for planting, fresh and sufficiently moist from the recent snow; this year it had been baked hard by the wanton Libyan wind. The surface resounded like a sheet of metal under the attack of the peasants' hoes; the solitary plough moving over it was as effective as a tooth-pick. In the dry afternoon heat I found it tiring even to look at such unrewarding labour.

While the police-sergeant disappeared into the mountains with his dog and gun, Daphne and I wandered about the plain in search of *ampelitsa*, a variety of tree which is confined to these slopes round the Omalo. Since it grows nowhere else in Crete, the walking-sticks made from its wood are particularly prized. Almost everyone in Lakkoi has one, and ownership of such a comparative rarity adds to the natural swagger of that village. I decided to add to my own swagger, now that I was here, by getting one of these sticks for myself.

But I had no idea where to look, or what to look for; I had never, as far as I knew, seen the tree; or if I had, I certainly could not have identified it now. Perhaps the policemen could help me; I asked them if they would be able to recognize an *ampelitsa* if they saw one. Oh yes, they said, they know all about *ampelitsa*, they would show me one at once. Simultaneously two of them pointed in triumph, one at a pear-tree, the other at a clump of hawthorn. *"Ampelitsa!"*, they both insisted. The third, more cautious but equally inaccurate, suggested that it might be a cross between the two.

It was by pure accident, and months later, that I solved the *ampelitsa* mystery. I happened to pick up an old copy of *The Journal of the Royal Horticultural Society*, which featured an illustrated article on Crete by the celebrated botanist, George Baker. One photograph showed a group of men from Lakkoi, each holding a walking-stick as contorted as Harry Lauder's—*ampelitsa*, unmistakably. The caption underneath stated that these sticks were made from *zelkova cretica*, a tree related to the elm family, of which the Cretan variety is confined to the White Mountains, all other species of the genus belonging either to China, Japan, Arabia or the Caucasus.

So that was the answer: *zelkova*—unless, of course, I had made a mistake and the sticks in the photograph were not *ampelitsa* after all; I had only assumed that they were from their appearance and from Baker's description. But the connection between the two words, *zelkova* and *ampelitsa*, was finally established when I learnt of an alternative name for the tree—*zelkova abelicea*, or Bastard Sandalwood—the name under which it is described in Clusius's *Planta-rum Historia* from the following information supplied from facts furnished by Onorio Belli in 1594: "A large tree with abundance of branches . . . the wood is hard with a slight degree of fragrance, in so much that its sawdust resembles the scent of sandalwood."

If only I had known all this when I was on the spot!

But I did make one discovery that afternoon. The surface of the plain was sown with dead plants, which the snow's weight had flattened into the shape of starfish; acre after acre was covered with these corpses, which looked more animal than vegetable. I hardly expected a sensible answer but, for the sake of conversation, I asked the policemen what they were. "*Vrovios*": their reply was unanimous.

I hoped it was also correct. If these dead leaves really did belong to the *vrovios*, I would soon be able to identify the most delicious pickles I had ever eaten—pickles that looked and tasted something like an onion, but an onion etherealized and magically refined, a regular Holy Ghost of an onion, sheer ambrosia. Michalis of "The Seal" had first introduced me to them, but had been unable to tell me anything about them except their name: *vrovios*. And further enquiries had only revealed the obvious fact that they were a bulb of sorts. "Yes, but *what* bulb?" I would ask. "Oh, the bulb of a plant," was the invariable reply.

Now, at last, I was faced with the plant itself. I still did not know what it was, but Daphne at once enlightened me: "Grape-hyacinth."

So at last the pickle mystery was solved.

The police-sergeant was an enthusiastic shot. He was also a poor one. His day's bag was one small partridge.

"Isn't this the close season?" I asked him.

"Of course," he assured me, "I mistook this bird for a pigeon."

Close season or not, we appreciated the forbidden food. There was nothing else to eat in the hut where we had gathered for the night, apart from yoghourt; the cheese being made there was still unripe. But the shepherds gave us all the milk that we could drink, ladling it out from an enormous copper pail, while the sheep which had just provided it wandered around in the moonlight looking like silly white ghosts. The inside of the hut felt colder even than the sudden cold outside, until the milking at last was over and the fire was lit for the cheese-making to begin.

The smoke and glare of the flames at once transformed this simple interior, heightening the air of mystery which always surrounds—at least, so it seems to me—such elemental activities as bread-baking or cheese-making. Bread, the symbol of life; and the miracle of milk— I was more than ever conscious of their mystic significance in the firelit atmosphere of the hut, compounded of church and clinic and laboratory; I felt that I was attending a divine service, assisting at a birth and witnessing a chemical experiment at one and the same time. A wonderful process was at work inside that steaming cauldron over which the cheese-maker presided, all unconscious of the triple role he played of priest and surgeon and alchemist.

I was brought back from this flight of fancy to the realm of facts and figures by the cheese-maker's own conversation. With pride he announced that his cauldron contained no less than ninety-five okes of milk (the equivalent of about two hundred pounds in weight). This liquid was brought up to a temperature of 40° C. (48° for *graviera*, the Cretan version of gruyère) before the curdling agent was introduced. After that, the work consisted of stirring the mixture with a swizzle-stick of the same size and shape as a caveman's club, but made of wood. The milk would then break up into a more or less solid mass, ready for the primitive press weighted down with boulders.

It was as simple as that. Yet apparently there was room for error; for a whole year a large proportion of the cheeses made in Crete had turned out poisonous. The Government had forthwith issued an order: cheese-makers were to wash their hands before handling the milk. Our host on the Omalo had observed this order to the letter. Before settling down to his task, he had scrubbed his fingers, finger-nails, palms, wrists and fore-arms with soap and water for at least five minutes; then wiped them dry with the dirty old sweat-rag which he had worn round his head for the last three months.

Cheese-making is a tiring business which leaves little time for rest. Wrapped up in a shepherd's cloak on my couch of thorn, I dropped off to the sound of the splashing cauldron. Six hours later I woke up to the sound of the creaking press. Two gigantic cheeses had been produced during the night. But their creator meanwhile had not slept a wink. And the sheep were due to be milked again in the morning.

17

ST. PAUL'S

I WANTED TO SET OFF for Samaria at once, but the police-sergeant had disappeared again during the night; we could hear his shots echoing round the hills. He returned, empty-handed, several hours later. It was almost midday by the time we reached the top of the Xyloskala and faced the dizzy drop into the gorge.

The view from that startling cliff on a clear day can be described only by the sort of romantic epithets popular in the eighteenth century; perhaps, then, it would be better not to describe it at all. At the time, I must confess, the tritest expressions of awe sprang to my mind with shameful facility; repeating them here would only cause embarrassment. During our previous visit to this spot, in the autumn, the mist had camouflaged but not quite concealed the outline of the crags; contours could be divined, but no colour. For the first time we now noticed the astonishing dark-blue of the rocky face sinking sheer on our right; and opposite, where the separate mountain forms grappled like wrestlers, the convulsive red of bruised and broken stone. Well below us, in the gullies which no sun could penetrate, incipient glaciers meandered downwards, each to its own individual melting-point. Many of these defied the summer by persistently continuing to exist even during the heat of August; tucked away in the deepest clefts, they preserved themselves throughout the lethal season—hibernators in reverse. Sometimes their frozen inactivity would be disturbed, not by nature but by man. Until quite recently these hidden sources of ice were regularly tapped, and their

contents packed in straw and transported by mule-convoy, to cool
the drinks of the thirsty metropolitan populace. The modern refrig-
eration plant in Canea has since given them a new lease of life.

The descent seemed steeper and more difficult than it had the
first time, and not only because we were now able to see every precipice. Winter had broken the path in a number of places; we had
to negotiate gaps and screes which before had never existed. Damage by rain and flood was evident, too, when we reached the bottom. The stream was swollen into a vicious torrent. At water-level
the friction of pebbles had worn the bark from every sound tree; all
hollow trunks along the bank were miraculously rendered whole,
their cavities filled not with wood but silt. Only the giant cypresses
guarding the Chapel of St. Nicholas remained untouched; against
them the torrent called off its overt attack and, as though to avoid
an encounter with such preternaturally superior forces, continued
the running battle underground.

The little grove was no longer deserted. Half a dozen shepherds
were encamped there for the summer under the largest overhang of
rock, converted now into a cheese-manufacturing centre more primitive even than last night's hut. That had been untidy; this was cha-
otic. Unrestricted by the normal confine of four walls, the natural
Cretan aptitude for disorder was here given full rein; the ground surrounding St. Nicholas's had the cheerfully littered appearance of a
bank-holiday picnic site. The building itself looked as if it was now in
regular use—and so it was: as a cheese-store. The entrance was fitted
with an ingenious home-made burglar-alarm which, when the door
was opened, released a noisy cataract of tins on to the stone below.

The first milking of the day had just finished when we arrived.
Already a fire was ablaze to receive the blackened cauldron propped
up between two rocks. Ladles and wooden platters, pieces of clothing
and bits of old rag lay scattered round about; it was impossible to tell
whether these were the tools of a trade or the accumulation of several people's personal rubbish. The shepherds were transformed into
busy housewives by this open-air domestic activity; in spite of their
beards they would have looked more in keeping with the kitchen atmosphere had they been dressed in skirts instead of breeches.

If they felt any resentment towards the police, they certainly did
not show it. Our escort was cheerfully included in the invitation to
sit down and share the bowl of yoghourt which was immediately
produced. Three of the present company I had last seen when I vis-

ited Vangelis Viglis in prison—a meeting which they now recalled
with unembarrassed chuckles; none of them, it seemed, had expected any tangible result from my efforts to intercede on their behalf. They had been punished—unfairly, so they thought—but they
had taken their punishment. As far as they were concerned, there
was nothing more to be said. No complaint, then; the silly business
was over. Far from embittering or breaking them, their experience
seemed to have invested them with a sort of philosophic power that
owed nothing either to resignation or revenge. It was with a distinct
sense of superiority that they entertained our escort; they could afford to be ironically gracious.

The inexperienced policemen with us appeared to be fully aware
of this; they must have realized that, for all their insignia of authority, in spite of their uniform and arms, they were no match for these
jovial ex-victims of theirs whose very kindness was an effective mark
of scorn. Certainly the last battle in the war of nerves waged round
the yoghourt bowl was a victory for the home team. As we got up to
leave there was a shout behind us:

"Hey, youngster! Don't you want this thing? Or have you left it
behind for us to shoot an ibex?"

The youngest of the gendarmes, in the flurry of departure, had
forgotten his rifle.

Vangelis, whom we met half an hour later outside Samaria, showed
the same sense of humour. He seemed almost happy to have spent the
winter in exile. "It was nice and warm on Gavdos," he told us, "and
at least I avoided the catastrophe here. Come and see what the floods
have done."

The village looked as if it had suffered a direct hit in an air-raid.
There was no longer a bridge over the stream; this had been washed
away when its rocky supports, each weighing several tons, had capsized under the pressure of water during the early autumn storms;
in a single season the banks, which had withstood the continuous attrition of centuries, had fallen to this one sudden onslaught.
Swollen now by the melting snows, the river was again threatening
the planks and tree-trunks laid across the gap which it had already
formed. As though Samaria was not sufficiently cut off from the rest
of the world!

"I suppose the Government will help with the repairs," one of the
policemen hopefully suggested. "Old Manoussos will see to it, he's
a good man."

"Politicians! The only time a politician comes to visit us is when he's after an extra vote or two."

There was some truth in Vangelis's remark. I do not suppose that Greek politicians are much more unscrupulous than those of any other country; they are simply more open to the temptation of working for themselves at the expense of their constituents. And for that the system, not the individual, is to blame. For if, as the Cretan peasants claimed, an M.P. is entitled to a life pension from the Government once he has managed to retain his seat in three consecutive elections, it is reasonable to suspect that he might have a secondary, and more personal, motive for contesting it in the first place.

Below Samaria, as far as the passage of The Gates leading into the Ayia Roumeli glen, there was more water than dry land at the bottom of the gorge. Where before we had crossed the stream over stepping-stones, we now had to paddle. To begin with, we all put our shoes and socks on again each time that we reached the opposite bank. But we soon found that we were spending more time in the water than out of it; it was less of an effort, then, to walk barefoot even over the short stretches of pathway still showing. The rocks there cut into the soles of our feet, but we could not feel them; the first touch of the water had rendered us numb from the knees down.

At Ayia Roumeli our escort left us. If we had ever been in danger of attack in the gorge, that danger presumably existed still. But the sight of the coastline induced a sense of security; the bandit menace, it seemed, was calculated according to our height above sea-level— the risk decreasing in direct proportion to our descent. Without questioning the police-sergeant's logic, we said goodbye and thanked him for his pains.

We intended to spend the night with my godbrother, Yiannis Tzatzimas, but neither Daphne nor I could remember where he lived. We enquired at the first house we saw.

"But which Yiannis Tzatzimas do you want?" we were asked; "There are three or four of them, you know—Yiannis George's son, Yiannis the son of Anthony, Manolis's Yiannis."

I tried to describe the Yiannis whom we had last met when we came through here with Vardis Paterakis. We were told that he was away in Canea. Our informant, an old woman dressed in conventional black, asked us to stay with her instead. "Yiannis is a nephew of mine," she explained. "In his absence we must do our duty to his friends."

Chairs were brought out for us into the courtyard; a bottle of *tsikoudia* was produced and as we sat there enjoying our first drink in two days, we were greeted by our first visitor of the evening. Surprisingly, it was Yiannis Tzatzimas—not one of the strangers, but my godbrother, the man who was supposed to be in Canea. "Why didn't you come to my house?" he at once demanded.

It took us quite a time to get to the root of the misunderstanding. In the first place, the old woman had thought that the Yiannis Tzatzimas whom we wanted was her nephew who had gone to Canea—a reasonable mistake; for, apart from having the same name as my godbrother, he also, apparently, had the same looks. My description had only added to the confusion. In the second place, my godbrother was also a nephew of hers; and a further similarity between the two nephews was their age; they were contemporaries. And finally, my godbrother was not known in the village as Yiannis Tzatzimas; I should have asked for Katsoulos.

The *paratsougli* system in use in Cretan villages is identical with the Italian *contranome* habit which so confused Norman Douglas in Calabria. In a small community containing several people with the same Christian name and surname, the use of a separate nickname for each is, I suppose, a sensible means of distinguishing one from another. But the means sometimes defeat the end; how was I to know that my godbrother, who was Yiannis Tzatzimas to everyone outside his village, had a completely different identity at home?

"Never mind," he said, echoing the old woman's words, "you're in the same family here. My aunt will do her duty towards my friends. But you must call on me before you leave—when are you leaving, by the way, and where are you bound for this time?"

I told him that we wanted to visit St. Paul's in the morning, and then go on to Loutro.

"Look out for the mine in the church," he warned me, "those cuckolds of Germans planted it—at least, we think they did. It wasn't there before. It's under a great big pit of sand in the middle of the floor—at least, we think it is. Something's there anyway. But none of us dares to investigate; it would be silly to get blown up just out of curiosity."

St. Paul's sounded more intriguing than ever; I pictured it now as a Ming vase containing a time-bomb. Here was an additional threat to its existence even more immediate than the gradual encroachment of the sands. Our urge to see the potential victim increased; Daphne and I both felt a longing to get up and leave then and there.

Had we done so we should have been spared a more than usually uncomfortable night. The food that we were given—pancakes filled with cream-cheese floating in honey—was delicious. The wine was ample and adequate—any wine would have been after the two days which we had spent with none. And we slept in beautiful lace-trimmed sheets—relics of the fine dowry which Yiannis's aunt must have brought with her when she first came to this house as a young bride. But these were symbolic objects rather than articles of daily use; stored away for years and now half-rotten, they were almost as irretrievably lost as their owner's former pride in her home.

For our hostess was a widow; since her husband's death she had condemned herself to a life-time of mourning, and her house to a life-time of decay. In spite of the embroidered sheets, which she had specially brought out for us, Daphne and I both slept badly. The cockroaches that scuttled over us as we lay in bed were tolerable; they distracted our attention from the fleas. What neither of us could bear was the threatening sound of the rats, which kept us awake all night, yet turned those hours of wakefulness into a long, continuous nightmare.

The morning, when we were out again in the open air, seemed even brighter than it was. Before leaving the village we called at my godbrother's house for a final *tsikoudia*. He wanted to outline for us the route which we would have to take; he also wanted to show us his latest acquisition: a baby ibex which he had caught a few days previously. And his wife wanted to know if we had any penicillin; she had cut her hand rather badly. As I leant over her to examine the wound, I realised why the ibex which she had just been fondling smelt so strongly of the Paris *métro*. The poor woman had been eating as much garlic as possible "in order to clean the bad blood." Her hand was swollen and the cut looked filthy. But what I had at first taken for suppuration proved to be resin—an alternative to the usual village unguent of honey and ashes. There was nothing that we could do, alas, except wish her a speedy recovery.

Yiannis had told us that we could not lose our way. From St. Paul's onwards there was a second path, harder to find; but as far as the church all we had to do was follow the coastline. Trudging along those three miles of shingle would have been a tiresome business had we not by now become accustomed to the steep inland roads; compared to these, the beach felt wonderfully comforting as it yielded underfoot. More than ever I realised that for me the delight of mountains was exclusively visual. I had allowed myself to be fascinated by a mere idea; the splendour of peak and precipice, which I had made a habit of exaggerating, was nothing but a romantic illusion. What I really appreciated was this maritime atmosphere, in which I wallowed as I walked along.

It was pleasant, too, to be on our own again. The shingle gradually gave way to an expanse of dark grey sand which looked, and in summer felt, as hot as ashes; there was no-one in sight on this natural cinder-track which, after the hampering horizons of the gorge, seemed to stretch onwards to infinity. Nothing ruffled its surface but a single trail, so light and regular as to be barely perceptible— the rubber-soled footsteps of some solitary traveller who had forestalled us.

But in Crete it is impossible to travel far on the flat, least of all along this southern coast; the cliffs soon intervened, and we found ourselves veering inland to circumvent a rock-red barrier camouflaged with pine and oleander, wild lilac and dwarf broom—a luxuriance which seemed to have been purposely planted there to soften the blow of the landscape beyond. The church which we had come to see lay somewhere at the foot of this gigantic breakwater, which, breached only by the single chasm of Aradaina, extended all the way to Sphakia.

I am not quite sure now what I had been led to expect from the description that I had heard. I believe that I had pictured St. Paul's as a sort of landmark, something as obtrusive as an obelisk on an otherwise denuded sky-line; I may even have imagined it as a miniature cathedral completely buried except for the cross protruding from its dome, an isolated outpost of Christianity constructed by man and symbolically swallowed by nature. Whatever representation I had formed in my mind's eye was at once erased by the actual sight of it. I had not been prepared to come upon it so suddenly. I had thought that it would be visible at a greater distance and that we would approach it—though I cannot explain why or how—from below. For this reason alone, perhaps, I was disappointed to find it a few yards off at our feet, its engineered angles and curves worn away into an asymmetrical shape barely distinguishable from that of the stony slabs surrounding it.

The most apt description of St. Paul's comes from Professor Dawkins, who compares it to a valuable casket accidentally dropped on the shore. There is, indeed, a metallic quality about the little chapel; its walls gleam against the green of the pine-trees, as though hammered out of tarnished copper and silver sheets, their predominating tints of blue-grey and pale-orange not easily associated with stone. But it is the size more than the colour of this delicate edifice that reminds one of a trinket carelessly mislaid and in danger of being lost forever. That danger, however, if it exists at all, is certainly not immediate. Far from lying half-buried in the sands, St. Paul's stands on a platform of rock at least ten feet above the beach, which in any case consists not of sand but shingle. Unless it falls a victim to the usual Cretan vandalism, this church will stand for centuries to come, unaffected by sand or any other Aeolian deposit.

We scrambled up the rough flight of steps to the door and peered inside. Some goats had been here before us—whether of their own accord or forcibly introduced to test the alleged mine, it was impossible to tell; though the quantity of droppings all over the floor might have been an indication of their fear. At all events their weight had not detonated the mine—if there really was a mine underneath that pile of sand patterned all over with their footprints. I doubted it myself and so did Daphne, but neither of us was prepared to convince the other by boldly stepping forward. We might, of course, have inadvertently stepped backwards while viewing the wall-paintings; but these hardly warranted such a conventional gesture of admiration.

Still, St. Paul's had been worth the journey. Daphne and I felt almost triumphant at the ease with which we had got here after so many self-imposed setbacks; we decided to celebrate our success by squandering a whole reel of film on the church. But the camera apparently did not share our enthusiasm; there was no answering click to the pressure of Daphne's thumb; the shutter had jammed. Not a great catastrophe—a minor repair by an expert was all that was needed—but it seemed overwhelming at the time; we felt that the church had cheated us in a secret conspiracy with the camera. The shutter had never behaved like this before; it had always clicked merrily, even when faced with dull demanding models like those people in Canea, complete strangers, who would stop us in the street and ask us to take their photograph. Metaphorically St. Paul's, too, was begging to be taken—a perfect subject—yet Daphne, for the first time, was unable to comply with the request.

The church is said to have been erected here to commemorate the island's liberation from "wild beasts and noxious animals."[1] It is on this site, too, that the saint is supposed to have baptized his first converts; presumably, then, there once existed a copious spring in which those early Christians were immersed. The only sign of it that remains today is the water that bubbles up through some pebbles at the very edge of the sea. Had we not been told about it, we should never have found it; on a rough day it is swamped by the breakers. Even now Daphne and I could only detect it by lying down in the sea and lapping our way along its fringe as each wave subsided; until we found the salt water turned, as though by a miracle, to fresh.

This was our first bathe of the year. We felt that summer was really here, although the sun managed to push only an occasional beam through the blanket of haze which hung from the cliffs. Every bit of land five hundred feet above sea-level was blotted out, invisible; the sky seemed to be right on top of us. Our path, however, lay only a little way uphill; we should probably avoid the mist.

The first part of the gentle ascent led through a forest of pine-trees, their needles on the ground providing a soft, if somewhat slippery, carpet for our feet: a welcome change from rock and stone. What we could see of the landscape was no more indomitable than the tamest stretch along the Riviera. But just as we were congratulating ourselves on the prospect of such easy going, we found the path blocked by a forbiddingly deep crevasse of boulders. There was no direct way across it. My natural inclination was to work downwards to the sea, since Yiannis had told us that the general direction of our path was along the coast—all except a short uphill stretch which was necessary to circumvent a steep promontory. There was a promontory in front of us now. I also thought that I could see a way across the scree further up; this seemed to answer to Yiannis's description of the path which we were meant to take. "You can't miss it," he had cheerfully assured us.

But we did miss it. I had stupidly forgotten my map, and so had no means of checking the route that had been outlined for us, All

---

1. St. Paul's local representative, Titus—Crete's first bishop and patron saint—is likewise credited with ridding the island of snakes. He appears to have been less successful than St. Patrick in Ireland; snakes, though not poisonous ones, are still found in Crete.

Sphakians are wonderfully fast walkers in these mountains. All Sphakians think that they are faster than they actually are; or even if they do not think so, they say so. How, then, was I to judge what Yiannis had meant by "a little way uphill"? The distance, say, that he would claim to cover in half an hour? That was as good a yard-stick as any. It meant a distance for which he would require well over an hour; so that Daphne and I could be calculated to cover it in just under two.

Long before that time was up, we had reached the level of the mist. From down below it had looked like a static blanket, heavy and windless; but as soon as we stepped into it we were buffeted by the cross currents of air that seemed to be trapped inside. Although the coastline was now blotted out, the visibility was still unhappily good enough for us to see not only the precipice that we happened to be scaling, but also the next one which we would shortly have to scale. This was discouraging enough, but more frightening still was the sudden cold. It increased our sense of being hopelessly lost, in the same way that darkness intensifies claustrophobia.

Yet there was one comfort: the unmistakable path. In spite of the landslides which we had to cross, in spite of the angle of our ascent which at times seemed almost vertical, the path loyally persisted; it persisted in spite of the threat of ending in mid-air at every turn on its zigzag course up the cliff. It persisted, although I was no longer confident that it would ever lead us to Loutro. Still, it would obvi-ously lead somewhere; those large slabs of stone cunningly laid to form a staircase up the side of the mountains were slippery and pol-ished with use; they were identical with those that I had seen on another main mountain route—the one from Souyia up the Selino valley. So long as it continued uphill, we could easily follow it. We did so, for almost three hours. Then, suddenly, it came to an end as it had threatened to do—not, it is true, in mid-air, but almost. We walked off it not into space but on to the flat. We had reached the top.

The mist here was thicker than ever. It surged upwards and over us like a wave, to break into foam-like particles on the level ground beyond. But I felt as though we had, indeed, reached shore; I could hear the bells of a nearby shepherd's flock. I gave a high-pitched shriek, then followed it up with a shout: "Where are we?"

This shriek was not intended as a signal of alarm, but as the con-ventional opening to a conversation conducted in space. Like a "hello" on the telephone, it attracts the hearer's attention and prepares him for the words to come. This method of telolaly is widely used in Crete and, on a clear day, is extraordinarily effective. I once heard two shepherds conversing in this manner across a distance which would have required more than an hour to traverse on foot. Their words bridged the gap in a second; I fancied I could see as well as hear them as they winged their way across in a trajectory as visible, to the mind's eye, as that of a tracer-bullet. In this mist, however, my shout was devoid of all piercing power; as though the bullet had been fired into a sandbag. Yet promptly there came an answering yell, then distinctly the two words: "Ayios Ioannis!" The sound seemed to drive a tunnel through the surrounding haze; for an instant the curtain of mist was shredded, and through a clear rift I saw not only the owner of that lonely voice but also, far behind him, the village which he had just announced by name.

18

Ayios Ioannis

THE MIST PROVED to be no thicker than the wall of a fortification, breached now by the sound of the shepherd's call. We passed through the opening and emerged on to a sunlit plateau dotted with rock and scrub. Snarling with alarm at our sudden appearance, a dog came bounding towards us.

Cretan dogs, according to Pashley, are all of one race and are peculiar to the island; "they are smaller than the greyhound and have a longer and rougher coat of hair: their head is somewhat like that of the wolf. . . . I feel no doubt that these dogs are the undebased descendants of those mentioned by ancient authors." The Cretan breed was rightly celebrated in times of remote antiquity, but I doubt if it has since been preserved. Tournefort refers to the dogs that he saw here as "*des lévriers bâtards.*"

I could see no trace of greyhound in the mongrel that advanced on us now; but *bâtard* it certainly was—in the colloquial English sense of the word. A stranger can keep most shepherd's dogs at bay by bending down and pretending to pick up a stone. This one was not so easily daunted. Even when it saw the stone in my hand it pressed forward its attack, even when it received the stone full in the ribs it faltered only long enough to let out an angry yelp before continuing the onslaught, which it might have kept up indefinitely had it not been called off by its owner.

The shepherd, a lad of fifteen, showed no surprise at the sight of two strangers appearing, it must have seemed, straight out of the sky. His blue eyes flashed a constant enquiry, but he waited for us to tell him who we were and what we were doing. Our explanation must have sounded unlikely: if we were really bound for Loutro, what on earth were we doing up here? But the lad seemed more amazed than suspicious as he told us that we were still as far from our destination as we were when we started from St. Paul's. Instead of following the coast we had climbed the Sellouda, the steepest entrance of all into the White Mountains. There was no hope of getting to Loutro that night.

"But welcome to Ayios Ioannis," he concluded. "We'll be milking shortly; come up to the hut and rest for a while, then we'll see what we can do for you."

Even though we had arrived by mistake, I was glad that we were here. I had planned to visit Ayios Ioannis some day, in any case; for I had heard that, besides being one of the most remote, it was also one of the prettiest villages in Crete. From the plateau not many of its houses were visible, but the few that I could see looked as though they were made of marble, white-clean against the wooded slopes behind. Cypress and fir-trees grew here even more thickly than on the undisturbed heights of Selino: relics of the huge forests which every early traveller to Sphakia had noticed and admired.

In those days the inhabitants were an easy-going people who had no need to till their poor soil in order to scrape a living. "Because of the aridity of their mountains," observed Belon, "they do not cultivate the ground but live by the sale of cypress timber, and on the milk of their herds of goats." Deforestation has put an end to wood-cutting as an industry; but the herds are still plentiful. Flock after flock of sheep as well as goats were brought into the pen where Daphne and I sat watching the milking—a lengthy process because of the numbers, which required six milkmen instead of the normal two. They converged one after another from all directions, their owners cursing and shrieking, waving their kerchiefs and hurling stones with wonderful accuracy to head them off—the only method of controlling the stampede since their dogs are not trained for the task.

It was almost sunset by the time the last herd was driven out, and the milkmen and shepherds sat down with us to rest from their efforts. Their work at least was over for the day. The milk was poured into goatskins and then carted off by a convoy of mules instead of being made into cheese on the spot. Rather than spend all night on that tiresome task, the men of Ayios Ioannis prefer to deliver their milk wholesale to a buyer from Athens—the first and only example of middleman enterprise that I had come across in these mountains.

This scheme had apparently been designed to afford the local population sufficient leisure for more profitable activities, the nature of which was made quite clear when the shepherds refused the cigarettes which we offered and instead asked us to try their home-grown tobacco. There was nothing unusual in this. Despite the Government monopoly and the laws against private tobacco plantations, almost everyone in the island grows enough for his own personal use. And the local weed tastes better, not only because it is forbidden—it is also delightfully harsh, with the same painful though comforting effect on throat and lung as massage on a muscle. The only nasty thing about smoking it is the old bit of newspaper in which it is usually rolled; cigarette-paper is not allowed to be manufactured in Greece.

But the shepherds here were well equipped with what they laughingly described as their "imports." "In this part of the world we have our own laws and customs," they explained, little realizing how pertinent was the play on the last word when translated into English. Rolled in good cigarette-paper smuggled direct from Egypt, the tobacco of Ayios Ioannis made a blissful smoke.

The Christian version of The Good Shepherd is, I suppose, responsible for the universal notion that pastoral activity is essentially innocent. The Cretans are too realistic to regard their national occupation through such falsifying rose-coloured glasses; they prefer to preserve, however unconsciously, their proud tradition of lawlessness. Their forefathers of old contrived to be pirates as well as shepherds; it is only fitting, then, that they themselves should maintain, in a manner more suited to the present day, a similar association with the sea and, above all, with the coast.

I found this cheerful disregard for the law a captivating quality; our companions at the pen were banded together in a brotherhood as firm and loyal as any founded for social or religious ends. And I felt flattered that they should have taken us so quickly into their confidence. Perhaps it was the atmosphere of truancy created by our illicit smoking that made me feel like a schoolboy again, proud to be "a member of the gang" and happy to have been noticed by its leader—in this case a crimson-faced, black-bearded comedian who introduced himself as Andreas Malephakis. With the sort of sensation that comes from requited hero-worship, I accepted his invitation to stay the night, and lightheartedly followed him with Daphne as he led the way up to the village through a waist-high swamp of yellow-flowering sage phosphorescent in the evening light.

It was too dark to see much of the village; the houses in the gathering dusk were no more than the ghosts of their sunlit selves. But in spite of their unsubstantial appearance, they gave an effect of permanence which was confirmed in actuality by the interior of Andreas's main room. Here, for the first time since my return to Crete, I was impressed by a sense of solid and enduring craftsmanship. The furniture was old and worn but not decrepit: the heavy chairs, built on a mediaeval Venetian design, looked as though they had been used for centuries and would last for centuries longer. The carved stand for the tiny oil-lamp was made of wood but felt as heavy as iron. And the rugs on the massive polythrone, although identical in pattern with all the others I had seen in Crete,[1] were shown to better advantage against a background which, for once, was neither newly jerry-built nor falling to pieces with age. The obvious care with which all these materials were preserved, apart from their actual quality, was responsible for the immediate sense of comfort.

Although we had no wine to drink—the nearest vineyards were in Anopolis—we spent a hilarious evening: Andreas was a natural comedian. He knew it and played to the gallery, which consisted of Daphne and myself and half a dozen visiting neighbours ranged along the polythrone like a theatre audience. Andreas performed his one-man act sitting in the centre of the room, while his wife behind him heaved on the rope of a swing hammock in which their child lay fast asleep. Throughout the performance this silent bundle described a sweeping arc through the air from one corner of the roof to the other.

---

1. The patterns for Cretan rugs date from remote antiquity—in the words of the women who weave them, "from always." Certain well-established motifs, such as the bird-on-the-tree, are no doubt based on fertility symbols handed down from the Minoan Age, since when Byzantine, Saracenic and Venetian (but no modern) designs have also been introduced. Cretan home-made ware has therefore been spared the self-conscious "arty-craftiness" due to false folk-revivalism which is noticeable in the peasant handicraft of many other parts of the Mediterranean.

The highlight of the evening was Andreas's attempt to read phonetic English from an American phrasebook issued by the E.C.A.
headquarters in Athens. If everyone else in Greece finds as much
difficulty in mastering it as Andreas apparently did, then this useful
little publication must, I am afraid, be considered yet another waste
of Marshall Aid. The whole room spluttered with Danny Kaye
noises as Andreas tried to curl his tongue round the fugitive consonants and elusive diphthongs, his moustache curling in sympathy
with the effort to capture the unpronounceable words.

Even in his own language the sounds that he made were strange
enough; his crackling Sphakian syllables were delivered as though
scrambled through a defective microphone. As much nonsense
has been talked about the Sphakian dialect as about the Sphakian
race. It has been referred to alternatively as "pure Greek" or "pure
Doric," and peculiarities have been attributed to it "which may have
descended from the days of Minos." If the citizens of Knossos spoke
Greek in the same sort of way that an uneducated Chinaman is supposed to speak English, then the claim to Minoan descent may be
justified; for the Sphakian even today seems unable to distinguish
between an 'l' sound and an 'r.' But this confusion is the only extant
peculiarity of the modern Sphakian idiom.

There are, admittedly, certain words and phrases exclusive to this
remote and mountainous province; but then everywhere in Crete,
even in those districts near the capital which are most of all liable to
linguistic reform, there are vestiges of purely local vocabulary. In the
prefecture of Canea alone, a walking-stick is known under five different names, which are used respectively and independently in five
separate geographical areas.

Andreas's manner of speech fascinated me, not because his conversation sparkled with phrases that were new, but because he made
a novel use of those that were already familiar. Every sentence of
his was cluttered with the recurrent verbal trinity "*me to sympa-
theion*":[2] three words of apology which are invariably inserted before
any noun which might be considered to give offence, such as "donkey," or "pig." I have never heard it used, as Pashley did, in front of

---

2. Untranslatable: the nearest English equivalent would be "begging your pardon." Language snobs afraid of soiling their lips with such a "genteel" phrase
would have to use a more cumbersome alternative, such as: "If you'll forgive me
for saying so."

the word "Jew"; but time and again I have witnessed its accompaniment to the simple gesture of raising a forearm in order to denote the size or length of an object under discussion—in case, I suppose, this erect limb should be taken to represent not a measuring-rod but a rod in the English slang sense of the word. Andreas never once made this gesture. Nor, as far as I can remember, did he mention a pig or a donkey in the entire course of the evening. Yet he used the conventional apology so frequently and incongruously that everything he said sounded comically contrite. It was only when we were going to bed that he broke out into a vernacular that was completely strange to me.

"What time do you have to leave tomorrow?" he asked.

"As early as possible."

"Then I'll wake you up 'at hand-day.'"

This idiom, translated here quite literally, defeated me, until he explained that he meant the time of day when the sun was a hand's breadth above the horizon.

In these clockless and watchless villages the sun is the only time-piece; its splendid variability suits the nature of the congenitally unpunctual inhabitants, many of whom are still unable to make much sense of a couple of pointers moving round a dial. A young bride, who was recently given a watch as a wedding-present, tried to hide her ignorance, when asked the time, by glancing surreptitiously at the sun before pretending to consult the strange toy on her wrist. Then she looked up and proudly announced: "Just a little before the mid-morning break!"

I had no idea what time, by my watch, the sun rose above the horizon at Ayios Ioannis. Though we knew that we would have to start early in the morning if we wanted to get to Loutro by daylight, Daphne and I were both tired and in need of a long rest. We went to sleep hoping that the crags to the east would somehow double their height in the night, or that Andreas would wake up miraculously transformed, with each hand as broad as a tray.

———————

It was long past "hand-day" when we woke up—of our own accord and not to the summons of Andreas, who had left the house before dawn to see to his flocks. He returned just in time to share our nine o'clock breakfast—a repetition of the evening meal: bread and rice-pudding—and as soon as we had eaten, we got up and left. No

Sphakian ever remains at table once the food is finished—I suppose because there is no wine for him to enjoy at his leisure.

I wish we could have stayed longer in Ayios Ioannis, but we had to be back in Canea on the following day: Daphne was once again returning to England. We had no time for more than a casual glance at the village; but even that was sufficient to confirm the impression I had had of it in yesterday's twilight. The houses here withstood, and even seemed to defy, the most searching scrutiny of the sun's direct rays. Individually, they were not much better designed than those of any other mountain village; the usual ugly features were in evidence, such as poky little windows all innocent of glass, but they were less obtrusive in their present setting which was not so uncompromisingly utilitarian as most. These buildings had been made to be looked at as well as to be lived in; and not only one by one, but as part of a general visual effect. Whether accidentally or with intent, the separate masses of masonry were so grouped as to form a harmonious whole—a unique achievement in a country with no inherent architectural sense.

But the most attractive quality about Ayios Ioannis was a negative one: the complete absence of decay. There was not a ruin in sight. The village, admittedly, had never in its history been destroyed. Snug behind its natural defences—the mountains to the north, the coastal cliff to the south and the two gorges of Aradaina and Samaria to the east and west respectively—it had eluded the depredations both of Janissary and Nazi. But so had other villages, which nevertheless were still littered with ruins caused not by the passage of any invader but by the negligence of the native population. Elsewhere abandoned houses would be looted till only the shell—and sometimes not even that—remained; churches, unless in daily use, would be left to crumble where they stood. In Ayios Ioannis the disused monastery of St. John, which gave the village its name, was not only intact but restored—another example of communal pride which I had noticed nowhere else.

For our benefit, Andreas drove his flock across the plateau as far as the point from which he would be able to put us on the path for Loutro. Our progress was retarded by his animals, which kept blundering in senseless panic at the sound of two strange voices behind them. Sheep, of course. But there was one goat as well: a solitary black kid which, in what must have been a moment of juvenile aberration, had deserted its own kind in favour of these bleating brutes.

The stampede which I expected to break out from one minute to another was only averted by Andreas's constant whistling—an irritating noise from which they, however, seemed to derive comfort. It was amazing that such stupid beasts should be able to distinguish one voice from another—as amazing as the ability of these shepherds, almost all of whom are exceptionally unmusical, to distinguish the sound of their own sheep's bells from those of their neighbours' flocks.

But Andreas's shrill instructions were not completely understood; or if they were, they sometimes went unheeded. One or more of these trotting bundles of wool would occasionally dart away in the wrong direction, to be headed off by an accurately aimed stone. Not once did Andreas's missiles either hit the sheep or fail to turn it; every stone landed exactly where it was required—a few feet to the side of the straying animal, close enough to frighten it back into line. But this stone-throwing was a tiring business; by the time we reached the far side of the plateau Andreas was redder in the face than ever and dripping with sweat. No wonder! Under his black silk shirt he wore a garment which no self-respecting shepherd ever thinks of doffing, even in the height of summer: a woollen vest as thick and hairy as a Hebridean sweater.

It was typical of Andreas's hospitality that he should have gone to the extra trouble of accompanying us so far in order to give us our bearings. He explained the route which we had to take in detail, describing each feature which we should encounter on the way; so that there was little risk of our getting lost again. "But I hope you do," he told us as we said goodbye, "then you'll have to come straight back here. And next time I shan't let you leave so soon."

It was just as well that he did come with us; without his instructions we should never have found our way. Scarcely anyone goes to Loutro direct from Ayios Ioannis—the high road in this district passes through Anopolis and Aradaina—so the path which we took was out of use and overgrown. Plunging down towards the main gorge a mile or more away, it soon petered out in a tangle of boulders and undergrowth. The surface of this winding watercourse was like that of a shattered ice-rink; my worn-down hob-nails skated over it. Daphne, in tennis shoes, fared scarcely any better; the jagged rocks pierced those thin rubber soles of hers in no time.

I have never been able to make up my mind what form of footgear is best suited to the mountainous paths of Crete. The shepherds here once used to wear boots with ridged soles made of leather. They now prefer to nail bits of discarded motor-car tyres on to the bottom of their shoes—not only as a novelty but for the sake of economy; any tyre-manufacturer would be delighted to hear the unsolicited testimonials of durability which his product provokes all over the island. A tyre certainly lasts long enough, as anything so horribly heavy should; I used to walk tyre-shod during the war, but I was tougher in those days; I had to be, with what felt like a hundredweight clamped to each foot. Nails, though lighter, are no better, as I was now beginning to realize after wearing them for almost a year. With each skidding shrieking step, I longed more and more for the comfort and security of rope—not round my waist but on the soles of my feet. Espadrilles, I felt, would be a god-send in Crete; so long as one was prepared to wear out at least one pair every day.

We reached the bottom of the gorge at last, and there, a little way up the opposite side, was the spring which Andreas had described: a pool of water bubbling gently from a moss-lined cavity in the rocks. Shaded by giant delphiniums, it was mercifully situated just where it was most needed: a few feet off the path. We only had to lie down in turn and insert our head into this cool cavern to feel our cheeks cushioned against the fern inside as we lapped the water seeping up through them.

Once on top of the cliff, we emerged again on to the familiar lunar landscape of the Sphakian littoral. The path led over vast stony downs, at one time inhabited but long since abandoned; each isolated ruin was a monument to nature's victory over man. The soil here must have broken the hearts as well as the plough-shares of those forgotten pioneers who made the first hopeless attempt to till it. Nothing grew here now, not even goat-fodder; the ground we trod was as curved and bare as a gigantic Byzantine dome—a sim-ile which automatically suggested itself when we found ourselves, at the top of a rocky rise, walking over the roof of a church. We had reached the village of Livaniana.

The houses here, built into the side of the coastal slope, seem to lie one on top of another rather than side by side; the front door of each can only be approached across the roof of the building below it. But we devoted no more than a glance to this architectural novelty; the western bay of Loutro was now in sight; our aim was to reach it as quickly as possible and plunge into the beckoning sea.

The remaining hours of daylight, which we spent in and out of the water, were sufficient reward for the decision we had taken to return by the longer route instead of through Aradaina and Anopolis. It was not only the lure of Loutro that had dictated our choice. Had we taken the easier highroad to Sphakia, we should have been forced to stay there for the night; and I was sure that the Douroundous radio was still in working order. Instead, we were enabled to spend our last evening on the coast in more congenial surroundings. The Athitakis family welcomed us home, and their welcome lasted until dawn, when Andreas dropped his nets and rowed us on to Sphakia in time for us to catch the morning bus.

19

FRANGOKASTELLO

Dᴀᴘʜɴᴇ's ᴅᴇᴘᴀʀᴛᴜʀᴇ coincided with the arrival of another friend from England, Hugh Farmar, an amateur botanist, who had chosen Crete for his summer holidays. Hugh was also interested in ibex-preservation, so I arranged for Costis Paterakis to show him the lairs above Koustoyerako. Unfortunately I was unable to accompany him myself; I had a date with some ghosts which were said to materialize only during that one week in the year. I could not afford to miss them. So, while Hugh made his way from Canea down to Selino, I prepared for my journey in the opposite direction to Frangokastello,[1] the scene of the alleged phenomenon. We had agreed to meet again in Sphakia in a week's time.

No one seems to know exactly when the ghosts of Frangokastello made the first of their annual appearances. They were certainly an established feature by the end of the last century. Manoussos Koundouros mentions them in his *Diary of the Cretan Rebellion of 1895* and explains what they are meant to be—the regimented materialized souls of the 385 soldiers led by Hadjimichalis Daliannis, who were killed in a battle against the Turks towards the end of the Greek War of Independence. Clearly, then, they were already a familiar

---

1. This so-called "Castle of the Franks" was built by the Venetians. "Franks" was once used in the same way that "European" is used now, to denote a Christian of a nationality other than Greek. Further instances of this loose terminology are "Turk" (a Moslem of any country) and "Arab" (anyone from Africa).

phenomenon, although they had not yet been given the name by which they are known today—the *Drossoulites*, or Dewy Shades, so-called because they appear only when the dew of early morning is still on the ground.

Since my return to Crete I had spoken to several people who claimed to have seen them—mostly peasants from the village overlooking the old Venetian fort which commands the one-time battle-field. Their individual descriptions were so vivid and unvaried that I could not dismiss the alleged materialization as a "tall story" based on popular superstition. Besides, there was the written evidence—admittedly somewhat out of date—of a completely disinterested witness. A government official called Psyllakis had recorded his impression of the *Drossoulites*, which he saw in the summer of 1904 during a walking tour in the White Mountains. Since then no one, apart from the local villagers, has ever observed the phenomenon; so the field was still clear for a little amateur investigation. I decided to go to Frangokastello and see for myself whatever there was to be seen.

From the bus stop far above Sphakia, the only building visible on the coast is Frangokastello itself, an isolated block of masonry of which the ruined parts are concealed by distance. The late afternoon light in which I first saw it transformed it into a gleaming landmark—a direct target for the rays of the setting sun. But mere reflection, I felt, could not alone be responsible for such luminosity; it looked as though a whole day's sunshine had been captured and stored within those walls, impregnating the very stone and mortar, which gleamed all the brighter, like the phosphorescent hands and figures of a watch, the more that darkness threatened.

The fort is separated from the main road by what at first glance seems to be a gently sloping plain. But there is no path diagonally across it. I realized why as soon as I started walking. The track which I took—the only one visible—was sandy and soft. I assumed that it would lead me in less than an hour to Patsianos, which lay in a fold of the mountains, out of sight but only three miles away. I had advanced only a few hundred yards, however, before I came to the first of the many rifts which slice the ground between the foothills and the sea into a series of parallel strips. I saw then that the fabric of the plain was not the smooth material that I had imagined. It was corduroy.

I should have known at once that the promise of easy going was bound to prove false. The apparent evenness of this bit of country had been too good to be true, too utterly unlike the rest of the Cretan littoral. Here the familiar cliffs split by chasms were to be found not on the coast but a mile inland. As though to make up for their absence by the sea, these rifts splitting the plain existed instead, each one a chasm in miniature, so neat and regular as to appear man-made: a sort of elementary and purposeless irrigation system. Some were only a few yards across—almost, but not quite, narrow enough for an athlete to take in his stride—yet dropped sheer to a lethal depth in the centre of the plain, where a succession of bridges would have been required to carry a path across. For economy's sake, therefore, the only track was built along the northern fringe, skirting the root of the foothills where the rifts present less of an obstruction.

There was also, I noted, another reason for the position of this main local thoroughfare; the villages which it serves stand not in the open country but half-concealed against the mountain slopes. No community in Crete, other than an exclusively sea-going one, is situated on the coast, for fear of a sudden attack from pirates. Even so, the villages which I now passed a mile inland looked as though they had lately fallen victim to an unexpected raid. They were not damaged but deserted, and the silence of so many houses left intact was more eerie in the evening light than the atmosphere of any ruin. I knew, of course, that in theory all lowland villages are evacuated during the summer, but nowhere had I come across total evacuation; in Sphakia and Loutro life still went on. Here, in Vouvas and Nomi-kiana, nothing stirred, the exodus was complete. Even the gold-and-green grasshoppers which blazoned the scrub and thyme on either side of the path avoided the shadows thrown by the gaunt abandoned buildings. I began to wonder if I would find the same hand of death laid on Patsianos.

But I was soon reassured by the sight of nearby cornfields—the harvest was in progress; somewhere, then, there were harvesters—and, from a distant olive-grove, the sound of voices. And when the first houses drifted into view a little later, I could sense rather than see—for there was no visible sign—that they were all inhabited.

Were it not for the sweep of the coastal plain in front of it, Patsianos would be indistinguishable from a mountain village. Turn your back to the shore and the houses appear to be hugging the knees of crags which, for all their difference from those above Asi Gonia or Koustoyeroko, might be miles inland and thousands of feet above sea-level. But the village of Patsianos has one peculiarity, it contains no coffee-shop. For their evening relaxation, the inhabitants have to cross over an old stone bridge to the sister-village of Kapsodasos.

I had never been here before, but since I had at one time or another already met a number of the villagers in Sphakia, I was immediately welcomed by friends. The coffee-shop of Kapsodasos fully compensated for the absence of one in Patsianos. The terrace outside was canopied by a vine-trellis; geraniums grew in ranks of white-washed petrol-tins around it—a pathetic attempt at a garden, but nevertheless an attempt, the first I had come across in a Cretan village. But more delightful than all this was the view. The empty plain with its single wide horizon was a comfort to my eyes, which had so long been bewildered by predominantly vertical landscapes. In the mountains I was always in a state of apprehension, tensed to meet the constant visual shock of precipices and jagged skyline. Here, where nothing in sight was higher than the tower of the fortress, I would drop my guard and relax.

The village schoolmaster, a surprisingly erudite young man who looked like Fernandel—like his colleagues in Anopolis, he was clean-shaven—pointed out in turn each feature before me as it cropped up during the conversation. The topic, of course, was the local phenomenon. This was the time of year when the *Drossoulites* made their annual appearance; any day now we might see them. "But they're not always punctual, I'm afraid," said the schoolmaster. "If they really are the ghosts of Hadjimichalis's men, you'd think they'd turn up promptly on May the 18th, wouldn't you? That was the date of the battle. But they don't; some years they're almost two weeks late."

"Perhaps they don't realize the changes from the old calendar to the new,"[2] I replied, and was amazed to see how readily my facetious suggestion was accepted.

"Yes, that's quite a reasonable explanation," one old man admitted. "Sometimes I get confused between the two myself."

But there was no confusion in anyone's mind about the *Drossoulites* themselves. Several men who came into the coffee-shop that evening claimed to have seen them, and the individual descrip-

---

2. It was not until 1923 that Greece abandoned the Julian calendar in favour of the Gregorian, which had been adopted in some parts of Europe as early as 1582.

tions of what they saw tallied in every detail. The ghosts, it seemed, always materialized at the same time of day, a few minutes before the sun came over the eastern curve of the crags behind us. They were invisible from the village itself but could be seen quite clearly from a section of the plain known locally as "Thyme Field." They appeared as a vast column of armed soldiers, some on foot, others on horseback, and all a little larger than life-size. They emerged at first from the neighbourhood of St. Charalambos (a ruined priory which, in the darkness mounting around us, could be distinguished only as a distant patch against the lighter background of the uncut corn) and would then move, slightly above ground-level, in the direction of the fortress, where they vanished as soon as the first rays of the sun struck the fields.

They appeared most clearly, it was noticed, when the weather was unusually damp and when a north wind was expected. In these conditions their swords and helmets could be easily distinguished, and one shape, even taller than the others, could be seen—the phantom of Hadjimichalis himself.

The clearest apparition of all had been in 1928—which, of course, was only to be expected, since that year was the centenary of the battle. On that occasion the *Drossoulites* had seemed so life-like that a woman working in the fields had mistaken them for a gang of harvesters arriving from another village. Later still, during the occupation in the last war, they had again been mistaken for a living crowd; the German coastguards stationed on the plain had fired at them on the assumption that an Allied landing was under way.

So much for the movements of the *Drossoulites*—on that point everyone was agreed. But the nature of the phenomenon was not so easily settled. The younger men in the coffee-shop ridiculed their elders' belief in ghosts. They could not, of course, deny what they themselves had seen with their own eyes, but they refused to admit the possibility of a psychic materialization. One of them, who had obviously acquired the correct vocabulary from some pseudo-scientific article in an Athens magazine, proudly announced that the whole business was simply a question of mass auto-suggestion. But this sophisticated solution did not explain why the apparition should occur at regular yearly intervals and during one season alone. Another suggestion was tentatively put forward: perhaps the *Drossoulites* were nothing more than the expanding shadows of the crags moving across the plain? A sensible, though somewhat prosaic, explanation—which could only be valid, however, if the sun rose in the west and set in the east. For at the time of day that the *Drossoulites* were said to appear, the shadows of the crags would not only be diminishing but moving in a direction exactly opposite to that of the alleged advance of the phantoms. And even supposing the solar system to be miraculously inverted for a few specific seconds every year, why should the consequent shadows be visible from Thyme Field alone and nowhere else?

The third argument I heard, which at first sounded the most far-fetched of all, was probably the nearest approach to a reasonable solution. The *Drossoulites*, it was suggested, were indeed shadows, but not of the crags; they were the projected shadows of a caravanserai crossing the African desert, which lay due south of us across the sea. Stripped of its more obviously illogical aspect, here was a suggestion which openly declared what the others had only hinted: the *Drossoulites* were simply a mirage, an ordinary optical illusion. Everything pointed to that; the atmospheric conditions required for the apparition, the position of the sun at the specified hour of the day, both were climatic factors which drove one, however reluctantly, to a clear scientific conclusion. The *Drossoulites* of Frangokastello were to be explained in the same terms as the Fata Morgana of the Straits of Messina or the Spectre of the Brocken in the Harz Mountains.

A disappointing solution, too facile, too technical. But more disappointing still was the attitude of the local youths, all of whom instinctively groped for an up-to-date "progressive" explanation, although they were not yet sufficiently eloquent to put it into words. Eventually, I suppose, every schoolboy in Patsianos and Kapsodasos will be equipped with the correct terminology and will dutifully describe the phenomenon as "caused by progressive but sporadic variations in the refractive indices of adjacent layers of the atmosphere," or something of that sort. All very right and proper, too. But I could not help feeling glad that the time had not yet come and that there were still people here, like the old men, who preferred superstition to jargon.

An absurdly romantic outlook, of course; I had to fight against it. As I started back to Patsianos with the schoolmaster, who had invited me to stay with him, I contrived to assume the "no-nonsense" expression of a determined, clear-headed investigator. "We'll look into this matter tomorrow," I said in a tone of voice intended to con-

vey the exact degree of supercilious confidence which I felt was expected of me.

————

We were up and out on the plain well before first light. Leaving
my bed so early had been no hardship. I thought that I was by now
quite immune to fleas; Patsianos had proved that I was not. In spite
of the D.D.T. which the schoolmaster sprinkled all over our blankets—even he, a native of the village, took precautions against the
particularly vicious bite of the local vermin—I had hardly been able
to sleep at all.

In Thyme Field the harvesters were already assembling in the
darkness and, as the sky gradually faded above the crags in the east,
the surrounding fields also slowly took shape and I began to distinguish the individual features of the landscape. It was too early yet
to be aware of any colour in it, but every outline was finally clari-
fied. The darker shapes I could recognize as women—as with the
olive-harvest, only women are employed on the arduous task of harvesting the corn—and as they stooped and bent at their work, their
curved backs rose here and there like playful porpoises above the
billowing expanse of the fields. It was hard to imagine such a peaceful, pastoral scene disturbed by a visitation.

Yet it was now or never that the ghosts would appear if they were
to appear at all that day. The sun was already approaching the sky-
line and announcing its approach indirectly; the crags were thrown
into sharper silhouette, as the hump of a road is sometimes outlined
by night against the glare of ascending but still invisible headlights.
I peered across the corn in the direction of the ruined priory, and
kept peering—until I saw the first rays of the sun glint on the parch-
ment-coloured stones. Too late in the day now for the *Drossoulites* to
put in an appearance. I was disappointed, but not surprised; in that
utterly un-spooky atmosphere I had hardly expected them to materialize. There was no point in waiting any longer; the schoolmaster
offered to show me around the one-time battlefield and together we
made our way down to the coast.

From Patsianos the plain looks almost completely deserted. Frangokastello dominates the view to such an extent that the neighbouring buildings, most of them in ruins like the fortress itself,
are all overshadowed. I had no idea, for instance, of the number of

churches that were prodigally scattered about the corn-fields and near the shore, until we came upon them one by one.

Suitably situated right on the sea was the chapel of St. Pelagia, patron saint of sailors. This insignificant building would scarcely have been worth a glance had it not been for the surroundings. Accustomed as I was to the usual Cretan coastlines of rock and cliff only occasionally relieved by a narrow stretch of sand, I was surprised to find vegetable gardens growing a few feet away from the waves. The ground here was so lush that the wild fig and palm-trees sprouting from it looked more like decorative features than living growths normally associated with a parched soil. But even more delightful than the sight of this patch of green, which seemed to challenge the adjacent expanse of blue, was the sound of running water: not the punctuated surge of the sea—for the waves were little more than ripples—but the bubbling chorus of countless streams.

An adequate water supply is the first essential for any village; these countless streams, properly canalized, would serve a whole town. Meanwhile they are exploited only by a handful of villagers who camp here during the summer. For the Cretan still prefers, as Spratt observed, "the free life of shepherd, pedlar and pilgrim to that of a settled agriculturalist"—or, for that matter, of a settled seaman. The Venetians once planned to build an artificial harbour on this site. Had they done so, Patsianos might have become a port to rival Sphakia and Loutro. But in that case the fortress would probably have been dismantled long ago; no Cretan of a later generation could have resisted the urge to lay his hands on such a convenient source of stone already cut and prepared for building. Frangokastello then, owes its present state of preservation to its distance from the nearest habitation.

Even so it has not escaped altogether the customary vandalism. It was already in need of repair over a century ago, at the time of the battle; but during the action itself it suffered no damage at all. It was not until years afterwards that the peasants stripped it of its more easily portable features. The roof, if it was supported by beams, was probably the first bit to be pulled down and carted off: timber is always in demand. Fortunately the enormous stones which went into the construction of the walls and turrets were considered too heavy to tackle. They are still so considered; so that Frangokastello remains today the most complete example of Venetian fortification in the whole of Sphakia.

We entered it by the sea gate, beneath a carved architrave from which a life-size lion of St. Mark snarled down at us in a posture of exaggerated ferocity, as though to distract our attention from the mangy condition of its body; its stony flank was worn away and pitted by the weather; wind and rain had devoured its tail. The innocent, naked appearance of its hindquarters made a mockery of the animal's chiselled attitude; this was no lion, but an overgrown Manx cat posing as one. Still, it was the liveliest feature, the only comic relief in the stony desolation.

Roofless, the interior of the fortress was monastic rather than military. The rectangular corridor formed by a pair of parallel inner walls resembled cloisters, in which a monk would have looked more appropriate than any soldier; age had endowed this ruin, the scene of hectic action, with an atmosphere that was now essentially calm and contemplative. The light, I suppose, was largely responsible for this transformation. Now that they lay uncovered, even the areas of stone inside were sun-drenched and glowed—orange, pink and biscuit-coloured—in the same way as the external walls. Within them I felt I was standing at the centre of a huge, inverted lamp-shade.

The unfiltered glare dazzled us as we stepped outside and walked along the beach below the fortress. A deserted windmill, which the Germans during the occupation had converted into an observation tower, lurched drunkenly against the dunes; without their support it would probably have capsized into the sea, to join the lichen-covered millstones, rusty chains and other disused nautical impedimenta which cluttered up the shallows. A solitary rowing boat, uselessly anchored and half submerged, proclaimed how much the villagers loved the sea.

"Not much fishing on this coast," said the schoolmaster, as though to apologize for the sight, "but look, there's plenty of shooting"; and he pointed out the sandy slope behind us, crisscrossed with the tracks of hares. The idea of these mountain animals running wild all over the shore at once dispelled the maritime atmosphere; when I turned my back to the sea I felt that the fields which separated us from the Priory of St. Charalambos, although only a hundred yards or so inland, might have been in the middle of a continent.

Uncut corn almost engulfed the priory, lapping the base of its walls like water in a moat; a barricade of thistles encircled it for extra protection. I made them an excuse for not visiting the church inside. I did not want to disappoint my guide; but I was getting a little tired of these little ruined chapels, all in a state of similar collapse and all, therefore, more or less identical. The marble pillars in the church of St. Evstratios had been looted—"they made perfect roof-rollers," the schoolmaster explained—while the columns in the church of St. Niketas had been removed from their original position at each corner of a tessellated pavement to make more room for the congregation; apart from that, the difference between the two—and the interest I felt in either—was negligible.

What did intrigue me, however, was how all these churches came to be here. What purpose did they serve in such numbers? And where did the material come from, with which they were built? There was only one logical answer to these questions: the plain was the site of an ancient town, not a trace of which survives—except, perhaps, for the floors of the churches themselves. The community must have been a large one, to warrant so many places of worship— assuming that the present sites were used as such—yet it vanished completely; and in the middle of an open plain. But the presence of Frangokastello and the surrounding buildings affords an explanation to this apparent mystery: the masonry of the ancient houses must have been used as material for the new—the fortress alone would have required at least half the stones available—and the remainder probably lie buried six feet below the corn.

This, I admit, is a *simpliste* theory, which I put forward with all the humility proper to an amateur. It is unsupported by any professional opinion; the two chief English authorities, Spratt and Pashley, who conscientiously investigated other sites along the southern coast, are both disturbingly silent on the question of this one. Neither of them even mentions it as a possibility. But I once came across, in a long-forgotten Cretan song, a reference to some athletic meetings— a local version of the Olympic Games—which used to be held in early Christian times "at St. Niketas." The chapel, then, must have been a recognized centre which served as a focal point for those ancient assemblies; is it too unreasonable to suppose that it also served as the parish church of a town to which it gave its own name?

The schoolmaster and I discussed the matter as we strolled back to the village, but soon abandoned the quicksands of conjecture for the safer ground of modern history; the famous battle at least was an established fact. Yet even here we could not be certain of the details. As on so many other points where Cretan parochial loyalties are involved, the versions of the same account differ. No two historians are in complete agreement either on the political background to this particular phase of the war or on the course of the battle itself. And what is known about the personality of the central character is based on a popular ballad, which is noted—and with reason—for its patriotic sentiments, but not necessarily for its accuracy. At least one of Hadjimichalis's descendants has recorded an impression of his illustrious forefather; but these personal opinions are no more reliable than the descriptions of the battle given to me by two elderly villagers of Patsianos, who drew for their information on the dimly remembered and probably garbled evidence of contemporary eyewitnesses.

In the absence of all authority backed by chapter and verse, the best I could do was to gather together these separate slabs of legend and verisimilitude and, after rejecting the obviously unsuitable pieces, fit the remainder into a mosaic which might conceivably bear some resemblance to the original pattern of scattered and disrupted facts.

By the beginning of 1828 the standard of revolt which had been raised to some purpose on the mainland had become, in Crete, a tattered banner of despair. The islanders were almost completely cut off from the main insurgent movement, and their remaining line of communication, through Grabousa, was being threatened as much by the Greek rebel authorities themselves as by the French and British naval patrols. The local leader had fought hard for possession of the old Venetian fortress, their last link with the mainland. Unfortunately, as soon as they had secured it, they began to use it for piratical as well as patriotic purposes: a habit which they had inherited from almost every resistance movement in Cretan history. Grabousa once more became a nest of corsairs; the provisional government of Nauplia under Count Capodistrias condemned it as such; the Allied blockade was intensified; and the fortress was quickly taken over by a British squadron who subsequently surrendered it to Mohammed Ali.[3]

3. The British frigate *Cambrian* was sunk during these operations—an unimportant event in itself, but significant of this British official attitude to the Greek bid for independence and to Cretan aspirations to union with the mother country once the independence of the mainland had been achieved. The romantic

But not before a relieving force of 300 foot-soldiers and 85 horse-men from Epirus, under the command of Hadjimichalis Daliannis, had safely landed on the rocky promontory. Two months later, after waiting in vain for further supplies—for by that time Crete, though nobly refusing to acknowledge the fact, was out of the struggle—Hadjimichalis withdrew through the White Mountains to join the local chieftains beleaguered on the plain of Frangokastello.

For the Cretans, it was the most critical stage of the war. Apart from this narrow strip of land between the sea and the inland cliffs, the whole of the inland was now dominated by the Turks. Patsianos and Kapsodasos could barely support their own inhabitants; yet the whole remaining resistance movement was concentrated on them. Food for the troops could only be obtained by traditional klephtic methods, and the neighbouring villages were consequently victimized; all the livestock in the area was commandeered, and the crops looted. And a Turkish attack was imminent.

In these circumstances the plan which Hadjimichalis adopted was probably dictated by his upbringing and career more than by any sense of strategy. The outbreak of the war had found him in Trieste. He returned to Greece at once with a cargo of arms bought with his own money, and promptly presented it to the insurgents. He then organized a cavalry force, eight hundred strong, again at his own expense; and with this private army sailed to Beirut in the hope of persuading the Emir governing the Lebanon to revolt against the Sultan. His rough-and-ready troops, however, were under the impression that they were landing as an army of occupation, and immediately started to behave as such. Hadjimichalis managed to withdraw them just in time to avoid a disaster. Back in Greece he took part in the relief of Karystos and served on various other fronts all over the country—in the Peloponnese under Nota-ras, and with Karaiskakis in the fighting round Athens—before he was finally promoted to the Cretan command. He was therefore an experienced irregular soldier.

But not an experienced general. Although he knew he would be outnumbered—for the Turkish commander, Mustapha Pasha, had

---

conception of Great Britain as the champion of Greek liberty, for which Byron's poetry and legend are largely responsible, is apt to blind one to our Government's pro-Turkish policy which continued, at least with regard to Crete, right up to the present century.

openly announced his intention of advancing with a force of at least ten thousand—Hadjimichalis insisted on basing his own troops on the untenable Venetian fortress and meeting the enemy on the flat ground outside. The local leaders advised him to take up a defensive position with them in the hills; a counter-attack launched against the Turkish flank under cover of the gorges and clefts behind Patsianos would have the advantage of surprise, if nothing else. But he refused to listen and even accused them of cowardice. "I'll do the fighting, then," he is reported to have said, "and you can sit up there and look on."

A willfully stupid attitude, of course, but typical of a *pallikari*. Hadjimichalis obviously underestimated his enemy. He had been used to fighting real Turks and not Islamized islanders; he therefore had no idea that the "Turks" in Crete had the same fighting qualities as their Christian compatriots—that, at least, is the explanation given by one historian. Another claims that Mustapha's troops were not Cretan at all, but Albanian. But whatever their nationality, they had won the battle in advance, thanks to Hadjimichalis's headstrong decision.

In the early hours of May the 18th, the large Moslem force that was expected poured into the plain from the east and surged up against the walls of the fortress. In the smoke and confusion of the fighting the Cretan defenders on the hills were unable to distinguish between friend and foe, and so could offer no support. By the end of the day the small Epirote garrison had been wiped out. Hadjimichalis himself, an easy target on his white charger, had been brought down and beheaded. His body was later recovered by the Prioress of St. Charalambos and secretly buried in a corner of the convent; those of his troops were placed in a common grave beneath the sand dunes—the very spot from which the *Drossoulites* are supposed to appear.

But they still would not appear for me. Day after day I got up before dawn and went down to Thyme Field. Every morning I changed my position, watching the plain from various heights and at different angles; I still saw nothing unaccountable. I soon became a standing joke with the harvesters. But they saw nothing either—that, at least, was some comfort. If the *Drossoulites* had been visible to them while remaining invisible to me, I should have been forced to conclude that I was not sufficiently *elephroiskiotos*[4] to see the things of the spirit which are hidden from mortals of duller wit and sense.

After almost a week of these early morning vigils I began to lose confidence as well as patience. The chance of seeing the *Drossoulites* was the only attraction that Patsianos held for me; the days, made longer by my early rising, began to drag unbearably. I was glad when the time arrived for me to meet Hugh in Sphakia. On that day, instead of returning to the flea-bitten tedium of the village, I made my way down to the sea and headed westwards along the coast.

I could find no proper path by the shore, which was broken at regular intervals by the opening of the rifts in the plain. These ditches were wider here but less formidable than a few hundred yards inland; it was easy to scale their walls, which capsized into the sea to form a long succession of sandy coves dotted with oleander and hedged in by thyme, over which bees hummed in the sun like telephone-wires. I was tempted to plunge into the water at the sight of the very first of these bays; but to increase the eventual pleasure, I walked deliberately fast for an hour at least, through a barrage of crickets and grasshoppers which bounced off my face and body like harmless shrapnel, before clambering down to bathe.

It was almost midday when I reached the main road about a quarter of a mile outside Sphakia. I had no idea what time Hugh would be arriving. If everything had gone according to plan, he should have reached Ayia Roumeli last night and arranged for a caique to bring him here this morning. At the moment there was no boat out to sea; but as I descended the last slope into the little harbour, I noticed a vessel at anchor which I had never seen there on my previous visits to Sphakia. Then I recognized it as a Palaeochora boat: Hugh must have got here before me. Sure enough, as I came into the street leading to the Douroundous tavern, I saw him approaching with Costis Paterakis from the opposite direction.

"How long have you been here?"

We asked the question simultaneously; each of us thought that he had kept the other waiting. In fact, we had both arrived at exactly

4. For this word I am indebted to Professor Dawkins, who discovered it during his extensive research into Cretan folklore. I use it here in the original Greek since there is no word in our language to describe this ability to see phenomena such as *Drossoulites*, which occur *in the present*. "Second-sight," the nearest English equivalent, can be applied only to signs of future events.

the same time. Pure coincidence, of course; but the villagers who witnessed our meeting did not think so. "There's organization for you," they applauded. The English have such a reputation in Crete for always "being on time," that the very phrase has been altered locally to "being on English time." Hugh and I must have appeared to them as paragons of punctuality; we made no attempt to shatter the illusion.

Over lunch we discussed our respective expeditions and made plans for the next few days. Hugh's holidays were almost over; he had to be back in Canea that week to catch a homebound aeroplane. My days in Crete were also numbered; I should be leaving soon afterwards. It would have been useless to spend the little time that was left in Patsianos; the *Drossoulites* were late already. But I was determined to give them one more chance, and persuaded Hugh to come back with me for a final dawn vigil.

I was surprised by his enthusiasm. He woke me up next morning at least an hour earlier than was necessary. It was still pitch dark, but he shook me and kept repeating: "Come on, we'll be late." Then I saw the reason for his urgency: he could not stop scratching. The fleas of Patsianos had found a new victim.

For the last time I went down to Thyme Field, with no conviction at all. I realized now that I should never see the *Drossoulites*; that they would never show themselves to me. It was almost as if they resented my presence there and were only waiting for me to leave before consenting to appear before an exclusive audience of harvesters. They had behaved like this once before. In 1928, the year that they showed themselves more clearly than ever, two Englishmen from the Society for Psychical Research had travelled all the way from London to investigate. They had reached Frangokastello in good time and had stayed even longer than I had—all to no purpose. But as soon as they had packed up and left, the *Drossoulites* marched out in all their splendour—several days late, admittedly; by then it was the 4th of June—but by way of compensation they repeated their performance twice, on the 6th and again on the 7th.

I subsequently learnt from Anthony Baynes that my own investigations had a similar sequel. Weeks later, when Anthony visited Frangokastello, he was told that the *Drossoulites* had appeared three days after my departure.

"What did they look like?" he had asked.

"Armed soldiers—the usual."

"On horses?"

"No. That's what's so strange. Before—but always—some of them appeared riding. This year they came on foot, every one of them."

No doubt that was why they came so late. But then the Greeks, who admire punctuality in others, have never made a virtue of it themselves—neither in this life nor, I now realized, in whatever life there is to come.

20

KALLIKRATI

THE QUICKEST WAY back to Canea, of course, was by bus from
Sphakia. But I was getting a little tired of that route; besides, neither Hugh nor I was in such a desperate hurry to return. We therefore decided to walk right over the main range and make our way
down to the north coast on foot. For me this plan had an additional
attraction; our path would lead up the Kallikrati Gorge immediately behind Patsianos—the only entrance to the stronghold of the
White Mountains that I had not yet tackled. This final journey,
then, which was also inevitably in the nature of a self-conscious farewell, would neatly round off my twelve months' visit; our last night
would be spent at the very centre of my year's activity, in the highest
part of the area which I had surveyed. Even if this had no particular
significance, it would be less of an anti-climax than the alternative
trundling departure along a main road.

The impact of the Kallikrati Gorge is even more immediate than
that of Samaria. At Ayia Roumeli the mountains yawn invitingly; a
traveller entering them at that point can enjoy the sunshine of the
glen before being swallowed up. But at Patsianos their jaws are set
in an expression of stubborn determination; we had to force our
way upwards through the clenched teeth of the cliffs, which seemed
to snap behind us as soon as we set foot inside them. The winding
shaft (instinctively I found myself thinking of our surroundings in
terms more appropriate to subterranean passages) presented a series
of Salvator Rosa landscapes with which by now I felt quite familiar:

there, in front of us and behind us, on either side and occasionally, it seemed, even on top of us, were the usual rocks telescoped like parts of a train which had petrified in a collision.

Although it is not so narrow nor so deep as Samaria, the Kalli-krati Gorge gives a greater impression of severe confinement; no single stretch of it is long enough to embrace more than a few successive areas of cracked stone. It was only after climbing a mile or more that we had our first sight of an horizon further away from the eye than a few yards; looking back, we could see, at the base of a V-shaped open space, a smaller wedge of blue: the sea. Then, as we turned the next corner, even that tiny light was extinguished and we were once more pacing a patch of ground which, apart from its slope and roughness, might have been the floor of a cell. In this gloom the shade that any tree might have afforded would have been superfluous; but there was no tree large enough to cast a shadow of any size. The harsh contours of Samaria had been softened by cypress forests; here an occasional stunted maple served to emphasize the aggressive insistence of stone. Only a trained eye, like Hugh's, could make out the miniature plant world which existed in the crannies of the rocks and under the thorn-bushes.

An encounter in this gorge would have been as dramatic as the discovery of a new species of human life. The path was only too palpably terrestrial, but so remote that I felt as though I was voyaging upwards through inter-stellar space; an entity approaching from above would have appeared as strange as the denizen of another planet; for the moment Hugh and I seemed to be the only beings alive on this one. The mule-boy who was with us could hardly be counted as a third person; he was so unusually taciturn for a Cretan that I looked upon him simply as a combination of our two shadows following close behind us. During the ascent only one word passed his lips; pointing out a rampant stink-lily a few feet off the path, he grunted and said: "Turk"—a local name given to that flower on the supposition that it marks the grave of a Moslem killed in battle.

But we did see someone else before we reached the top of the last slope: a ghostly figure, with head and shoulders draped in a net, creeping along a bridge high above us. A ladder made of a slotted tree-trunk showed us how this apparition had climbed up there, but we could not tell why it should have wanted to reach that improbable perch until we noticed the object of its attention—a row of wicker baskets enclosed in clay: primitive beehives. Such an isolated apiary did not necessarily portend the presence of a village round the corner—the bees of Koustoyerako, for instance, are kept in an equally inaccessible position, at the base of the Tripiti chasm, at least a mile from the nearest habitation—but the clambering phantom shouted as we went by: "Welcome to Kallikrati," so we knew that we were near our destination.

In one stride we reached simultaneously level ground and open country. Though we were now at the top of the pass and five thousand feet above the sea, we were still in the mountains rather than on them; visibility was restricted to the one mile diameter of the circular plain on to which we emerged—sometimes even to less than that; for the whole area was covered in cornfields, vineyards and dense orchards; and from certain angles the tallest trees eclipsed even the loftier crags which reared and curled like fossilized breakers all round us. In this tilled and tended jungle we had to look twice before we could distinguish a single house.

During the Venetian occupation Cretan society could be roughly divided into three main classes: the indigenous inhabitants or so-called "ancients"; the "Romaic[1] nobles," that is to say the descendants of the Byzantine colonists who settled here when the Saracens were driven out at the end of the tenth century; and the "Frankish" oligarchy drawn from the ranks of the *nobili Veneti* who administered the island. Sphakia at that time was populated mainly by "ancients" owing allegiance to the original Byzantine overlords, such as the Kallergis and Skordylis families, who had transformed the province into a virtually autonomous state independent of the foreign forces of occupation. But with the fall of the two fortresses of Grabousa and Souda, which caused the immediate dissolution of the *khainides* and a general exodus from the plains to the hills, the neatly balanced social system was overthrown. The mass migration must have given rise to economic and administrative problems even more acute than those caused today by political refugees from behind the Iron Curtain; the native mountaineers, enjoying an isolation that was more smug than splendid, could scarcely have wel-

1. In the Middle Ages a Greek was known as "Romaic" to distinguish him from "Frank," or "European." For further reference to this form of nomenclature, see note on p. 271.

comed the arrival of so many dangerous and discontented outlaws. Fugitives are presumably popular only so long as their numbers are limited; once they become excessive the very name by which they are known seems to reflect the opprobrium in which they are held by established society. Twentieth-century bureaucracy was required for the invention of such an equivocal term as "displaced persons"; the Sphakians of the seventeenth century were more forthright and referred to their refugees quite simply as "ill-bred."

This social distinction was universally applied throughout the province, until the passage of time and inter-marriage erased any difference in birth or upbringing which might once have been noticeable between the "well-bred" indigenous population of the mountains and the "ill-bred" *parvenus* from the plains. Kallikrati was one of the last villages to abandon this elementary and harmless snobbery; until quite recently the older families there were aware of their particular "breeding," though not one of them knew its historical significance. Today not one of them knows that such a distinction ever existed—and a good thing too; for otherwise there might even now be Cretan peasants boasting that their family "came over with Nikephoros Phokas" in exactly the same way that bores in this country mention their own ancestral link with William the Conqueror.

My friend Kokolis, for instance, might easily have made such a claim; his family, the Manousellis, were direct descendants of those "Romaic knights" who had first ruled Sphakia. Half the present population of Kallikrati still bear the name; so I was not surprised to find that the first house at which I asked for Kokolis belonged to one of his relations. I had forgotten where he himself lived, and in any case could no longer recognize the village, for since I was last here it had been burnt down by the Germans. The ruins were now happily concealed by the vegetation, and since the original buildings were scattered all over the plain, the consequent destruction had been spread over a correspondingly wide area. Kallikrati thus looked less desolate than it would have done had it been a more compact village. But the few houses that had been rebuilt were still incomplete; the one where we stopped contained no more than a bed and a table; its owner seemed to be camping out rather than living in.

We learnt here that Kokolis was "in trouble again"—an ambiguous phrase, but one which perfectly described the almost permanent state of revolt in which he lived. During the occupation he had been "wanted," and not only by the Germans. Since the war he had evidently become still more in demand. The authorities, it appeared, would have given a great deal to "have a little word with him"— if only they had known his whereabouts. "Is he in hiding then?" I asked. "Well, no, not exactly in hiding," I was told, "but he does avoid the village as much as possible. You'll probably find him up on Rodare."

It was on Rodare, a mountain further inland, that Kokolis had his cheese-hut. He was by far the best cheese-maker in the district, so I was glad to hear that he was managing, with typical Cretan ingenuity and compromise, to combine his professional career with the purely amateur conditions of an outlaw. I was also glad on another account: his absence gave us an excuse for leaving our present embryonic shelter and pushing on at once in order to reach the hut by night-fall.

So, after a quick meal of hard-boiled eggs and fried potatoes which our temporary host insisted on giving us, Hugh and I set off once more, crossed the plain and climbed out of the basin over rocks set like spume along the topmost edge of a petrified whirlpool. Like divers surfacing, we emerged on to a choppy sea of limestone from which the real sea was visible both to the north and the south. At this point we straddled the very backbone of the range, yet we were still far below its highest peak; wave after wave of stone extended all round us, culminating in distant pinnacles; but despite the view of the sea shimmering far off on either side, the landscape was limited to our level; there was nothing immediately beneath us; the whole world seemed to lie suspended more than five thousand feet up in the air.

Any path which might once have been traced over this lunar surface existed now only as a theoretical route between two given points; there was no visible track, but the direction in which we had to move was clearly marked by the contours of the land, so that we could not lose our way. Even so, I asked the first shepherd that we met whether this was right for Rodare. My superfluous question provoked immediate suspicion; it was only after I had introduced myself and explained that I was an old friend of Kokolis's that the man stopped behaving like an interrogator to become an informant. Kokolis had evidently organized a sort of sentry system in the neighbourhood.

As soon as I sighted Asi Gonia, I recognized our position. From the ridge on which we stood the village, which had always appeared so high and inaccessible when approached from the northern plains, seemed now to lie even further down than it actually was. Acclimatized to our present height, I had come to regard anything below this level as a subterranean feature; even the Church of the Holy Cross, which from Petros's house could only be seen by directing one's gaze high up the opposite slope, now looked like a pebble lodged in a fissure underfoot. This view of the village had been a familiar one during the war, when I had often stopped at this very spot to admire it; I knew now exactly how far we were from Rodare, and this knowledge made the distance appear negligible. In less than no time, it seemed, but in fact half an hour later, we rounded the last bend in the ridge which separated us from Kokolis's hut.

———

The night that we spent there was as uneventful as our journey during the day had been. There was nothing to distinguish the hut from any other, except, perhaps, the rifle hanging from a peg on one wall, and the sheets spread over the brushwood couches; and these two incongruous features—twin guides to their owner's character—were the only signs which distinguished Kokolis from any other cheese-maker. His fair hair and beard, his voice constantly raised in the sort of tone more commonly used for addressing a flock of goats—these might have belonged to any one of a thousand other shepherds. His conversation, too, was similar to any other peasant's; I had listened to these war-time reminiscences so many times before. And even the food that he offered, the milk and the cheese, was the same that I had eaten in a score of other huts of this kind. Yet that night everything seemed, if not different in itself, then at least charged with a different, deeper meaning.

The difference, of course, was in myself. Sentimentality, provoked by impending departure, had blunted my critical faculty; I was prepared to see in anything Cretan a significance which was probably quite imaginary. And as I lay awake, shivering slightly under a sky which held the stars in a grip of ice, I found myself agreeing with Sir Walter Raleigh's[2] romantic belief "not in refinement and scholarly

---

2. Not, of course, Sir Walter Raleigh, the Elizabethan adventurer, but the twentieth-century scholar of the same name. Only a professor protected by the cotton-wool surroundings of a Common Room would be capable of voicing such an ideal.

elegance, those are only a game, but in blood feuds, and the chase of wild beasts and marriage by capture . . ."

Crete provided all these requirements, and I knew what a bore each one of them could be—how many times during the last year spent in their midst had I longed instead for what Sir Walter affected to despise as "only a game"! Yet here I was regarding them with nostalgia, missing them even before I had left them.

I tried to analyse these conflicting sentiments of mine. The idea of Crete had haunted me ever since my departure after the war; I had pictured it as an unattainable never-never land. That conception had been modified during the last year, during which idea had given place to reality; the ghost had been laid in the daylight of tangible fact. But only, it seemed, temporarily; for the original picture was once again being projected on to my mental screen; the phantom was re-materializing—even before the darkness of absence and distance had fallen.

I knew then that I should never be permanently exorcized.

Epilogue

W<small>HY SHOULD</small> the island's primitive conditions, sometimes so unbearable when applied, seem so desirable in retrospect? The answer is not to be found in a subconscious "back to nature" yearning, nor in self-conscious wonder at the "noble savage." For the Cretans are not natural in the formalized Western sense of the word; nor are they savages in any sense. Parts of Sphakia, admittedly, are even today as remote as the Middle Marches of sixteenth-century England, and some of the inhabitants still live in much the same manner as the moss-troopers of that time; yet the standard of hospitality there is higher than in this or in any other more progressive country. It was the Greeks who gave to the world the term *philoxenia*, while leaving other races to construct out of the elements of their language the word *xenophobia*; and nowhere is this "love of strangers," which they universally preach, practised with more conviction and intensity than in Crete.

But their hospitality alone cannot account for the nostalgia which the Cretans inspire; its aggressive quality is more often responsible for feelings of irritation. Admirable in theory, in practice it impresses one as alien. And that, I suppose, is the only way in which the retrospective impact and memory of the island can be explained. By-passed by history, its inhabitants are outstanding in the evidence which their customs and traditions afford of the survival of an unspoilt people of the Heroic Age; but however admirable it may be, that age is alien to contemporary civilization and not necessarily a comfortable one in which to live today.

No argument, moral, romantic or realist, is capable of deciding whether such a survival can or should be encouraged. Artificial means are now being applied to preserve and increase the island's exclusive flora and fauna; Cretan dittany, which used to be collected from the steepest crags, is today being grown commercially in the valleys and the plains; and the Cretan ibex, whose natural home is the mountain peak, has found a manmade sanctuary on the island of St. Theodore. Both these measures are justified. But such methods, luckily, are not yet needed to prolong the existence in its present state of the island's most important exclusive feature of all: the Cretan people.

Bibliography

C. ALBIN, L'Ile de Crète (Paris, 1898).

S. C. ATCHLEY, Wild Flowers of Attica (Oxford, 1938).

Pierre BELON, Les Observations de Plusieurs Singularitez et Choses Mémorables Trouvées en Grèce (Paris, 1554).

Ralph BREWSTER, The Island of Zeus (London, 1939).

BUONDELMONTE, Liber Insularum Archipelagi (1422). Published in Creta Sacra (Venice, 1755).

Paul COMBES, L'Ile de Crète (Paris, 1897).

D. O. DAPPER, Description Exacte des Iles de l'Archipel (Amsterdam, 1703).

Μ. ΔΕΦΘΝΕΡ, Ὁδοιπορικαὶ Ἐντυπώσεις ἀπὸ τὴν Δυτικὴν Κρήτην (Athens, 1918).

Charles EDWARDES, Letters from Crete (London, 1887).

M. N. ELLIADI, Crete, Past and Present (London, 1933).

EVLIYA EFFENDI, Narrative of Travels (English Translation, London, 1834).

Ζ. ΖΑΜΠΕΛΙΟΣ, Κρητικοὶ Γάμοι (Turin, 1871).

ΖΑΜΠΕΛΙΟΣ and ΚΡΙΤΟΒΟΥΛΙΔΗΣ, Ἱστορία τῶν Ἐπαναστάσεων τῆς Κρήτης Συμπληρωθεῖσα ὑπὸ Ι. Κονδυλάκη (Athens, 1894).

Ernst GERLAND, Histoire de la Noblesse Crétoise au Moyen Age (Paris, 1907).

John HARTLEY, Researches in Greece (London, 1833).

Christopher KININMONTH, The Children of Thetis (London, 1949).

Π. ΚΡΙΑΡΗΣ, Ἱστορία τῆς Κρήτης (Athens, 1930).

L. LACROIX, Les Iles de la Grèce (Paris, 1881).

V. LAMANSKY, Secrets d'État de Venise (St. Petersburg, 1884).

A. de LAMARTINE, Voyage en Orient (Paris, 1832).

Ch. LAROCHE, La Crète Ancienne et Moderne (Paris, 1897).

W. M. LEAKE, Researches in Greece (London, 1814).

W. LITHGOW, Rare Adventures and Painfulle Peregrinations (London, 1632).

Ι. Δ. ΜΟΥΡΕΛΛΟΣ, Ἡ Ἐνετοκρατία ἐν Κρήτῃ (Athens, 1939).

H. NOIRET, Documents Inédits pour servir à l'Histoire de la Domination Vénitienne en Crète (Paris, 1892).

G. A. OLIVIER, Voyage dans l'Empire Othoman (Paris, 1801).

Robert PASHLEY, Travels in Crete (London, 1837).

Γ. ΠΑΠΑΔΟΠΕΤΡΑΚΗΣ, Ἱστορία τῶν Σφακίων (Athens, 1888).

Μ. Μ. ΠΑΠΑΪΩΑΝΝΟΥ, Ἡ Κρήτη ὑπὸ τοὺς Σαρακηνούς (Athens, 1948).

John PENDLEBURY, *The Archaeology of Crete* (London, 1939).

Georges PERROT, *L'Ile de Crète* (Paris, 1867).

Richard POCOCKE, *A Description of the East* (London, 1745).

Bernard RANDOLPH, *The Present State of the Islands in the Archipelago* (Oxford, 1687).

Victor RAULIN, *Description Physique de l'Ile de Crète* (Paris, 1869).

Κ. ΣΑΚΑΒΕΛΗΣ, Δασκαλογιάννης (Herakleion, 1952).

George SANDYS, *Travels Containing an History of the Original and Present State of the Turkish Empire* (London, 1615).

Claude SAVARY, *Lectures sur la Grèce* (Paris, 1798).

Γ΄ώργος ΣΕΦΕΡΗΣ, Ἐρωτόκριτος (Athens, 1946).

C. R. SCOTT, *Rambles in Egypt and Candia* (London, 1837).

F. W. SIEBER, *Reise nach der Insel Kreta* (Leipzig, 1823).

J. E. Hilary SKINNER, *Roughing it in Crete* (London, 1867).

C. S. SONNINI, *Voyage en Grèce et en Turquie* (Paris, 1801).

Εἰρήνη ΣΠΑΝΔΩΝΙΔΗ, Κρητικὰ Τραγούδια (Athens, 1937).

T. A. B. SPRATT, *Travels and Researches in Crete* (London, 1867).

Ν. ΣΤΑΥΡΑΚΗΣ, Στατιστικὴ τοῦ πλυθισμοῦ τῆς Κρήτης (Athens, 1890).

Theodore STEPHANIDES, *Climax in Crete* (London, 1946).

Erwin STURZL, *Kreta: die Insel im Herzem der Alten Welt* (Vienna, 1948).

J. M. TANGOIGNE, *Voyage à Smyrne* (Paris, 1817).

André THEVET, *Cosmographie du Levant* (Lyon, 1554).

J. P. de TOURNEFORT, *Relation d'un Voyage au Levant* (Paris, 1717).

A. TREVOR-BATTYE, *Camping in Crete* (London, 1913).

Β. ΨΙΛΑΚΗΣ, Ἱστοριά τῆς Κρητης (Canea, 1909).

Articles by various authors in Ἐπετηρὶς Ἐταιρείας Κρητικῶν Σπουδῶν (Athens, 1938–41).

A series of articles in Ψυχικαὶ Ἐρευναι (Athens, 1929).